Harsh Realities

ADVANCE PRAISE FOR THE BOOK

'I have known Harsh for several years, and the inspiring story of how he discovered his purpose of "making a difference", of scaling up, failing, learning and striving to succeed—as he puts it—makes for a very insightful read. I enjoyed how he weaves in many other stories too, including the genesis of Marico, the evolution of a family business and the changing industrial landscapes, all of it underscored by the importance of grounded, values-based leadership. Prof. Ram Charan's reflections on Harsh's personal growth journey are a wonderful addition'—Adi Godrej, chairman, the Godrej Group

'The story of Harsh Mariwala is a fascinating tale of a man born in a traditional joint family, finding place and meaning in the family journey, using his instincts and natural intelligence to grasp opportunity, in passionate pursuit to understand the customer, and navigating his way to create a unique and ethical consumer company, Marico. I have known Harsh since his Kanji Morarji days, seen him carve out his consumer business from the traditional trading business and transition to a fully professional company. Marico is an outstanding example of an Indian multinational comparable to the best-in-class global consumer companies'—Uday Kotak, managing director and CEO, Kotak Mahindra Bank

'Harsh Mariwala's love for innovation, process orientation and building organizational culture is absolutely inspiring, and Marico is a glowing testimony of this. As revealed in this finely penned memoir, Harsh is a combination of spice and calm, as the two major products in his business, pepper and coconut oil. There is a mystical balance in him—traditional yet cutting-edge, searching yet grateful, restless yet transcendent, observing yet couldn't-care-less, loving yet impatient, and it is this potent mix that has helped nurture an outstanding organization and a fine human being. This book is the real "What they don't teach you at Harvard"'—Harsh Goenka, chairman, RPG Enterprises

'Harsh has many exceptional abilities. The one that I have found almost unique—having known him for a long time—is his capacity to learn and absorb from everyone and everything, and then to convert this learning into something useful—small to big to huge. We can all learn this from him. And what better way than to read this book, which is in your hands'—Azim Premji, chairman, Azim Premji Foundation, founder chairman, Wipro Ltd, and chairman, Wipro Enterprises Ltd

'Running a family-run business is no easy feat. And to take that to heights is a success story beyond one's imaginations. Harsh makes each of his struggles so relatable in this memoir. Superbly inspiring'—Rajiv Bajaj, managing director, Bajaj Auto

'Harsh Mariwala's inspiring entrepreneurial journey is an interwoven story of how he created a world-class company from a small part of the family business that was entrusted to him. His business philosophy of innovation and differentiation on a strong foundation of values and professionalism has made him one of the most admired and respected business leaders in twenty-first-century India'—Kiran Mazumdar-Shaw, founder, Biocon

'This memoir is like reading three books in one. Firstly, there is the incredible story of Marico, its birth and how Harsh grew it to today's success. Second, Harsh's own thoughtful reflections on the journey he has been through. And finally, there are insights from the legendary Dr Ram Charan himself. An enriching read!'—Nandan Nilekani, chairman and co-founder, Infosys, and founding chairman, UIDAI (Aadhaar)

'*Harsh Realities* beautifully takes us through the journey of a family-owned trading set-up to a professionally managed global consumer brand house built by Harsh with a strong focus on quality and governance. It reveals how Harsh dealt with obstacles and learnt from each failure—rich takeaways that helped him grow his company and also as a person. A must-read for entrepreneurs as well as business scions who aspire to shoulder the dual responsibility of taking their family legacy forward while scaling it to newer heights. Harsh has created Marico with governance, transparency and a passion for innovation and giving back to society'—Anu Aga, former chairperson, Thermax Limited, and philanthropist

'A truly riveting story of how an iconic leader with purpose, persistence and passion leverages customer-centric innovation driven by uncommon thinking to create a world-class enterprise. An inspiring "must-read" for all'—Dr R.A. Mashelkar, National Research Professor, and former director general, Council of Scientific and Industrial Research

'*Harsh Realities: The Making of Marico* is a very personal and captivating journey of how Harsh Mariwala built a world-class company highly admired by others. It is also a heart-warming story of the making of Harsh as a human being, who, through sheer determination and learning from failures, transformed himself from an ordinary to an extraordinary person. The book is a pure joy to read!'—Professor Jagdish N. Sheth, Charles Kellstadt Professor of Business, Goizueta Business School, Emory University, USA

'There are many youngsters who inherit their family-run business and manage it through their lives. It's one thing to sit in fancy air-conditioned offices and oversee the business. It's yet another to actually go on the ground, travel the lengths and breadths of the country, understand your consumer, understand your distributors, and then take all your stakeholders on the ride of their lives. Harsh's journey is a story that created history. And it has been a real learning and joy to read about it. Lots to emulate here for youngsters'—Rajiv Kumar, vice chairman, NITI Aayog

'Before reading the book, please remember that "Harsh" in Hindi means joy. Read it, and read the joys of a journey. A journey of grit and determination. Of living and learning by personal experience and from those of your predecessors. Look for new destinations, but don't forget where you came from. Before reading this book, I thought I knew a lot, but now I have more food for thought. Thanks, Harsh. I'm sure your journey will lead to thousands of new journeys by young women and men'—Piyush Pandey, chief creative officer, worldwide, and executive chairman, India, Ogilvy

'Harsh rolled up his sleeves and went into the field and learnt the business from the ground up—starting with the consumer and then led the company to where it is today through a combination of genius and toil. A must-read'—Sanjeev Bikhchandani, co-founder, Naukri.com

Harsh Realities

The Making of Marico

Harsh Mariwala and Ram Charan
(As told to Archana Mariwala and Jeswant Nair)

BUSINESS
An imprint of Penguin Random House

PENGUIN BUSINESS

USA | Canada | UK | Ireland | Australia
New Zealand | India | South Africa | China

Penguin Business is part of the Penguin Random House group of companies whose addresses can be found at global.penguinrandomhouse.com

Published by Penguin Random House India Pvt. Ltd
4th Floor, Capital Tower 1, MG Road,
Gurugram 122 002, Haryana, India

Penguin Random House India

First published in Penguin Business by Penguin Random House India 2021

10 9 8 7 6 5 4 3 2

ISBN 9780670094783

Marico History Wall photos by Himanshuu Chandrakant Sheth

Typeset in Adobe Garamond Pro by Manipal Technologies Limited, Manipal
Printed at Thomson Press India Ltd, New Delhi

To all the entrepreneurs who are creating economic prosperity for the country and all the stakeholders

Contents

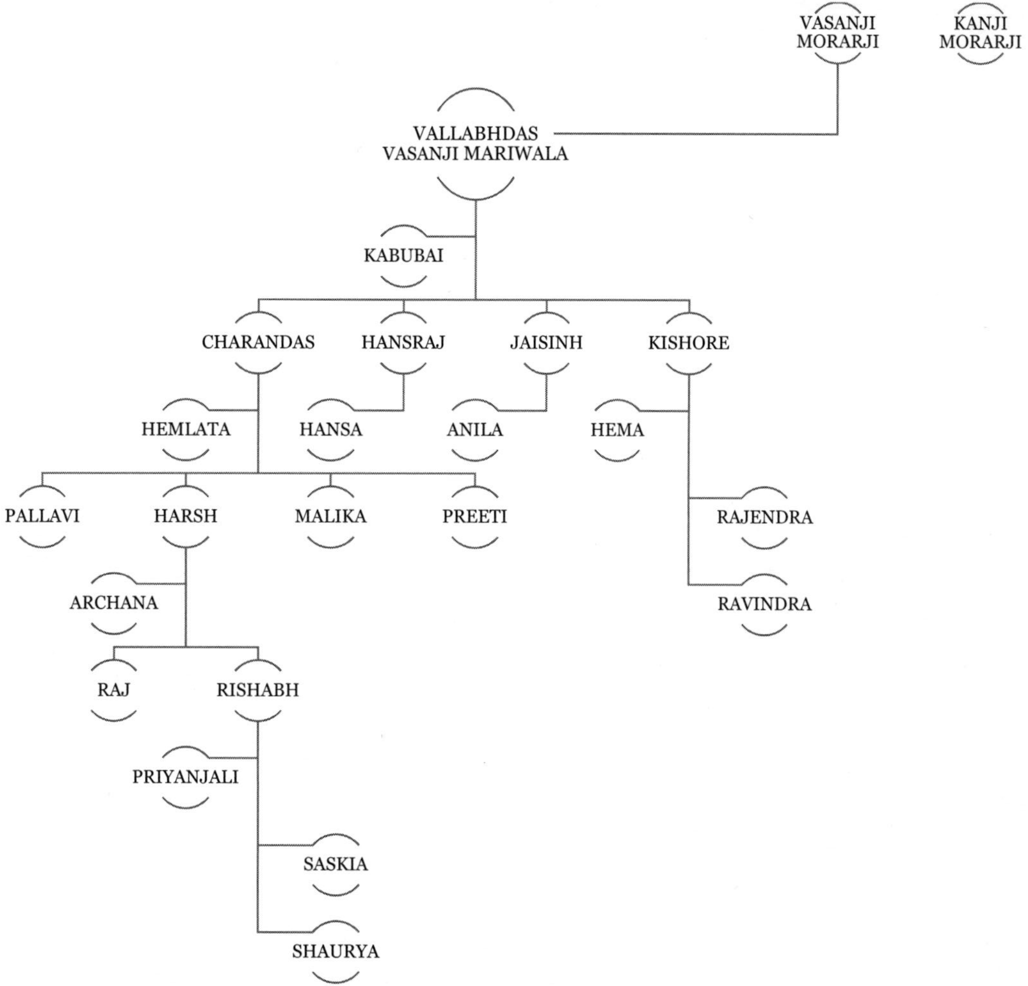

VASANJI MORARJI
KANJI MORARJI
VALLABHDAS VASANJI MARIWALA
KABUBAI
CHARANDAS
HANSRAJ
JAISINH
KISHORE
HEMLATA
HANSA
ANILA
HEMA
PALLAVI
HARSH
MALIKA
PREETI
RAJENDRA
ARCHANA
RAVINDRA
RAJ
RISHABH
PRIYANJALI
SASKIA
SHAURYA

Foreword

Underpinning my philosophy of life is the truth that you come into this life with nothing—and leave with nothing. It is the period in between that belongs to you. Learning begins at birth and ends with death. And in the interim, the journey is what you make of it. Some may contend it is destiny that determines your path—and that you merely flow with it. I disagree with that premise. I believe you steer your own course. Drive your future. That opportunity knocks on every door. It is for you to heed that knock.

What determines success? Luck at being there at the right time? Partially, maybe, but beyond that, it is the ability to visualize, create opportunity and overcome the hard yards that follow.

My story is about scaling up. About failing. Learning why I failed. And then understanding how to deal with failures. And striving to succeed. It is about taking challenges head-on. It is about how to create a right-to-win on a perpetual basis. My memoir here captures the basic truth about not only building a business but also the impetus to give back to society. To make a difference.

This book then is a narrative of the genesis of Marico and how it fielded the curveballs it encountered on its journey. Responses that were often unconventional and contrary to popular wisdom. It is also the story of the influences that shaped my leadership thinking and my motivation and drive to succeed against all odds. It recounts the transformation and growth of a family owned and managed commodity-manufacturing business to a publicly owned and professionally managed consumer goods company, and now an institution that has the capacity to successfully survive time and new challenges.

Success is a double-edged sword. It brings admirers as well as critics, both equally keen to know the story of how you achieve success, and thereafter, draw their learnings and conclusions from these experiences. Many start-ups flounder and remain small while others fold up in time. Only a few show the imagination and tenacity to break through the clutter and go the distance in terms of size, spread and returns, and grow into institutions.

World over, nearly 70 per cent of companies are owned and run by families. India ranks third globally in terms of number of family-owned businesses (*Economic Times*, 14 September 2018), and these contribute to over 70 per cent of India's GDP (*Business Today*, 9 September 2019). Almost all family companies, at some stage of their continuation, face a quiet, not-so-spoken conflict, as the next generation with new aspirations come of age and challenges older constructs—constructs that have fared well thus far. A dominant and successful father, who is larger than life, unwittingly breeds a family environment of awe and fear. The younger generation, then, is hesitant to raise issues that are perceived to contradict the elders. Open discussions do not take place. This silent struggle continues till something gives.

I too struggled with these dynamics for a long time before I found a constructive way out. Scions of business families may obtain some insights from how this path was traversed, from my experiences. Given rapidly changing business and work modes, the tradition of offspring stepping into their fathers' shoes and carrying forward the mantle of their family business, is declining. Keeping pace with current times, it is vital that today's parents be cognisant of their child's aptitude and inclination and provide a facilitative environment for it to blossom. When that talent is combined with passion and perseverance, it becomes a potent mix for success.

Prof. Ram Charan, global advisor to CEOs and a best-selling author, has been my coach and mentor over the last twenty-five years. Born in India and educated in the US, and despite more than half a century of living there, the professor remains fundamentally Indian in his values and thinking. After graduate and doctoral studies at Harvard Business School and years of professorship at Harvard and Northwestern University, the professor pursued his passion for consulting, coaching and mentoring CEOs and boards across the world. He is instrumental in shaping my leadership philosophy. In this narrative, Prof. Ram Charan frequently incorporates his timeless insights and truths about leadership and management. His perspectives on company boards, corporate responsibility to stakeholders and society, as well as top leadership coaching and organizational processes, are nuggets of wisdom that readers will find illuminating.

Harsh Mariwala

27 JANUARY 1990
THE DAY THE TIDE TURNED

The journey that culminated that day had been long. Very long and emotionally breaking.

A journey that demanded two never-ending years of innumerable and endless meetings with family elders.

Meetings seeking to unravel the convoluted maze of financial, legal and economic tangles. Replete with confusion, doubts, suspicion. Meetings that struggled to achieve common grounds and fair solutions. Infinite hours of wrenching helplessness, lost tempers, emotions running amok. Until . . .

Finally.

The journey ended.

And began.

And so, it was on this momentous day that the demerger of the consumer products division of Bombay Oil Industries Pvt. Ltd led to the birth of a new company.

M A R I C O.

Under a new stewardship.

Helmed by Harsh Mariwala as its managing director.

1

The Mariwala Roots

This story harks back to a time long, long ago and an era now obscured in the sepia tones of yesterday. An era when bullock carts, horse carriages and palanquins were the modes of transport and steam locomotives had just begun chugging their way around India. British India.

It was in this milieu, in 1872, that two young brothers from the distant village of Vinjhan in Kutch set out for far-off Bombay. Traversing the then huge distance of 140 km by bullock cart to the port town of Mandvi, they boarded a 'country craft' or sailboat—a journey that took seven days on the Arabian Sea. Both youngsters, Kanji Morarji, aged seventeen, and Vasanji Morarji, aged fifteen, eked out a humble living by the docks in Bombay, hand-stitching gunny bags. Thereafter, they moved to Cotton Green, where cotton bales were packed for export. Their jobs were to hoist these bales onto the weight balances. Both Kanji and Vasanji were quick to learn the ropes and soon began brokerage of cotton. The enterprising duo then formed their first firm in 1887: Kanji Khetsi & Co. (in partnership with Khetsi).

Meanwhile, on the family front, Vasanji's son Vallabhdas (Harsh's grandfather) was born in 1896. Unfortunately, Vasanji died soon after, leaving Kanjibhai to raise Vallabhdas, his young son (much later, Kanjibhai would come to be regarded as grandfather by Vallabhdas's children, all ten of them: four sons and six daughters).

In 1916, two major events occurred in Vallabhdas Vasanji's life. First, he got married, and second, the firm of Kanji Khetsi & Co. was dissolved. In its place, a new firm, Kanji Morarji, was established by Kanjibhai and Vallabhdas.

Their initial line of work was as commission agents. Their job was to receive and sell goods that were shipped from the Malabar coast (Kerala) by local traders. The railroad had not yet reached Kerala. So all commodities and spices, like ginger, turmeric, copra and pepper, from that state, would be transported to the port of Bombay via sailboat. The commission agents' job would then be to sell these commodities to traders from the big cities that were connected by railway, like Delhi, Calcutta, Amritsar and Karachi (pre-Partition). All for a princely brokerage of 1.5 per cent. Given the absence of any form of long-distance daily communication (phones were a rarity then), the traders in Kerala had to depend on the word of the commission agents regarding the prices at which their goods were sold. Therefore, the integrity and honesty of the agents were crucial criteria for them being entrusted with the goods. Regular contact with the traders from Kerala led the uncle-nephew duo to yet another enterprise: they opened a spice shop and then a firm in Kerala under the same name, 'Kanji Morarji'. Following this, a spice processing plant was set up on the palm-fringed backwaters of Alleppey, Kerala.

In those days, Kutchi families did not have surnames. The name of the individual followed by the father's name declared a person's identity. Thus, it followed that Kanjibhai was identified as Kanji Morarji and Vallabhdas, known as Vallabhdas Vasanji. The census of 1911 led to the British government giving surnames to all. Traders were anointed with the name 'Merchant'. And thus, Vallabhdas Vasanji Merchant it was. Again, 'Merchant' became an extremely common name. Since one of the mainstays of Vallabhdas's trade was pepper, he earned the sobriquet of 'Pepper Man'. Pepper in Gujarati is *mari*. And therefore, 'MARIWALA'. The name stuck. Vallabhdas Vasanji Mariwala.

2

1947

The dawn of a new era for India.

A country, its people, tasting freedom, breathing freedom.

The jewel that finally broke loose from the tyranny and slavery of British rule and regulation. In every walk and mode of life: communal, religious, social, economic and financial.

Among the many edicts and mandates of the British was their stranglehold on trade and export. No 'native' was allowed the right to export any goods or merchandise out of India, which privilege belonged only to the ruling tyrants.

Upon the exit of the British empire, Vallabhdas lost no time in gaining a foothold as an exporter. He was very ably assisted by his first son Charandas (born 1921), who by then had been inducted into the business while still pursuing a degree in college. The exiting British gave outstanding references regarding the father and son pair to their trade clientele in Europe, based on their integrity and the superior quality of their commodities. By the mid-forties, Vallabhdas had entrusted much of the decision-making to his eldest son, Charandas.

The father and son duo set up offices in Alleppey, Cochin and Calicut, buying raw pepper. This was then dried, cleaned and graded before being exported to Europe. Charandas was a visionary and foresaw the potential of stepping up from trading to manufacturing. Around 1945-46, he had already started a small oil mill converting copra[1] into coconut oil. So, when Independence was declared in 1947, he was well prepared.

1 Copra: Coconut meat.

3

Bombay Oil Industries

In 1948, Vallabhdas and Charandas formalized all business operations under the name 'Bombay Oil Industries Pvt. Ltd'. With the blessings and support of his father, Charandas proceeded to set up a crushing plant to extract coconut oil from copra. He also set up a refinery to refine edible oil and an oleochemicals[2] plant, as well as a spice extraction unit. He determined that spice extracts could be exported to developed markets like the US and Europe instead of shipping the spices in bulk, thereby saving substantially on freight costs. By that time, spice extracts were being used by the processed food industry overseas.

Of the four factories that Charandas set up, three were in Bombay: two edible oil units and one oleochemicals unit. The fourth was a spice extraction plant in Kerala. He then handed over the manufacturing of the oleochemicals as well as the spice extraction plant to his youngest brother, Kishore Mariwala, who had earned a master's degree in

[2] Oleochemicals: Chemical manufactured from oils.

chemical engineering from MIT in 1957. The same year, a vanaspati[3] factory was acquired in Porbander, Gujarat, as was a solvent extraction plant to extract residual oil from oil cakes. This had a huge export market. Charandas's eldest brother, Hansraj, a science graduate, took charge of this factory, which was called 'Shree Jagdish Oil Mills'. The finances of these various companies were handled by Jaisinh, Charandas's second brother.

Reminiscing, Harsh says, 'Basically, my father was a visionary. He anticipated, then actioned trading operations into manufacturing. By converting raw materials into finished products, he was able to add value to and expand our traded commodities business. A powerful personality, he also headed various trade and industry associations.'

Bombay Oil's reputation for quality came from the ground up. Company inspectors tested samples of coconut oil for aroma and clarity. The 'noses' sniff-tested every batch, and based on their determination of quality, the batch was either returned for further processing or made the cut and qualified for consumer use. One of the brands of Bombay Oil, Parachute Coconut Oil, was sold wholesale in 15 kg tins and larger barrels. It soon established itself as one of India's superior quality oils. The brand derived its name, obviously, from the then novel parachutes of World War II. These were a novelty in the Indian subcontinent at that time. A parachute denoted safety and reliability and the connotation was, therefore, so did the oil. In local lingo, Parachute Oil was also referred to as '*chhata*[4] brand'!

In the 1960s, medical research identified safflower oil as beneficial to heart health due to its high content of polyunsaturated fatty acids.[5] However, unrefined crude safflower oil has a bitter taste. So every month, the family would receive postcards (then the common means of communication) from people with heart issues requesting that a few litres be refined for them. Empathizing with this need, the family complied and would specially make the required amount monthly. This demand kept increasing and eventually, Vallabhdas

---

[3] Vanaspati: hydrogenated vegetable oil.

[4] Chhata: umbrella.

[5] Polyunsaturated fats help reduce bad cholesterol levels in the blood, which lowers the risk of heart disease and stroke. They provide essential fats like Omega 6 and Omega 3, which help lower cholesterol.

along with Charandas and Hansraj decided to launch safflower oil. This, the second brand of Bombay Oil, named 'Saffola' by Hansraj, was launched in 1965. In those days, 'ola' was the preferred suffix used by manufacturers to brand packed oil (such as Mazola). As would be obvious, the first part of the name came from 'safflower'—i.e., 'saff'—followed by 'ola'. Thus, 'saffola' it was.

While the various plants and factories were situated in different locations in India, the headquarters were based in Bombay in an area called Masjid Bunder. Located near the docks, it was at that time the largest wholesale market and truck transport hub in India. The area was further serviced by a railway station, which was just one stop away from the main station of Bombay, the majestic, neo-Gothic Victoria Terminus Station, or VT, as it is better known.

Masjid Bunder was a scene of utter chaos. Not only did its narrow roads and gullies house the grains and spices wholesale market and transport operators, it also hosted attar[6] shops by the dozen as well as small-time vendors selling spices from their *thelas.*[7] Added to that was the profusion of *haathgaadis*[8] laden high with goods, street hawkers on the narrow pavements, their wares spread out in front of them. *Dabbawalas*[9] doing their balancing acts with 20–30 tiffins in holding trays atop their heads, ungoverned tumultuous traffic, horns blaring non-stop ad trucks belching black smoke. Cattle wandering where they would or just standing stock-still, unmindful of the bedlam around them. And last but not least, pedestrians by the hundreds ably supported by the Masjid Bunder Station, spewing out commuters hour upon hour.

In the midst of such unmitigated turbulence stood Kanmoor House (short for Kanji Morarji), which was built and owned by the Mariwala family. The offices of Bombay Oil were located on the fifth floor. One side of the office saw traditional Indian-style *gaddi* seating[10] while the other half saw staff seated on regular desks and chairs. The family, headed by Vallabhdas, an imposing figure in his crisply

---

[6] Attar: perfume.

[7] Thelas: handcarts.

[8] Haathgaadis: pushcarts.

[9] Dabbawalas: men who deliver lunchboxes from homes to offices.

[10] Gaddi seating: where people sit cross-legged on mattresses laid out on the floor with custom-built desks in front of them.

starched white dhoti[11], *daglo*[12] and Gandhi topi,[13] and his four sons sat in closed door cabins. The only others entitled to cabins were 3–4 trusted family acquaintances, handpicked to help with the business. There were no professionals at that time. All decisions pertaining to the business were taken jointly by the family. In the 1960s and '70s, communication happened via telegrams, teleprinters and post. At Kanmoor House, every morning, all correspondence that had come in through the night would be collected, filed into specific folders and circulated within the family. The office also housed a dining room, to which the family members would convene at 1 p.m. daily to partake of a strictly vegetarian lunch prepared by a maharaj[14] in the office kitchen. Following this, the brothers would assemble again in the patriarch's cabin for tea, at 2.15 p.m. And then again for coffee at 4 p.m. It was at these sessions that business updates and issues were discussed and resolved. All the family members were involved in the day-to-day running of the business. Concentration on short-term tactical issues led to a neglect of long-term strategic planning. Thus, over time, business performance fluctuated due to various factors.

In the '60s and '70s, oil was sold in tankers, barrels and 15-kilogram tin containers. Most of it was not branded. Though the 15 kg tins were sold under their brand names, Parachute and Saffola, an extremely meagre amount had been invested in building those brands. Thus, neither of the brands could command a significant volume and market share. If raw material rates dropped, selling price had to be reduced accordingly, leaving a very slender profit margin. The fluctuations in raw material prices were influenced by the size of the agricultural crop (coconut and safflower) and its demand and supply. This, then, impacted the performance of the business from year to year, leading to erratic profitability. Another key factor contributing to the erratic graph of profit was the failure of Fritche, Dodge & Alcott, US-based buyers, who failed to honour their commitment. They defaulted on their guarantee to buy substantial quantities of spice extracts, causing the oleoresin plant to operate at a much lower capacity while continuing

[11] Dhoti: a piece of fabric tied around the waist to cover most of the legs.

[12] Daglo: typically a black Indian overcoat.

[13] Topi: Indian caps, obviously named after Gandhiji, popularly worn at that time.

[14] Maharaj: a Gujarati cook.

to incur fixed costs. Overall, some years saw profits while others saw losses.

To add to this, there were no proper management information systems in place, resulting in a lack of awareness regarding the profitability of each business. The annual statutory audited financials would run beyond the permitted six months to be finalized. Cash flow planning was carried out on a daily basis, often resulting in delayed payments to vendors. This would in turn hamper the future supply of raw materials by the vendors. Moreover, accounts were maintained in manual ledgers: time-consuming to prepare and prone to errors. There was an absence of annual budgets or forecasts. Other systems too were missing, some cases in point being a lack of appointment letters for employees, performance and evaluation systems, etc.

On the family front, all four brothers and their families resided in the family bungalow at Haji Ali, which faced the Arabian Sea. It overlooked the lush green golf course of the prestigious Willingdon Sports Club on one side and faced Haji Ali Road, which led on to Pedder Road and Tardeo Road on the other side. All three roads were just single lanes. The bungalow gardens also had a tennis court and extended well into what is today the centre of one of the busiest crossroads in Bombay. Bit by bit, the garden was taken over by the municipal corporation in order to widen all the roads.

Though each brother had a floor to himself, they all shared a common kitchen on the second floor, where the head of the family, Vallabhdas, resided. Roughly 20–25 family members, children included, dined every night in the large dining room, the children around 7.30–8 p.m., followed by the elders. As with the business, where the profit and loss were shared equally, on the home front too, with the ladies and children, everything—be it running the huge kitchen, other household responsibilities, cars and meals—were shared. There was no question of individual likes or demands at mealtimes or otherwise, no 'I, me, myself' insistence. Unity and bonding within the family was absolute. Engendered and encouraged by the patriarch, Vallabhdas, and the matriarch, his wife, Kakubai. Through the day, the doors of all the homes remained unlocked, and family members walked into each other's houses at will—even after the kitchens were separated post-1965.

Though the ladies of the house were not allowed to work or attend office, all had diverse interests, which ranged from stitch-craft and making bead-*batuas*[15] to Ikebana, Indian classical music and even golf. In fact, one of the bonding factors for the entire family, including the men, was their shared passion for Indian classical music. Music permeated the entire building, playing in all homes through the day, well into the evening. Another common interest was their fondness for dogs. Additionally, the men too had diverse hobbies: sailing, horse-riding, golf. The latter too could be pursued a stone's throw away at the Royal Western India Turf Club (RWITC) or the Racecourse and the Willingdon Sports Club. Peace and harmony were the order of the day.

Says Harsh:

'Those were the days . . . even though we were a large joint family, we were extremely cohesive and bonded. The whole family acted as one—peace and unity prevailed.'

[15] Bead-batuas: women's embroidered cloth purses or reticules.

4

Harsh and the Third Generation

Taking It All in . . .

This, then, was the environment which Charandas's second offspring and only son, Harsh, grew up in. Born in 1951, he was Vallabhdas's first grandson. The birth of a male child, in those days, called for celebration. An elated grandfather announced the birth of his grandson and celebration and ceremonies followed. The entire household staff, too, were gifted gold coins. The family astrologer reading his birth chart at his naming ceremony declared that this child would achieve great success. In keeping with the emotions of the grandparents and parents, the baby boy was named Harsh. Meaning, 'Joy'.

Harsh was educated in the preferred choice of the Gujarati and Kutchi communities, the New Era High School. His parents as well as his uncles were alumni of the same school. Along with him in the same school were his three sisters as well as the entire third generation of the Mariwala cousins.

Time passed, and the astrologer's prediction stuck in the minds of the father and grandfather. Their expectations ran high and the youngster was frequently reminded of what the stars foretold. This weighed heavily on Harsh—in fact, it had a detrimental effect on him. As the years passed, the shy young boy, and then the teenager, became even more shy and reserved. The expectations of the elders preyed on his mind and he grew up unsure of himself and lacking in confidence. This stayed with him throughout his college years and for a long time after he joined business.

He went on to attend Sydenham College, which was at that time the most prestigious college for commerce in Bombay. Wanting to pursue management at the postgraduate level, he applied to the Indian Institute of Management as well as to the Jamnalal Bajaj Institute of Management Studies, not really expecting to be admitted to either.

He wasn't.

Notwithstanding this, he broached his keenness to pursue an MBA at a business school in the US to his father, who promptly dismissed the idea—probably from the apprehension that he would lose his only son to either marriage to a 'foreigner' or to pursuing business and settling abroad, or both. Concurrently, post earning his BCom degree, Harsh and his close friend Pradeep Harlalka planned a trip to the US and Europe. This was the norm at that time: a junket overseas before one buckled down to business. This trip, unknowingly then, laid the foundation of things to come. The seed for the future was sown.

Meeting his friend at the airport—both wearing bell-bottomed trousers, broad belts and long sideburns, as was the rage in those days—Harsh was taken aback to see his friend empty-handed with absolutely no luggage. 'I will buy everything once we land,' declared Pradeep. At that time, the craze for anything 'foreign' was huge. On arrival in New York, they set off to the stores and malls to buy daily essentials and other items for Pradeep. The convenience stores and shops displayed a huge array of options and brands, as did the malls. The store and mall layouts were extremely well-organized. Product displays showcased merchandise attractively. Consumer brands, ranging from breakfast foods, snacks, cookies, cosmetics, grooming and hygiene products to household goods and appliances, offered innumerable choices. Any and every category presented a huge number of brands and variations. The range was eye-popping, especially when compared to the Indian market, where choices, when available, were extremely constrained. Branded consumer goods were limited and, in many categories, non-existent.

Fascinated, Harsh was taking it all in, from the vast selection of goods and brands, the marketing with diverse displays showcasing merchandise, to the seductive advertising and the range of different and eye-catching packaging. Harsh returned to India with memories of these diverse facets of enticing the consumer etched vividly in his mind.

Early Years in Business

Harsh was among the first of all the eight boys of his generation, and the eldest of all the Mariwala grandsons, to join Bombay Oil Industries in 1971. BOI, as it was called, was a traditionally run company, where the family took most of the decisions. At that time, in the 1960s and '70s, most family-run businesses were exactly that—managed by the family. Qualified professionals were not employed except in specialist functions like manufacturing. Bombay Oil was no exception.

Harsh had not been allocated any particular responsibility, assigned to any specific department, or placed under the supervision and guidance of any one of the seniors. He was left to his own devices, which afforded him the freedom to do as he wished. This, in hindsight, proved to be a blessing in disguise.

And thus, his self-education began.

He visited the factories at Sewri and Mazgaon in Bombay, tagging along with Mr K.N. Mehta, the general manager, who was in charge of overseeing them and who also handled the purchase of raw materials like oils and oil seeds. Possessed of an extremely curious and inquiring bent of mind, he would continually interact with the office staff in various departments, questioning, seeking information, asking their advice. Accompanying the person responsible for liaison and sales, he would engage with customers, thereby gaining insight into quality, pricing, customer service, delivery schedules and complaints. He obtained comprehensive information about competitor strengths and weaknesses. He pored over ledgers, delving into finances.

During his market visits, Harsh observed first-hand the placement of company products and watched sales being handled. Bombay Oil's key markets then were Saurashtra and Vidarbha. However, no one from Bombay Oil had ever visited cities like Nagpur and neighbouring towns in Vidarbha to get first-hand insight into what the competitors were doing and what opportunities could be gained in the marketplace. Hiring a car, Harsh travelled to small and large cities across Maharashtra and Gujarat, studying the markets and visiting the distributors there. He drove for days, stopping in towns like Akola, Amravati, Jalgaon and Yavatmal. In smaller towns, where hotels were of very poor quality, he stayed at the homes of Bombay Oil distributors. These market visits also extended to different states like Madhya Pradesh, Uttar Pradesh and Karnataka. Where air travel wasn't possible, he undertook train journeys, especially into the hinterland. Some of which were not without their share of apprehensions. His train journeys in the interiors of Uttar Pradesh and Madhya Pradesh saw him sharing the commute with dhoti-clad locals—many of whom, very matter-of-factly, wore bullet belts and had rifles slung over their shoulders. A done thing at that time in those regions. He saw how people lived across a wide band of rural India, from the west to the south, where the company sourced its copra from. Later he covered the north and east of the country. These forays afforded Harsh a clearer understanding of consumer behaviour and mind set along with regional preferences. He noted how people in different regions used coconut oil differently. South India saw a majority of consumers use the oil for cooking. In some regions, people used coconut oil following the ancient Ayurvedic ritual of 'pulling'. In others, it was used as garnish to add flavour to dishes. In the colder north, it was applied on the body to prevent dryness of the skin, while in one of its manifold avatars, also used as a lubricant in cycles and other machinery. So, to some extent, various regions offered diverse business opportunities. Harsh's gleanings from all the above explorations and probing paid off. No teaching, no books would have been an adequate substitute for the in-depth learnings he had imbibed through observing trade, the consumer, the different practices, and most importantly, the ethos and cultural inclinations that prevailed in the country. Priceless insights, which no MBA degree would have equipped him with.

Back in Kanmoor house, sitting wherever he could find a vacant spot in the general area of the office, or sometimes even in a temporarily unoccupied cabin, Harsh set up 'shop'. In order to gain exposure to various facets of management, Harsh also attended short training programmes. He knew Homi Mulla, who headed a personnel department at Monsanto and worked out of Wakefield House in Ballard Estate. Harsh would catch a train from Masjid Bunder to V.T., walk to Ballard Estate and sit with Mulla to learn all about HR, or the 'personnel department', as it was known in those days. Says he, 'An assiduous learner, he would delve into different verticals of HR like policies, procedures, systems and structure. He would also sit in with me on interviews and if I was busy, he would sit with my secretary Lorraine Laporte and learn from her as well. To date, she harbours fond memories of a very hungry-to-learn young man.'

Harsh's exploratory mode having provided him an overall ground-up perspective of the workings of the business, he now began implementing changes. He endeavoured to make improvisations in the productivity and automation of the factories, thereby rationalizing costs. Setting up management information systems to prepare monthly profit and loss statements, he strove to expedite the annual closure of accounts. Human resource systems and processes were also instituted. All these initiatives received support from his seniors, who guided and encouraged him to expand his horizons and take up more challenges. When he needed guidance in specific areas, Harsh would tap office seniors like Chandrasinh Danthi, who oversaw sales and manufacturing. He also consulted friends from the corporate world, like Bharat Patel (former managing director of Procter & Gamble), whose expertise lay in marketing. Dr Labdhi Bhandari, professor of marketing, IIM Ahmedabad, too was a guide and a source of knowledge for young Harsh. The professor's daytime schedules involved lectures at the university so during the day, he had no time to spare. Therefore, Harsh would take evening flights out of Bombay and stay through the night with the professor for one-on-one consultation, often till 4 to 5 a.m., returning only by the early morning flights. So, based on his interactions with various mentors, distributors and customers, he established a sales information system to tap into newer opportunities and track sales and market shares. Visits to the wholesalers provided feedback on why Parachute was the preferred brand and why it commanded a premium over other 15 kg competitive brands. The answer was simple: the superior grade and aroma of the oil, which was the outcome of retaining only the finest grade of copra, thus persevering with quality, a basic requirement set by Kanjibhai, Vallabhdas as well as Charandas.

Following which the processing, treatment and rigid quality control during the manufacture ensured that an extremely premium grade oil reached the end consumer. All the above value adds served to identify Harsh's preference in terms of which area of business he had a leaning toward. His earlier exposure to the American supermarkets and his explorations at Bombay Oil served to identify his preference in terms of which field of business he would enjoy most. With all the seniors focused on the other family businesses, Harsh realized there was an opportunity in the consumer products business. He began to explore ways in which he could exploit the same.

Harsh Reminisces:

'In hindsight, my father not sending me to business school abroad proved to be a blessing in disguise,' Mr Mariwala reminisces. 'Had I gone to one, I may have returned with lofty notions regarding management and would immediately have run into conflict with the way things were being done. That I had to learn business virtually by the seat of my pants, gave me first-hand knowledge of how traditional Indian businesses were run. The change in thinking and approach, as it evolved, came in small incremental steps, hardly perceivable as it happened. I learnt quickly that if I had to influence the change process I had to, in a way, live with the two opposing realities of tradition and present-day trends, until time would cause these realities to converge. Often, I would wonder whether I was on the right path.

'Again, being shy and reticent, it was against my nature to engage in networking. I was not cut out for sweet talk, to grease palms or pamper egos to get my work done. Neither was I inclined to manage a business-to-business company, which would require a similar approach to succeed. As against that, investing myself in a consumer products business meant that I would have to deal with distributors and retailers and work on the basis of meritocracy. And transparency.

'The key learning here is to base your career and business on your strengths. The chances of success are higher if one leverages one's strengths and not because one's peers are pursuing an opportunity or opportunistic trends. Looking back, basing my business ideas on my strengths and interests, and staying away from areas where I could have been somewhat challenged, was probably what led me to success.'

Prof. Ram Charan Disserts:

'I recall 1978 vividly, when I was teaching at Harvard Business School. Attending the management programmes were youngsters from some of the biggest business houses of India. I learnt from these students that wealth creation was largely due to the ability of these business houses to obtain licenses from the government through influence. This was the "license raj" of that time, which led to further creation of their wealth. I know Harsh well enough today to surmise that this was something that would go against his grain. That he would never have bribed his way to procure a license. Rather, he would have stuck to legal channels and obtained his licenses by fair and transparent means.

'One does not need to have a formal brick-and-mortar classroom accumulation of knowledge. Harsh learns through seeing and observing. It is a pattern I have known him to follow throughout his life. In business, this translates to an undying quest to actively observe consumers and customers to be able to unravel emerging patterns and gain consumer insights. It is almost as if lens opens up in his mind, to see what others seldom see. He then converts his insights to address a need or solve a problem for the consumer. He perseveres through trial and error to find the right solution—and does not rest till the solution has been found. Apart from learning through observation, his lack of ego, coupled with astuteness, has led him to seek out experts for one-on-one tutoring to address specific knowledge gaps in order to enable answers. Harsh is a life-long self-learner.'

Kishore Mariwala Adds:

'Harsh's father and my eldest brother's outright refusal to give in to his ardent desire to pursue an MBA abroad would surely have impacted Harsh rather strongly. However, I think, so determined was he to learn, prove himself and succeed, that he adopted unconventional means of educating himself.'

5

Building a Consumer Brand

Harsh believed that his personal strengths and disposition were well-suited to the consumer goods industry. He started analysing what he thought would be the route to establishing a strong foundation.

He commenced by recruiting sales reps who would travel to appoint distributors, visit shops and sell company products. Next, he established a sales information system to gauge the effectiveness of the field force and distribution network. Then came the revamping of the packaging lines in the factories. Harsh also realized that to gain a better foothold in the market, the advertising quotient needed to be upped.

'Retailing our own brand in smaller consumer packs seemed the obvious answer to me then,' recalled Harsh.

Thitherto, the company sold oils in small volumes of 1 and 2 kg tins. Harsh learnt that the retailers were dispensing smaller measures of vegetable oil in 'loose form' from large tins to consumers who would carry empty bottles to fill the oil in. He was conscious and apprehensive of the dangerous and distinct possibility of adulteration leading to spurious quality. Another challenge he needed to buttonhole was—how could Bombay Oil make a dent and carve out a niche for itself in an otherwise disorganized market, to convert loose oil users to packed, branded oil in smaller packs? Harsh countered this situation with a series of small but strategic measures. He was among the first to introduce smaller packs of 100, 200 and 500 ml, well aware that it could be years before his efforts would yield any significant market penetration.

Bagging an experienced field sales supervisor from Hindustan Lever to be his new sales manager, Harsh leveraged the new supervisor's experience to build a more robust sales force. Recalling those days, Harsh says, 'I had to build national distribution over a period of time. As expected, it took eight to ten years to create an all-India network. With no one to guide me, I had to go it alone. I also had to show proof to the elders that it was working out. In those days, the family had a fixed mindset of not employing more people, since it would have meant incurring overheads. I had to scale up gradually. We began with the western region. It was only when sales showed positive results there that I could move on to the next region. With every step I took, I would test out a certain hypothesis and then take one more step—like moving from one region to another in India. In fact, my growth and strategy even today is a prototype approach rather than a "big bang" one.'

Harsh then went on to engage an advertising agency to create the first advertising campaign for Parachute. One of his uncles suggested that they drop the brand name 'Parachute' and adopt something more modern instead. Harsh declined and retained the name, and along with it, the image of the white parachute against the blue background of the bottle. His simple but crucial reasoning being that the majority of his consumers were unschooled and rural people, and their only means of identifying their favoured brand of oil was by pointing out to the single image of the parachute.

Along with a national distribution of Parachute, which was slowly but surely bearing fruit, Harsh grasped the opportunity to extend the other brand, Saffola, in the urban market as well. Though it was well-known in the medical fora that safflower oil had cholesterol-lowering properties, it was necessary to enlighten the public regarding the dangers of high cholesterol, and how Saffola could help reduce it. Another advertising agency was roped in to run a health education campaign. This was the first time an edible oil brand had chosen a health platform to endorse its properties. Brand Saffola was also promoted through doctors. Literature on heart care was freely circulated. Medical conferences and heart health camps were organized as forums to create awareness of Saffola's unique properties. Saffola recipe books based on cholesterol-reducing diets using Saffola oil were freely circulated and mailed to potential users. Harsh's approach paid off. From a point where there was low demand for refined safflower oil, the two-pronged strategy of mass education coupled with medical endorsements created a captive 'health oil' segment for Saffola. While all the other cooking oils were price-elastic, Saffola commanded a premium and had built up a strong franchise of loyal consumers in the edible oil market. None in the business could have then imagined that this prescient step taken in the 1970s would create the health and heart-care brand of the future.

The genetic code of uncommon thinking was perhaps seeded in this step.

It persevered further . . .

Opportunities to innovate with coconut oil were limited. Harsh had already made a significant first step by introducing small tin packs for Parachute, thereby converting a large number of consumers from loose to branded and packaged oil. He determined that he needed a strong differentiation to increase market share dramatically. To capitalize on brand Parachute and become a national leader, he deduced that innovation in packaging could be the next game-changer. Obsessed with consumer experience and how people used Parachute, he explained later, 'At that time, tin was the common material for packaging, used by all. I saw benefits in using plastic over tin for packaging the oil. Plastic containers would be easier to handle, to open and pour, and less messy than tins, which were not at all attractive. I visualized a more aesthetic, user-friendly pack that would appeal more to a consumer than a tin which has to be stored out of sight. Importantly, plastic packaging cost less, enabling us to offer it at a more attractive price point. Also, the improved margins that this packaging would bring in could then be invested in advertising, to promote the brand further,' recalls Harsh.

The marketing team then undertook consumer research which found that the buyer would definitely prefer plastic to tins, where they would no longer have to struggle with puncturing a hole in the tin or cut open a foil.

However, changing the profile of a product in those days was not exactly an easy proposition. The move to change to plastic met with stiff opposition from distributors as well as shop owners. They had, a few years back, stocked plastic bottles of coconut oil belonging to another company. This company's experiment with square white plastic bottles had proven to be disastrous. The square bottles had leaked, attracting dust and dirt. Even worse, the aroma of coconut oil attracted rats, who then gnawed through the bottle corners, puncturing the plastic. Coconut oil had leaked out and damaged the other products, making those unfit for sale as well. Shop owners would open their shops in the morning to find them trashed. The experience was an unmitigated disaster that no shop owner, distributor or retailer wanted to repeat. 'Please don't launch plastic packs. They will never work,' warned the retailers. Harsh heard this insistent plea from one of the leading retailers in Bombay, who had considerable influence among his peers. And whose support was much needed. Some members of Harsh's sales team were of the opinion that they could not afford to upset the retailers and they should stick to the current tin packaging.

Faced with these negatives, most entrepreneurs in Harsh's place would have abandoned the initiative.

Not Harsh. He persisted. And, along with his team, probed and studied the earlier team's efforts in minute detail. Their 'eureka' moment soon transpired. The failure of these plastic bottles lay in their shape. Square! The corners of these bottles were their undoing. The rats would bite off these corners. The answer lay in rounded containers that the rodents could not get hold of to bite. The team then worked with product designers and packaging experts to create a new, rounded container. To test the new packaging, the team placed the oil-filled bottles in cages, along with rats, for two days. And set up cameras to record what happened. Photo evidence proved irrefutable. The bottles emerged unscathed.

Now very confident that damage by rats was ruled out, the 'think tank' called the field force for a conference. They were briefed about the experiment and shown the recording. Further, they were handed out photographs showing the experiment and empowered to tell the distributors and retailers that they would be reimbursed in full for any damage caused. Moreover, the latter were also instructed to share with their consumers that the new plastic bottles would be priced lower than the tins. All this would additionally be backed by an advertising blitz revealing the new innovative and consumer-friendly packaging. Inspiring the field force was crucial, since, if they were not convinced, there was no way they would be able to make an impact and convert retailer mindset. All the above steps paid off, and retailer resistance was broken. Initially, a lot of them warily picked up small quantities to reassure themselves. Going forward, they found that they encountered no problems—added to which, the advertising was generating consumer demand. The field force was given monthly targets to accelerate the conversion from tin to plastic, and were also rewarded with incentives if they achieved their targets. Harsh would personally track market acceptance. Merely increased sales volumes were not enough. At the end of each month, he needed to know the percentage of sales contributed by the plastics range. 'What gets measured, gets done,' he told his team. Where the conversion rates did not match projections, they mapped corrective action.

However, the plastic bottles hit another snag. During the winter months, in most parts of India, the oil would freeze in the bottles. So, consumers started reverting to tins again, as they found it easier to scoop the now solidified oil out of the wider-mouthed tins. The narrow opening of the plastic bottles made it difficult to scoop. The bottles with frozen oil were required to be placed in hot water, allowing the oil within to melt. Back went the team to the drawing board and found their solution in wide-mouthed plastic jars. An add-on spout was also innovated, to facilitate convenient pouring out of the oil without opening the jar. All of this added to further 'locking in' the consumers to ensure that they would not shift loyalty or go back to tins. These successful initiatives also showed that innovation is possible even in a commodity-based product with low differentiation.

The initial changes in packaging from bulk to small tin packs and then to plastic bottles were the key to Bombay Oil's successful entry into the retail business. Sales soared. The blue bottle became synonymous with high quality coconut oil and Parachute. Bombay Oil sales multiplied more than five times during the 1980s, led by the success of Parachute.

Simultaneously, Harsh's earlier attempts to introduce new products in the mid-eighties had come a cropper. He had launched a tooth powder, 'Whistle', in a few test markets, targeting rural consumers.

This was driven by the opportunity to avail of financial incentives offered by the government. However, the product did not take off and had to be withdrawn two years later. Delving deeper into the failure of the tooth powder, the key lessons that emerged were:

a) consumer insighting and market research were poor
b) the product lacked a unique selling proposition, and therefore, was unable to make a dent in market share
c) should one stay out of 'me too' products?

Later, Harsh test-launched Parachute filtered groundnut oil in Gujarat. However, a major quality issue hit one of the consignments. A hasty withdrawal from a further launch of any new products followed. He would have to bide his time till he was better prepared. Harsh did not want any erosion to the equity of his two brands, Parachute and Saffola.

During the 1980s, within the incredibly short span of five to seven years, Parachute's market share had tripled from 15 per cent to 45 per cent. By the time others in the business responded to this new stimulus in the market, Parachute had stolen a march and built itself a platform of significance. The innovation culture was taking firm root as the team rejoiced in their success in introducing plastic packaging, the round design of the bottles, the sales story that overcame the trade objections, and the introduction of wide-mouthed plastic jars for winter.

During the fifteen-year period between 1975 and 1990, in spite of the change in the constitution of the business from unbranded large packs to branded small packs, value turnover had more than doubled every five years to reach ₹81 crore in 1990. The decision to change business strategy from vegetable oil trading to consumer packs was most significant in improving not only the overall business performance, but also the fortunes of Bombay Oil Industries. This would appear more relevant if the financial figures of the company, pertaining to the period between 1985 and 1990, were analysed. From a profit of ₹70 lakh over a turnover of ₹43.76 crore (i.e., a margin of 1.6 per cent) in 1984-85, the margin improved to 8 per cent on an average over the three-year period from 1987 to 1990. In 1989-90, Bombay Oil achieved a profit of ₹10.75 crore over a turnover of ₹103.20 crore. Thus, the consumer products division, headed by Harsh, was contributing substantially to both the turnover as well as the profits of Bombay Oil.

Harsh Reflects:

'My journey in consumer products evolved while learning the ropes. In the initial stages, progress was slow, as with each initiative I took, I had to stay the course very patiently and wait for positive results to prove myself to the older generation before I could take the next step. All of the above served to reinforce my belief that one may not have solutions to every issue. And to that end, you need to be open to learn from others and leverage their strengths.'

Prof. Ram Charan Comments on Harsh's Bent of Mind:

'Once again, we see the conviction that arises from observing the reality on the ground: experimenting, taking risks, thinking differently becomes the master foundation for building a business. The motive to change a mental template from a commodity business to a new archetype of a consumer-focused business, in order to bring in a new set of consumers, led to the introduction of small packs for Parachute Coconut Oil, as also leveraging the benefits of Saffola as a health brand. We will see this kind of "uncommon thinking" many times in Harsh's journey.

'Today, it is common for companies to say that we are customer-centric. However, being customer-centric transcends the normal focus groups, observing consumers' behaviour and identifying pain points. It also entails attention to critical details, such as the manner in which the consumer actually uses the product, and the persistence, through repeated experimentation, to solve problems.'

Prof. Ram Charan goes on to summarize the characteristics of successful leaders who did not go to formal business schools:

a) Undying quest to actively observe the consumer/customer.
b) Converting key insights into solving the problems for the consumer.
c) Never giving up: persevere till a solution is found.

'Today, it is essential to know the consumers "experience"—this is the pivot on which the success of any enterprise is based. Modern algorithms enable us to understand unique consumer experiences. Harsh drove through the country, observing. Point is, people may see the same thing, but most may not recognize what is essential. That is one of the distinguishing characteristics of a leader in the making. Of Harsh in his early age. Inbuilt in his DNA. He personally tracked market acceptance. Then executed further. His lack of both ego and arrogance led him to seek out mentors and guides like Dr Labdhi Bhandari. His "tin-to-plastic" story serves to highlight his persistence in the face of resistance, and early signs of innovation. Solving a problem causes innovation—consumer and customer observation-based innovation.'

6

Gen Next in Bombay Oil

In the meanwhile, through the 1980s, four more of the third generation of Mariwalas, Harsh's younger cousins, had joined Bombay Oil Industries. There were now a total of nine Mariwalas in the business: four of the seniors from the second generation and five from the third generation. Each of the newcomers joined the respective fields their fathers were involved in. Gradually, it became apparent that the scale of the business was not large enough to absorb the diverse aspirations of all the individuals or to allow for individual responsibility and growth. This lack of clarity and future opportunities resulted in a general stepping on each other's toes.

The presence of numerous family members in the business impacted the recruitment of good talent. Professionals were extremely reluctant to join a top-heavy family-managed business. Added to which, the location of the office, a crowded and unattractive one in the heart of the commodities market, served to be a further deterrent. Again, Harsh's proposal to shift the offices to a premium location in south Bombay was rejected outright.

Harsh was of the firm belief that he needed to engage professionals to grow the consumer products division that he was helming. Multinationals like Levers, Nestle, Procter & Gamble were offering top-bracket salaries to their managers. Harsh, too, could afford the same quality of professionals at comparable levels of compensation, since the consumer products business was churning out good profits. However, his aspiration to do so was met with stiff resistance from the other divisions. They were afraid that unnecessary comparisons of salaries would create an upward spiral of costs. This cost comparisons again was another deterrent to Harsh's desire to recruit quality talent. He was forced to make compromised staffing decisions. His hands were tied.

Furthermore, there were no clear systems and processes to draw up separate financial statements for each business. The need to accurately allocate costs to determine the profitability of each constituent business was not strongly felt by the seniors. This, then, led to a diffusion of responsibility and very importantly, accountability. It also resulted in sub-optimal allocation of capital. Accurate accounts were also not available. Despite this, it was obvious to all that the return on capital employed in the consumer business was clearly superior to those of the others. Even so, it would not qualify to receive priority in capital allocation.

Thus, it was almost impossible for Harsh to draw a future blueprint for the consumer products business in the absence of an inter-divisional capital allocation policy. Harsh also strongly felt that to attract professional expertise, it was crucial to improve the image of the company in the job market. For that to fructify, an extensive public relations campaign was essential. This, too, was met with stiff resistance from others.

Harsh felt extremely 'boxed in' and suffocated. On the one hand, he envisioned building a large and successful FMCG business and could clearly sense this opportunity. On the other, he was experiencing the drag of the structure of the Bombay Oil enterprise. Working through the complexities of multiple operating family members was extremely exhausting. His optimism and determination were often dampened by sheer frustration. In those days, seniority of age set the hierarchy in family led businesses. Not falling in line with the thought process of the seniors was frowned upon. Harsh would sometimes express his views on what he thought was needed for the consumer business to succeed, which would invariably end with deference to the wisdom of the older generation. Stonewalled and stymied at every step, Harsh realized he needed to do something drastic to be able to move forward. And to that end, began exploring different options. One of which was to initiate a dialogue with the younger cousins who had joined Bombay Oil. Like Harsh, they too had difficulties in realizing their business aspirations. They too felt that the business models created by their fathers were shrinking rapidly and a new, aggressive environment was taking shape. They had begun to feel the need to contemporize the business and diversify the product mix to meet the demands of the emerging markets and economic environment.

Deliberations began in the late 1980s among the five Mariwala cousins to chart out and resolve issues each one was facing. Ultimately, finalizing a roadmap forward, they decided that their interests were best served if they carved out the businesses of Bombay Oil into separate companies. Each of the family businesses had different customer types and was set in different market environments with dissimilar skills and technology needs. They analysed that each business could be spun off as a subsidiary, with Bombay Oil as the investment and holding company. All the four Mariwala families would hold equity in equal proportion. Also, each of the cousins would be clearly accountable for the business delivery commensurate with their responsibilities.

While this agreement among the cousins gave themselves the sense of moving forward, they were also aware that they were not the only stakeholders here. Bringing the seniors on board was a must. They had to not only convince the seniors that this was better for the businesses of Bombay Oil but more importantly, the seniors would hold meaningful roles as well. This new vision would have to get both the buy-in and the blessings of their seniors. They proposed that each cousin would take over the business that they were part of as CEO, along with their father as the non-executive chairman of the same. Thus, their fathers would mentor and guide them in strategizing the way forward. The youngsters knew that it would be no mean task to get their seniors to concede to their joint vision, as it would mean a sea change from what they had actively been doing so far. They convened a joint meeting with their fathers and shared their blueprint for the organization.

This was followed up with one-on-one meetings with their respective fathers to further influence the process of their acquiescence.

After huge effort, time and deliberations, the plan was approved. Over the next couple of years, statutory and legal issues involving the demerger of the businesses were ironed out.

For Harsh, this was a watershed moment in his business career. He could now take charge of his own destiny. And finally, proceed unencumbered to build the business and organization that he had envisioned for a long, long time. Better still, everybody involved felt equally empowered to chart their own fortunes.

And so . . .

One journey ended.

And a new one began.

Prof. Ram Charan Observes:

'World over, 70 per cent of businesses are either family-owned or are run by families. The number may be a little higher in India. These families may represent the second-third-fourth generations, presently. Almost all families face a silent struggle as new generations come in with new aspirations. The older generation holds control and commands obedience. They are not ready to pass on the baton in a hurry. The father looms large as a dominant and successful person, a colossus, and the youngsters live under his shadow. They are hesitant to raise issues that they perceive will contradict their father and so open discussions do not take place out of respect and even fear. And because of their reluctance not to rock the boat, the emotional drama may simmer for a long time.'

The professor adds that there's a lesson here from Harsh's life. 'Harsh could not influence his uncles' and father's old traditional beliefs all by himself. But he was able to pull together his cousins, who shared a common pain, and then promote an idea that would benefit all of them. Working together, they presented a transition model to their fathers. Harsh was looking for a win-win solution through a process of consensus and agreement involving all. It was a transition without tears. There is a learning on the part of the reader because he shows extreme patience, two years, to keep finding, exploring different solutions, keep talking to the cousins, leaving no stone unturned in his attempt to achieve his goal to gain independence and carve out his future.'

Harsh Reflects:

'Looking back, this was the most important milestone in my career. Had the consumer products business not been demerged, I would have had to operate in a highly constrained environment. The consensus building process, which took years, was fully worth the time and effort spent. I had finally broken free of the shackles that were holding me down. I had to let go of my frustrating and limiting past and look forward to a positive and happier future. One that *I* now held in my hands. A future that I could build, mould and develop.'

7

The Winds of Change

At long last, Harsh trod the path to freedom.
At long last, he was free to spread his wings.
And soar.
Free to helm his journey.

This freedom, a result of family deliberations with the elders, empowered Harsh to take over the consumer products business.

The new 'avatar' of this business, he decided, would wing its way into the future under a new name. The mental churn began. Only this time, it was different—and positive. He knew that some companies like Colgate, Dabur, Coca-Cola and Pepsi had adopted the name of their leading brand as their company name. Had Harsh followed their lead, he would have had to name his newly formed company using the words 'Parachute' or 'Saffola'. This, he reasoned, would have presented a restricted image to the market. Especially, given that he was already envisioning expansions as well as foraying into newer brands. On the other hand, companies like Hindustan Lever and Procter & Gamble carried the names of their founders. This was a far more appealing thought . . . a play on his surname, Mariwala.

And thus, the name **'MARICO'** was conceived.

MARICO – A Dream Come True

April 2, 1990 was a landmark day.
The day, the managing director of the newly minted 'MARICO', Harsh Mariwala, walked into his office.
It was the same office. Kanmoor House.
In the same place. The same milling crowds. The same unnegotiable traffic.
Yet, there was something magical, otherworldly, surreal about it.
It was a dream come true.

However, Harsh was very cognizant of the reality of his dream too. He was mindful of the fact that Marico had limited resources. It had only recently demerged from its parent with an equity capital of ₹0.90 crore (US$0.13 million in 2019), a high debt-equity ratio, no reserves and a turnover of ₹80 crore. The terms of demerger apart, the consumer business had been stretched for years as it kept covering the losses of the other Bombay Oil businesses. It needed to borrow heavily just to stay up and running, let alone invest in new growth. Marico was financially feeble and very vulnerable. Thus, it was an environment full of internal challenges that Marico had its beginnings: a baptism by fire.

Employees Walk Out of Bombay Oil

On taking charge as the managing director, one of the first tasks on Harsh's table was the need to tell the world that Marico was a new company. Not just that, he wanted to use the opportunity of the announcement to also attract great talent into the company. He had very limited resources and could not afford 'big splash' advertising, running into several weeks. Yet, it was imperative to reach far and wide in the corporate world and among business talent. However, the small budget he had could last only a couple of weeks. Thus, he chose the print media mix wisely to derive a 'bang for the buck'. He briefed his agency to develop a creative that would be able to break through the clutter of press ads, to convey his message in attention-grabbing advertisements.

Alok Nanda, then the creative director of Trikaya Grey Advertising, recalls that Harsh was looking for an interesting idea to announce the birth of Marico—and also attract expertise. Alok says he perceived Harsh as 'a man who wants to move out of a conservative family set-up, willing to risk doing something disruptive to catch the public eye. He wants to have attention-grabbing impact on the readers. Let's do it, shock with electrifying headlines, graphics and copy.'

And so, in April 1990, an award-winning three-part press campaign proclaiming the birth of Marico was announced.

With riveting headlines.

'200 Employees Walk Out of Bombay Oil'.

The copy explained that 200 employees were leaving Bombay Oil to join a new company: MARICO.

It was followed by sequels . . .

'Mass Killer Nabbed'

The above advertisement detailed how Saffola (as per medical data available then) benefitted the heart by arresting cardio disease. It told the story of the marketing insight that created brand 'Saffola.'

Lalitaji Boycotts Coconut Oil

Lalitaji, who was a fictional icon in TV commercials, portrayed a sagacious Indian housewife and was known across the length and breadth of India. A Hindustan Lever creation, she had become synonymous with the saving- and quality-conscious Indian housewife. The strategy of utilizing the popularity of the quintessential figure paid off hugely. The storyline went on to detail why Lalitaji endorsed Parachute Coconut Oil while rejecting all other coconut oils. This further enhanced the brand-building exercise for Parachute, while establishing in the job market that Marico as a company was a lucrative as well as challenging proposition, especially for those who were creative and defied convention.

These three advertisements served their purpose and created the required buzz. The well-heralded birth of Marico appealed to the senses of talented young managers.

Being short of resources, Harsh had learnt to do more with less. As the old maxim goes, 'Necessity is the mother of invention.' And so, it was in the case of Harsh. Managing to overcome the hurdle of limited resources, he succeeded in optimizing them. Learning from past experiences, he was very cognizant of the fact that constraints were a breeding ground for innovation to break through.

Says Harsh:

'Shock value helped us grab a lot of attention. It also underscored the innovative streak in our thinking.'

Prof. Ram Charan Observes:

'Harsh had a keen eye for big change. He saw the wave coming: the boom in consumerism fuelled by income growth. He was in a hurry to ride this wave and move fast to make Marico a pre-eminent fast-moving consumer goods company. Harsh's approach was unconventional in prioritizing talent over all else, as he knew that in a competitive marketplace, the fight was always going to be a battle of minds. He wanted to make sure that he had a head start in attracting talent and its synthesis into a high-quality team.'

8

The Hunt for Talent

Liberated from the shackles of being part of a larger entity with divergent talent expectations, Harsh was hungry for talent. The sort of talent that would help him build a large consumer goods company. He needed a new generation of professionals not just for his top team but right down to the front-line employee, so that there was a continuity of competence from top to bottom. He knew that professionals were more loyal to their career than to a company. He also knew that professionals were disinclined to work in family run companies, and if they did . . . were not known to be long-time stayers. But Harsh wanted the best the market could offer.

Home-grown companies faced a steep climb to catch up on the talent front. Hindustan Lever and a few other MNCs like Colgate and Nestle were the marquee companies to which talent gravitated. Being one with a progressive outlook, Harsh was decisively hungry for people who were pedigreed in the best schools and companies. Harsh knew that not having studied in a university abroad was not a limitation in itself. Steve Jobs was a college dropout but that didn't prevent him from being an inventor and a celebrated business leader. As was Bill Gates.

Harsh knew that he couldn't do everything by himself. He didn't want a centralized decision-making organization where nothing moved without his say-so. Rather, he envisioned an institution that would survive time. Harsh needed people who were experts in their disciplines and who could help him accelerate the growth of the business. So he was intent on inviting others more educated and capable, from whom he could learn and multiply his own competencies and those of the organization.

All entrepreneurs have a problem recruiting the first professional. They lack the experience of how to go about this. A mistake here can become a great setback for years. Harsh was clear about one thing: his first recruit had to be a human resources leader who, apart from specialist skills, would also bring credibility and be the face and voice of Marico in the talent marketplace. He reasoned that since human resources was central to his strategy, the chief human resources officer (CHRO) had to be a member of his top management team and be involved in all the internal high-table business meetings. It was his way of signalling to everyone else that the human resource function was high priority for him, and all people decisions were taken in the context of business and not based on likes and dislikes. Harsh was aware that in many family-managed and even in some professionally managed companies, the HR leader was seldom included in senior management meetings. To them, HR was a specialist department that practised its skills in isolation from business dynamics and decisions. In most companies, then, delivery expectations from HR departments were low and many times, the HR personnel were the lowest paid among other functional specialists.

Harsh was not the only young man with a similar vision. Jeswant Nair was a young manager who had a strong grounding with Asian Paints, the largest paint company in India, which had grown out of a family business. As part of his work, he had visited a number of factories in and around Bombay. Included was the Bombay Oil Oleochemicals factory. It did not leave him very impressed. Yet, one day, a few years later, an acquaintance suggested that Jeswant meet Harsh. 'Just go and talk to Harsh. He's got some plans that may be of interest to you.'

They met at the Willingdon Sports Club one Saturday morning in July 1989. Jeswant did not expect that anything much would materialize. After all, his only past experience with Bombay Oil was not particularly noteworthy. While at Blue Dart express, he had done much of the work that addressed the hard numbers and systems but was running into differences with the promoters on matters of human resource philosophy and policy. He was contemplating a change.

On his part, Harsh had done his homework. He knew that Jeswant was passionate about his work, as also that he had built a reputation as an upcoming human resources professional. He knew that Jeswant was well-regarded as a talent spotter and had access to talent sources. He had also learnt that Jeswant was opinionated and wouldn't back down easily. Harsh's own style of functioning was to empower. He didn't believe that his views were paramount and was open to the idea of discovery and co-creation. He had already done a considerable amount of thinking on his HR agenda with Homi Mulla, his then advisor on people matters. He had already drawn up the blueprint of the functioning of his organization when he met Jeswant.

Jeswant was impressed with Harsh, his preparation for the meeting and his earnestness. It was the first time Jeswant had encountered a business leader with the humility, simplicity and transparency to show a keen interest in a candidate. In his past meetings, he had experienced all his interviewers talking down to him. Instead, here was Harsh trying to excite Jeswant with the idea of building a new company together, an Indian 'Hindustan Lever' . . . the gold standard then. It was almost as if Harsh was extending an invitation to join the business. Jeswant was happy that the conversation was free-flowing and designed to find out more about him in a given role.

Harsh sensed that Jeswant found it suffocating to work under autocratic CEOs but could thrive if he felt a sense of partnership and mutual respect. He surmised that Jeswant's experience with thoroughbred companies would be a big plus in building a talent pool for Marico and that they could find a way to work together and create something new.

On his part, Jeswant felt assured that he would be able to add value to Marico's journey, in the way Harsh reached out to him. He saw that here was an opportunity to play a crucial role. Their conversations flowed and the chemistry seemed at a good take-off point. Jeswant came on board to lead human resources at Marico. However, Bombay Oil and, by inference, its off-shoot Marico, had no track record of hiring great talent. The naysayers would talk about the many problems in attracting talent. Though the insides of the office were a paradise, with impressive décor and a lawn to step out to for some thinking, the location was positively a put-off. Those who chose to drive to work were often confronted with the task of finding a place to park their car. Street-side parking would be available, with some luck, a few lanes away. That was the first challenge of the morning. The other big no-no was that Bombay Oil was a family business and professionals were disinclined to work with one. In such circumstances, trying to recruit competent senior professionals was a herculean task. The only saleable factor was Harsh Mariwala.

A recruiter could retreat into inaction presented with these factors. Having surmounted many issues in the past, this was just one more for Harsh to overcome. Fortunately for him, Harsh now had Jeswant as an ally, a person equally imbued with optimism.

Jeswant appointed a panel of recruitment agencies to target talent. Learning from his early meeting experiences with Harsh, Jeswant replicated and built a process of engaging potential candidates. The underlying philosophy in recruiting people was to make it an experience where candidates felt welcomed and valued, a social interaction that had pleasant outcomes.

Jeswant met the prospects first, professional to professional, mostly in a conducive 'cafe'-like environment away from the Masjid office. Once a mutual interest was established, the next step was a meeting with Harsh. Harsh was quick to spot talent. He reinforced the message of a new and exciting company where people were empowered to build the business and organization.

On another day in 1990, Harsh drove to the Willingdon Club to meet Shreekant Gupte. Shreekant, a mechanical engineer from IIT (Kanpur) and MBA from IIM (Calcutta), came with impressive credentials. He had worked with Sherwin Williams, Garware and Asian Paints. Harsh met Shreekant to see if he was willing to make the change to Marico. Gupte wasn't eager to return to an operations position. He was looking for a CEO role. But he too was struck by Harsh's earnestness and energy. Reflecting on his decision to join Marico, Shreekant said of Harsh, 'One thing that clinched it for me was when he said that he wanted to fill Marico with people who knew much more than he did.' The commitment to putting an enterprise above ego was very refreshing. Shreekant joined the team as vice president—operations.

Praveen Rattan was an engineer from BITS (Pilani) and MBA from IIM (Calcutta). He was a sales manager with SmithKline Beecham when he left to join Marico as its general sales manager. In the search for a business-oriented CFO, Marico zeroed in on Pranab Datta, a chartered accountant with many years of CFO experience with Tata Companies, including Rallis and Nelco. Datta had just returned from Alghanim, Kuwait, after the Iraqi invasion. He was contemplating offers from the Tatas, a group that he was familiar with. Initially wary of joining Marico, he was impressed by Harsh and charmed by his transparency. Commenting on his meeting with Harsh, Pranab said, 'Despite nearly twenty years of successful stewardship of the business, Harsh referred to the company as an entity outside of himself, making me think for a moment that it was not his own company.' Pranab joined Marico as its vice president for finance.

The last position on the top team was that of vice president—marketing. Raj Aggarwal (deceased in 1995), an IIT (Bombay) engineer and an MBA from Jamnalal Bajaj, was a marketing veteran who had worked on international brands like Singer and Colgate and local brands of Balsara Hygiene. Though he had spent a considerable number of years with MNCs, his approach was grounded and not straitjacketed. However, his many years at MNCs had left him with the formality that MNCs were known for. On his first day at work in Marico, he arrived in a proper suit and tie—something that was anathema at Marico. Harsh told him that Marico was informal, encouraged smart casual dressing and said that all employees addressed him as Harsh. 'Sir', 'madam' or 'mister' were misplaced terms at Marico. The top team was now complete, with Raj turning up in his smart casuals the next day.

Harsh had beaten all odds to assemble a team of seasoned professionals, sometimes on terms that bettered market pay. He had broken through the first obstacle of a conservative mindset and paid what it took to get the best. Not often heard of in small family-run companies in India. Now the task was to mould them into a team.

Likewise, following the same process, the next level of thirty managers were added: MBAs, chartered accountants and technologists from some of the best-known companies in India. Getting them to become part of the Marico team was not easy. Many times, it was necessary to convince them why joining Marico would be beneficial to their learning and careers. For one, they would be at the heart of creating strategy and making decisions—big policy decisions. Global brand decisions which included advertising, packaging etc. were usually dictated by global headquarters. Also, by and large, new local products and brands did not 'fit' into the brand baskets of MNCs as their focus was on creating only global brands. This allowed for limited career growth for the candidate; at best, executional skills were required. Whereas, in Marico, the employee was empowered with decision-making, thereby calling upon not just their marketing competency, but also enabling their entrepreneurial skills in creating something from the ground up.

The third step in the talent acquisition drive was to assemble a team of graduating MBAs through a management trainee scheme to groom future talent. So Jeswant went to the top business schools like the IIMs, FMS Delhi (Faculty of Management Studies), Bajaj and XLRI (Xavier's Labour Relation Institute) and made presentations to the graduating batches. The first batch saw five MBAs. A couple of years later, these MBAs went back to their campuses and talked to their juniors about what they had experienced and contributed at Marico. The few who had risked joining an unknown company in the early nineties opened up a flow that sustains to this day, and generations of young managers have walked the corridors of Marico, contributing to its growing significance as a business and a well-regarded company. The first few years of this talent acquisition programme were tough. Marico was an unknown employer and had to build a prominence with the student community. In later years, however, the pipeline building activity became more coherent. By building these talent pipelines, Marico successfully insulated itself from frequent market sourcing interventions and built a credible succession programme.

Harsh had visualized that one day, he would be steering a professionally managed and profitable consumer brands company. For Harsh, this vision was not a pie in the sky. He had a strategy. To break away from the small company mindset, he was willing to take risks like he did when he decided to pay competitive salaries to hire the best. Without taking these kinds of risks, he couldn't have built a business of scale, something most entrepreneurs find hard to do.

Says Harsh:

'Many entrepreneurs underestimate the impact good talent can create in building a business. Most of them recruit expertise as a reactive measure to cope with growth, rather than proactively investing in competency prior to growth. Entrepreneurs have to actively play a role to attract expertise in a highly competitive job market. A strategy which paid off when Marico turnover grew from ₹80 crore in 1990 to ₹648 crore in the year 2000: a CAGR of 24 per cent in ten years.'

Commenting on Harsh's Actions in Hiring Talent, Prof. Ram Charan Says:

'Many entrepreneurs and start-ups have a common anxiety that they cannot attract great talent from larger companies, and this can soon become a self-fulfilling myth.

'Harsh believed he could and fought the odds to create the conditions that would help him recruit great talent. He did this by creating a vision of the business and by painting a picture of what could be achieved. He was willing to pay what it took to invite talent and then empower them to lead and contribute.

'The first good employee then became a magnet for others. It happens to all young entrepreneurs: at some point they have to recruit their first major employee. This is one of the most crucial decisions for an emerging company. They will need to recruit people better than themselves, people who know more about key functions. Such recruits customarily come from overhead-intensive large companies, with high salaries and expense budgets.

'Harsh was determined to take that big step. His natural instincts of listening, drawing out the psychological world of the prospect and visualizing the prospect in action convinced Harsh to grab Jeswant. Harsh then persuaded him by painting a picture of the future prospects they could achieve together, things that Jeswant couldn't do elsewhere.

This ability to see that which is missing and build a narrative around it is a rare skill in Harsh's suite.

'Aspiring entrepreneurs can take a leaf out of Harsh's leadership playbook.

'There are talented people out there who would love to join entrepreneurs and businesspeople like Harsh. Will it to happen and it would.'

9

A Shared Vision: A Unique Culture

The year 1992 saw Marico moving its corporate headquarters to Bandra Reclamation, Bombay. Located about 20 km away from the then Central Business Districts of the ports (including Masjid Bunder), Ballard Estate and Nariman Point. The office, which sprawled over three floors, faced the Arabian Sea. A huge and extremely refreshing change from the closed and inward-looking office at Masjid Bunder. This location also addressed a key work-life balance issue: the commute became less tiresome for a majority of employees. An added positive was the availability of ample parking space.

Setting the tone for reinforcing the values of Marico, the brief given to the architect was that the office should mirror openness and transparency (among the core values of Marico). All cabins, including, of course, the managing director's cabin, were designed such that every worktable faced a glass wall. Each cabin had a separate round table at which the incumbent would sit across the visitor—symbolically doing away with a visitor having to face the occupant across an imposing desk.

One of Harsh's innovative ideas at that time, which met with much popularity within as well as outside the organization, was the introduction of a popcorn break daily at 4 p.m. The fragrance of butter popcorn wafting through the office was irresistible—and caused many a visitor to openly request for meetings at 4 p.m.—'popcorn time'.

Harsh was nearly forty years old when Marico was incorporated. The age group of his immediate team then ranged between thirty-four and forty years, most of them closer to him in age. Discerning this phenomenon, Shreekant said, 'The thing Harsh got right was to get a set of accomplished people with different skill sets and experiences. Each of them could have become prima donnas and pushed their own furrows. The fantastic thing about Harsh was his prescience. Instead of choosing to govern them, he created a shared vision, a set of values and a collective form of leadership that everyone would then live by.'

Also, by 1992, more than thirty managers had joined the company at the top and senior levels of management. They came from companies with diverse cultures, some multinationals and some home grown: Nestle, Unilever, Procter & Gamble, Asian Paints, Tata Group, Johnson & Johnson and Blow Plast, to name a few. Also present were the 200-odd old employees from the erstwhile Bombay Oil. It was a melting pot of cultures. Particularly, the senior managers, who had their own way of doing things, learnt from their past companies. There were frequent debates and arguments on the right process and the right action to be followed. Harsh, from his many readings, had some definite ideas but did not want these thrust down forcibly. How could Marico synthesize these many competing signals in the absence of a clearly articulated Marico approach? For instance, how should a manager deal with a team member falling short on performance? One manager fired the team member. Another shared their misgivings and gave the assistant time to pull up their socks. A third decided to guide and train as a way of improving performance. Harsh recognized this problem soon enough and discussed the issue with Jeswant. They concluded that the need was to design a culture by creating a set of shared values. A culture that was relevant to its business and managers and that which would characterize Marico's personality.

Defining Values

Harsh read books on management by the dozen. Among the authors who influenced his thinking on values and culture were Peter Senge, Dr Sumantra Ghoshal and Dr S.K. Chakraborty. He was particularly interested in reading the histories of successful companies and the biographies of well-regarded business leaders. It was his habit to highlight the insights he gained from these readings. He would often share these insights with his top team. These readings and his own ideas became the background notes from which he drafted his core beliefs. Harsh was, in his usual systematic and thoughtful way, thinking ahead and ruminating on how to instil some of these into Marico's work culture.

Harsh shared these notes with his top management team of five: Shreekant, Pranab, Praveen, Raj and Jeswant. Much of it resonated with the team. Others needed dialoguing, nuancing and alignment. All these notes that Harsh generated were debated and deliberated with this team for ten to twelve days over a six-month period, along with value additions by the team members.

A draft document was now ready. The team was deeply conscious of the fact that most companies spoke about 'culture' but there was no clear understanding of what it was or how to build it. In many organizations, culture was a consequence of a history of practices, some desirable and some not so. Sometimes the culture of an organization was at variance with any scripted document of vision and values. This typically happened when the statement was intellectually scripted and posted on company walls without due regard to the already existing culture. Often times, practices were not consistent with the values stated and what was practised, causing scepticism down the line.

Harsh and his team were clear that they would want the document, created over months of effort, to be a living and breathing one. It needed to be owned and proactively practised by one and all instead of being a mere set of buzzwords stored for posterity.

The next step was to deliberate the draft values with a wider team of senior managers. This team of thirty managers reported directly to the vice presidents. The thirty managers also joined Harsh and his top management team at a resort in Madh Island for a two-day workshop. Dr Mrityunjay Athreya, a former professor at IIM Calcutta, London Business School and Strathclyde Business School, Scotland, and later an eminent business and management advisor, led and facilitated the workshop. Dr Athreya was a popular teacher and management thinker, well versed in the concept of 'dharma', meaning righteousness, moral conduct and duty, drawn from ancient Indian teachings. In his well thought-out and inimitable style and amid exercises, flipcharts and small group discussions, the managers agreed on a set of values grouped under the 3 P's: People, Products and Profits. There was now a wider appreciation and buy-in of the company values among the top and senior leadership teams. The document, called the '3 P's of Marico', was then finalized and crafted. The challenge now was to make it a living philosophy and a descriptor of its culture.

At no stage were the company values forcibly implemented. Harsh wanted to make sure that every employee would voluntarily adopt company values and even be empowered to act on them as policies and processes were formulated and progressed. He stated that only when the senior management would adopt, practise and reinforce these values, would they percolate through the entire organization. He therefore encouraged and urged all members to call out the company or leadership, should any action of theirs contravene any of the stated values.

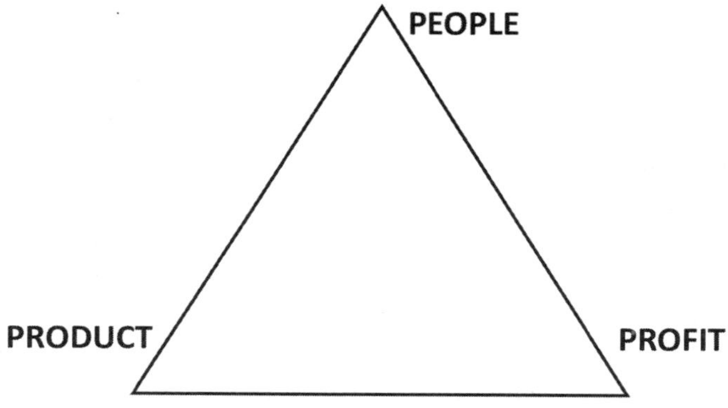

3 P's OF MARICO

PEOPLE

People are our greatest strength, be *they* our consumers, business partners or organization members. People buy OUR products, supply us with goods and services, and provide intelligence and energy in making things happen for us. People also create products and profits for us. We will invest in mutually beneficial relationships with people.

PRODUCTS

Consumer satisfaction from our products is the end result of all people endeavour in the organization. We shall create products of superior quality serving the needs of the Indian household. We shall offer to our consumers value for money. We will generate and sustain a desire in the consumer to continue buying our products. We shall be known by the products we market.

PROFITS

Profit is the universal indicator of how well we perform in satisfying the needs of the Indian household. Profits are essential for continuous reinvestment in expanding the market of our existing products, in creating new products, processes and markets, in keeping the organization revitalized and our people renewed. As a profitable company, we can invest in improving the quality of work life within and also provide to people opportunities for personal growth and prosperity. In short, profits will be viewed as a source of wealth maximization for all stakeholders.

The 3-P's are intimately interrelated. One cannot subsist without the others. The 3-P's can be visualized as the three cornerstones of a mutually reinforcing and synergistic triangle, each drawing from the other to create more of itself.

Harsh and a few of his top team members travelled to all Marico locations to communicate and discuss the company values with employees and launch the 3 P's document. Through such a cascade process, the 3 P's philosophy was explained to everyone in the entire Marico organization.

Following the communication process was a two-day training workshop where participants discussed case studies. The objective was to help the participants understand the nuances of each value as well as dilemmas when a stated value was sometimes seemingly at odds with another value. The purpose of these training sessions was to drive involvement, commitment and ownership towards values across the organization. The values document was prominently displayed and a published hand-out was made available to each employee. A more detailed values handbook acted as a reference guide for managers.

With the values well communicated, the onus was on the leadership to demonstrate its seriousness and commitment. Most companies craft a set of values and display it prominently. Some live by it partially. Others carry on doing what they did before, despite any statement of values. Marico approached it differently by carrying out a baseline survey to determine gaps between what was stated and what was actually practised. Where large gaps existed, a further discussion was triggered and problem areas were identified. Individuals or task forces were then asked to generate solutions to resolve the issue. Some 'big' issues were included in the leadership performance goal sheets so as to ensure that these received committed attention. These baseline value surveys were repeated each year for several years. This was meant to track whether the company leadership 'walked the talk' and whether the value gaps were being whittled down progressively. These deliberations also led to identifying gaps between stated values and current practices. Over a period of time, this led to many initiatives which ensured that ongoing processes which had deviated would fall in line with the values statement.

One of the biggest issues that got identified on the product value was that the factories were crowded and unclean and the output quality needed improvement. This was known to all but prevailing standards and a frugal approach to capital expenditure had left these issues unattended. It impacted all the values: people, product and profit. It impacted the people value as working conditions were poor, leading to a predisposition for workplace accidents. The product value was also compromised as finished packs were often smeared with oil, impacting product aesthetics, image and demand. The profit value was affected through re-work, market returns and wastages. The consequence of this feedback were new capital investments, resulting in the upgradation of the coconut oil factory at Sewri, Bombay, plans to set up a new greenfield coconut oil factory, the acquisition and upgradation of an edible oil refinery in Jalgaon, Maharashtra and the closure of the old refinery at Mazgaon, Bombay. This involved finding additional funds, term loans and loan servicing costs at a time when its equity leverage and reserves were poor. What appeared as poor working conditions led to a complete overhaul of the manufacturing set-up. Not just that. The company followed up by hiring Eicher Consulting Services and Qimpro to learn and implement Total Quality Management. This example of making huge capital investments, among many others, demonstrated unequivocally Harsh's commitment to setting right inherited errors and oversights, and to walking the talk on values.

Another dimension of values was to function in a **boundary-less** way and encourage multiple-way communication. Most organizations then maintained hierarchical distances between owner-promoters, leadership, senior executives, staff and workmen. Marico decided against adopting these artificial hierarchies. It flattened the organization, with the first level of CXOs focusing on the whole; the next level of managers focused on delivering functional outcomes; a third level of young managers focused on execution and the blue-collared members ran the production lines.

People addressed each other by first names. There were no 'sirs'. Harsh was 'Harsh' to all. There were no 'employees' at Marico. Terms like boss, subordinate, manager, staff and worker were seldom found in the Marico lexicon. All were **members**. Members had a voice in shaping the outcomes and future of the organization. The organization promoted team culture and multiple teams and forums were instituted. Almost all organization members were part of one team or another. **Participation** in teams ranging from planning to performance reviews to problem-solving projects, brought in **involvement** and **ownership** to the tasks at hand. The teamwork extended to organizing social and cultural events involving members and their families.

One such team was the Strategy Business Plan (SBP) Task Force. Each year, an eight-member team of functional experts was selected and tasked with creating a three-year rolling plan that included environment analysis, portfolio analysis, competition maps, growth areas, new products, cost efficiency opportunities and financial forecasts. The SBP team was led by a member of the top management. The task force worked through a period of six months to assemble a plan, which was then presented to a wider body consisting of Harsh, the top management team and a group of senior managers. After a process of rigorous debate and critique, the iterated plan was formalized.

The annual budget was cast as a sequel to this SBP and crystallized to 'Organization and Functional Thrust Areas' and 'Member Goal Sheets'. Each year, the composition of the SBP team changed, ensuring that more members got an opportunity to view the business in its completeness and brought this to bear on their regular work. An extract of the SBP and annual plan was used as a communication tool along with the Organization and Functional Thrust Areas.

The plans were then presented to all the members at different company locations followed by a Q&A. This ensured that every member of the organization knew what the expected outcomes were. The process of planning that started at the mid to senior levels of the organization, and later involved everyone else, ensured that each member was fully aligned and knew his or her share of the delivery. Importantly, it also meant also meant that Marico trusted its members with information that most other companies would hesitate to share.

Trust was another value inherent in the philosophy of membership. Stemming from this value, attendance records were done away with and members were encouraged to manage their own time. In return, the company expected its members to not compromise on performance and be accountable for the results as set in their performance goal sheets. Members were free to come to work or leave work flexibly. They could take a day off if they were unwell or had an important social engagement or a family emergency. The concept of sick leave and casual leave was discarded and members received salaries for the whole month despite unplanned absences. They only needed to keep their seniors informed and ensure that they made alternative arrangements for the day's deliveries. Likewise, members were empowered to manage their own vacation plans in consultation with their seniors. Complicated leave rules, leave application forms, issues of leave accumulation, carry-forwards and records were eliminated and there was no more need to administer these. The company had moved away from the idea of policing employees and bureaucratic procedures. Likewise, the system of authorizing expenses by members was also quashed. The norm in most organizations for claiming reimbursement of expenses incurred on behalf of the company, like conveyance, travel, telecom etc., would be raised through a claim to be approved by a superior. Marico defined clear policies regarding reimbursement. Approvals were not required. Self-authorization was valid, and thus, trust-generating values further reinforced. Random checks were carried out to detect any misuse of this policy.

Members appreciated the trust extended by the company and feedback received was that they felt liberated from the act of asking and being granted their requests by a 'superior'. The philosophy of membership implied that there were no bosses, but mentors. Any violations or subversion of the trust were few and far between and were dealt with severely and termination was instant. Trust was non-negotiable. This approach stemmed from the belief that people were by and large responsible individuals, and that the company need not have elaborate rules and procedures applied to all. A study carried out by the HR team reported that people actually behaved more responsibly and took less casual time off, than when they were under a system of leave quotas.

Harsh encouraged calculated **risk-taking**. Experimenting, doing things differently, questioning an existing wisdom were all sources of innovation. He would want his leadership teams to propagate this value as the planned and executed strategy. But he would caution against taking reckless risks. That is, taking risks without weighing the consequences. Making a mistake or a wrong decision was acceptable so long as due consideration was given to the pros and cons. It was all right to make a mistake, but it was also important that lessons are drawn. 'There is no shame in failing. Learn from failures; they teach lessons and are a route to success,' repeated Harsh time and again. Well aware that breakthroughs often were the result of experimentation, he didn't want his people to play safe and stick to the straight and narrow. Pulling up people for failure would shut down risk-taking and stymie growth opportunities, he felt.

One of the other values recognized that members had multiple roles in life. Only one of these was work. So, the stated culture encouraged the idea of **work-life balance**. By itself the statement looked fine, but sometimes, seemingly, came in conflict with another value, typically the one on meeting **performance standards** and deadlines. On one occasion, a deadline required team members to stretch their work hours to even include the weekend. A team member brought this up in one of the feedback forums. He complained that he felt compelled to put in extra hours over the weekend, as his colleagues seemed to voluntarily do so. He was reluctant to follow suit, as leaving late meant reaching home after his children had gone to bed and working the weekend meant that his family time was further compromised. He argued that the demand for extra work hours was not compliant with the spirit of the company's values. Another member then clarified that the company supported work-life balance as a principle, and this would be true most times. But once in a while there would be a need to stretch: to meet a larger goal that is important to the company. He reminded the complainant the company did not demand a 9–5 attendance and was flexible with its time, and that members too needed to be reciprocally flexible in return. The idea that values need to be understood holistically and not as a single strand became clearer as more such dilemmas began to emerge between the various statements covered in the 3 P's document.

Openness was another professed value. So when Marico moved its headquarters to Bandra, it had an open office plan that characterized transparency and openness. It was one of the first open office designs in India then. The cabins were partitioned with glass, enabling all to see each other. Harsh himself had a glass-walled cabin, clearly visible to all. The atmosphere in the office was relaxed. People walked across to talk to each other in preference to the intercom, be it work or chat over a cup of coffee or tea. All of this contributed to give the office a physical sense of openness.

Harsh was convinced of the need to bring in openness as he had heard from his corporate friends and employees of politics, lobbying, back-biting and games of one-upmanship that were deep-rooted in organizations where openness was absent. Many loathed these cultures for the insecurity and other dysfunctionalities they caused. So he wanted to create an organization that allowed for free expression and feedback. He encouraged the behaviour of critique in preference to the act of criticizing. Criticism is name-calling, directed at a person and leads to psychological hurt and damage, whereas critique is directed at observed behaviour with opportunities for improvement. Marico institutionalized openness and two-way communication through a series of initiatives.

An event called Organization Communication (OC) was designed and implemented at all Marico locations, once a year. Harsh and his top management team travelled to eight different conference venues to meet assemblies of Marico members there. At these gatherings, Harsh, addressing all members, would present an overview of how the company performed in the past year, following which he would share the plans for the coming year. Members of the top management then presented their functional accomplishments of the past year and their goals for the next year. It was almost as if the top management was reporting its performance to the rest of the organization. Like investors, members too would ask questions to the top management as well as to Harsh on strategy and performance. Harsh and his team would diligently respond to all these questions, respecting that member careers are intertwined with that of the company. A session on values followed where participants shared anecdotes of their successes and challenges on values practice. A values award was presented to the member who had overcome the largest odds. An open house invited the audience to share issues that impacted their association with Marico. The feedback included issues related to their career, work, human resource policies and bureaucratic delays in settling expenses and claims. Some of these found immediate resolution. Those reluctant to reveal their identity could voice their queries anonymously in a drop box. An awards night and dinner closed the day. Since the formation of Marico in 1990, these OCs have become a much-awaited event, and a single-point occasion to share, celebrate, rejoice and form new commitments. They are the highlight of the year at all sales regions and factories, including the international locations where Marico offices are based.

Introducing and making these changes signalled that Marico was standing by its word in the practice of values. Many momentous decisions and practices were implemented based on member feedback. The value survey scores improved significantly year-on-year, indicating that employee confidence was at a high.

Harsh remarked, 'The culture building process was time-consuming but laid a valuable foundation. The biggest benefit was that it aligned everyone. It created a culture of dialogue, candour and trust. It was a shared culture, so everyone had a stake in shaping it. People acted more responsibly. There was seldom an occasion to seriously admonish or discipline someone. The senior management had to lead from the front. The whole credibility would be lost if a senior manager behaved in a manner contrary to what was stated and understood by all. Culture creates results and motivation only if everyone believes in it and truly practises it. Openness, trust and empowerment, combined with a flat organizational structure, along with a diverse set of talents but devoid of hierarchy, further paves the road for innovation.'

The investment in culture-building made in the formative years, and the many organizational processes repeated year upon year, reinforced and ensured the perpetuity of the culture.

Pranab Datta, vice president—finance was a hard-nosed and result-oriented business manager. Ideas like culture building and values were esoteric concepts to him. Although Pranab went along with the body that scripted the values, he probably did not have as much faith in the company culture having the firepower to enable performance. He preferred to invest money in tangible outcomes. He would jokingly say at a closed-door top management team meeting, 'Hey, what do you want me to do? Do my job or practise values? I can't do both.' Much later, he was to admit, 'Working openly with each other in a hierarchy-less way has been enriching. In the past, I would begin with the premise of aggressively furthering my view or defending my actions. In doing so, I was saying that I know best and I am the expert here. Now I listen more and incorporate other viewpoints. I realize that I am a part of the whole and others too have a stake in the well-being of the company. Living this culture has changed me and I have begun to believe that an engaging and open culture actually delivers business results.'

The open office, organization communication, performance and career discussions, peer relationship reviews, values training and such other institutional mechanisms ensured that the performance and behavioural culture in the organization was internalized, nurtured and reinforced in perpetuity. As Marico moved geographies through acquisitions, it made sure that these very mechanisms were firmly implanted in the new organizations. The value surveys were another way in which Marico made sure that there was no dilution. A poor score led to diagnostics and corrective interventions. Harsh himself modelled the desired behaviour as it had become second nature to him. So it was with the leadership teams.

As the years passed, Marico built a legion of ex-Mariconians. These were people who left the company for newer challenges. From time to time they would come back to visit and sometimes Harsh would have chance meetings at social events, public engagements or during travels. They would tell Harsh of how they retained a fondness for the unique and innovative ways by which Marico worked and lived—the very things which made Marico thrum. The openness, empowerment and environment of learning were things that they valued most. Every few years or so, when Marico crossed major milestones, like it did in 2005 when it reached a turnover of ₹1000 crore, and again as it crossed ₹2000 and ₹5000 crore (US$715 million in 2019), Harsh hosted get-togethers for Mariconians that included the alumni. This was Harsh's unique way of expressing his gratitude to those who walked through, left a bit of themselves behind and took a bit of Marico with them.

They would tell Harsh and the rest that Marico was memorably the best company that they had worked for. A few of these reminiscences: 'Harsh, I have remained in touch with a number of my old colleagues and the unanimous conclusion is that Marico was the best company we worked at.' – Amit Nandi, ex-Mariconian.

'I was deeply touched at the farewell I received from my colleagues, as I left for a larger role in Britannia after seventeen long years with Marico. I was very happy to return when Marico offered to take me back for a bigger role: the culture, the people and the nostalgia clinched it for me.' – Jitendra Mahajan, currently back at Marico.

'As a young brand manager, I was presenting something on packaging. Harsh disagreed with my view. I refused to withdraw from my line of argument insisting that it was only me who had seen consumer reaction. He always tested our convictions and let us run with the ball.' – Sameer Satpathy, ITC Limited.

'I couldn't have gotten as far as I did without the learnings at Marico. It shaped me and helped me to become the president—farm equipment and member of the group executive board at Mahindra & Mahindra.' – Rajesh Jejurikar, executive director, auto and farm sectors, Mahindra Group.

'I have been appointed as the CEO and MD of ACC Ltd. Whatever I am is due to my experience at Marico. I will always be grateful to Marico.' – Sridhar Balakrishnan, managing director at ACC Ltd.

Harsh's innovative practice of consciously designing and building Marico's culture cemented a bonding and promoted a sense of ambassadorship among the Marico alumni. It was heartening for Harsh to note the many accomplishments of the company alumni.

The idiom that 'nice guys finish last' wasn't invented at Marico. Instead, Marico was a case of the 'nice guy winning'. It was both, a preferred employer and a sought-after scrip. No small wonder then that the Marico scrip delivered 850 per cent returns in the last ten years (source: ETMarkets.com, 21 February 2018). It was frequently among the top rankers of 'preferred employers'. It ranked twenty-first among Asia's Best Large Workplaces in 2019 (source: The Great Place to Work Institute). The foundations of the culture remained strong despite the passage of three decades and the company's growth in size and spread.

Behavioural Training

Most companies train their employees in technical skills and business skills. Marico, too, had its fair share of such 'skill' training programmes, with a large part of its training in behavioural areas that emphasized the 'will'. It was a deliberate strategy 'to do the right things the right way'.

Defining the values was the first step. Communicating them was the second. Addressing the value gap was third. Behavioural training, the fourth.

The overriding culture and the way in which people behaved and conducted themselves in the organization would rub off and eventually be internalized by newcomers. But that wasn't sufficient. So it was mandated that all newcomers should go through at least three training programmes in the first two years.

Management by Results focused on the process and motivational aspects of setting and measuring performance goals. It introduced the concept of basic and stretch goals. At the basic level was the result that the company had budgeted. The stretch levels varied, based on the potential and ability of a person to do a plus on the basic. The goal setting and performance evaluation process was accomplished through dialogue and agreement, and the training modelled this exchange.

Values Workshops introduced the concept and practice of values in the company. It helped newcomers understand the rationale and nuances of the values through caselets and anecdotal experiences.

Relationship Management Programme focused on leadership and relationships with seniors, peers and juniors. It helped identify individual styles of leading and relating with people and then helped participants to learn and practise more effective styles.

Apart from these, work teams were encouraged to explore and review the nature of interpersonal dynamics and effectiveness in the team, at least once a year. Called **Relationship Reviews**, these team building exercises aimed at improving the behavioural health of teams. Harsh and his top management team were also part of this annual exercise, dubbed TMT Retreat.

Some of these were led by internal trainers and others by external trainers. Harsh summed up the culture building effort best when he said, 'I am really pleased with the atmosphere in the company. Hard-nosed on performance, but convivial in the way people relate with one another. Importantly, owing to the various mechanisms and forums that have been instituted, differences and conflicts are amicably resolved.

'Some of my business-leader friends would ask me why I was wasting time and money on culture building and training. My reasoning was that the purpose of business organizations was not only about making goods and money. It was also about doing it joyously and ethically. I was convinced that a holistic approach to organization building was what was needed to build an institution that would survive generations.'

Values in Design

Soon after joining Marico, Shreekant Gupte, as the vice president—manufacturing operations, visited the two Marico factories in Bombay. From hearsay, he assumed that the factories needed refurbishing, but wasn't prepared for what he found. 'The winds of technology have not touched this company for years,' Gupte said to Harsh. 'The factories need an overhaul. We'll need to add capacities. The managers at the factories work hard and manage constraints as frugally as possible but stop short of asking for new investments'. This wasn't news to Harsh. He had already flagged it in his 'critical to-do list'.

As Gupte considered options for expanding and contemporizing Marico's manufacturing efforts, he cast a wide net. They could start a new factory anywhere in India—the field was wide open. He looked into options from Gujarat and Goa in the west to Pondicherry and Kerala in the south.

Since its beginnings, Bombay Oil procured its raw material, copra, from Kerala, which produced about two-thirds of India's coconuts. In fact, the name 'Kerala' means 'land of coconut trees.' Yet for generations, that region was notoriously averse to industry. Kerala was the heart of socialism in India, with a popularly elected Communist government. Among businessmen, Gupte said, the state had a 'very well-earned terrible reputation'. Gupte cited the popular saying that 'in Kerala, if you have three employees, you'll have four labour unions.'

So, when Gupte made his recommendation to build a factory in Kerala, everybody was horror-struck. 'They thought that I had gone off my rocker,' said Gupte. Harsh weighed the pros and cons. Marico had reasons to try something new.

First, the company would benefit from reduced transport costs by placing a factory close to the source of its raw material. Second, the Kerala state government offered financial incentives for a factory set up in the state, including land at a very low cost, electricity at subsidized rates and lower purchase tax on copra. Finally, the labour pool was top quality; Kerala had among the best educated population in India. For these reasons, Gupte made the case to go to Kerala with eyes open and do something completely different.

Ghanshyam Pant, a part of Gupte's operations team, had made a few trips to Kerala in order to identify potential sites where the factory could be located. While returning by train from one of these visits, he struck up a conversation with a fellow passenger. The gentleman hailed from Kerala and was returning to Bangalore after a short holiday in his home state. When Ghanshyam mentioned the purpose of his visit to Kerala, the gentleman was incredulous. 'Are you mad?' he blurted out. 'You will almost certainly lose money. Pack your bags and cut your losses. If you invest and commence operations, labour unions will begin agitating within a year and you will be compelled to leave and end up losing much more. Don't be foolhardy, abandon your plans now.' Ghanshyam said he was surprised that a person belonging to Kerala was discouraging investments in his state. To him, the explanation was obvious. 'Why do you think that most Malayalis work outside the state? Why do you think I work in a neighbouring state? There are so many negative forces in our state. They won't allow businesses to prosper in Kerala. You still have time. Go back.'

When Harsh shared the plan with members of the family, they advised against the move. The Mariwala family were already familiar with industry in Kerala and their personal experiences with running factories were none too good. Other well-meaning friends held a similar view. 'It is imprudent for a company to contemplate setting up a factory in a state known for its rampant labour troubles,' they cautioned.

The paradox of Kerala has long been that though it had the highest literacy rates in the country, it had one of the worst records in industrial development due to militant trade unionism. Consequently, the astute minds that grew up and got educated there were forced to seek opportunities in other places. They chose to go to cities like Bombay, Calcutta and Delhi and later to countries in the Middle East.

Harsh asked Gupte and Nair to work on the proposal and come back with why they thought they could make a success of it, despite the commonly held belief that factory operation in Kerala was a non-starter.

The project team conducted insight dialogues with people around Kanjikode, where the factory was proposed to be located. What they realized was that the root cause of the troublesome labour attitude was a feeling of being exploited and being merely used as a factor of production. Workers also believed that managements never really cared for their well-being and development and did not treat them with respect. To them, work was boring and monotonous. Later, in the after-hours at the villages where they lived, there was nothing much to do but indulge in idle talk. Included were local politics, work incidents of the day, complaints about inadequate remuneration and happenings in the neighbouring factories. Political parties, particularly the Communist parties, were an integral part of their growing up years, be it in high schools, colleges or at the panchayats and government departments. The agitation, protest and strike culture had become generic to the population. With nothing much to do and nothing much to look forward to in life, the spectacle of 'the idle mind being a devil's workshop' came into full play.

Gupte and Nair told Harsh that the benefits that could accrue would far outweigh the disadvantage of labour militancy. They argued that they could minimize this risk by eliminating the root causes that led to labour agitation. It was also a fond hope that Marico would, in the process, discover new paradigms in industrial relations.

Gupte envisioned a unique factory in Kerala that put worker interests, their families and those of the community on priority. To flesh out this vision, a task force of manufacturing and human resource managers worked over several sessions to develop a Kanjikode Vision Document—Continuous CARE (it was an anagram—**continuous** improvement in everything: Culture, Aesthetics, Reliability, External image). The Kanjikode vision was inspired by the 3 P's values document and drew heavily from it. Besides fair wage, workers would be encouraged to learn and practise multiple skills and perform a variety of jobs to prevent monotony and boredom. A planned job rotation would also help the company with a large, multi-skilled workforce. The factory campus would have recreational areas and employees could come in before work or stay after hours to enjoy sports. Since jobs changed frequently through job rotation, individuals would not be a permanent part of any departmental team. Their social environment at work and departmental identity would be in a state of flux. To obviate this, the task force innovated and came up with a 'house system', borrowing a paradigm from schools. They were organized into non-work 'house teams' that competed against each other at games and other cultural activities. They were also given opportunities to perform management tasks, be involved in shop floor operational decision-making and run the various social and welfare amenities in the establishment. The thought process behind this approach stemmed from the conclusion that regular rotation of jobs as well as extra-curricular activities would keep the member-employees engaged in multiple ways, thereby improving the quality of their life by providing diverse stimuli.

Before they made the final decision to set up the factory at Kanjikode in the district of Palakkad, Harsh visited the proposed site and listened to the Kanjikode vision presentations from the task force. The presentations plus the picturesque site with its surrounding mountains and stunning backdrop impressed him. He got a good vibe. So he encouraged the team to move forward.

Before recruiting a blue-collar member, a Marico officer would visit the prospect's home and meet the family. They would tell them about the company that their ward was about to join. The purpose of opening this dialogue was also to psychologically connect the family to the well-being of Marico. It was hoped that a good work and social environment in the workplace coupled with encouragement from the family would go a long way in averting militancy. During the course of the year, there would be scheduled occasions when the company would invite the families to participate in celebrations and festivities, including performances by members in music, dance and theatre. A bond between fellow members, families and the company was being nurtured through these interventions.

The hotbed for disgruntlement and union activity was typically in operations that demanded physically intensive work repeatedly. One such area was in material handling, which traditionally involved carrying gunny bags of copra to feed the mills. The engineering teams worked with an equipment manufacturing vendor to design an automated material handling system of silos for copra storage and conveyors to feed the mills—the first time such mechanization was attempted in copra milling. This eliminated labour-intensive work in the factory, particularly from stores to the mills.

The blue-collar members were in place a few months ahead of the factory being commissioned for commercial production and were trained in Marico values, work design and practices and plant and machinery operations. Probably the first time that a blue-collar workforce was being exposed to the idea of going beyond being a factor of production to taking on other responsibilities as members of the Marico community.

Vijayan, a valued senior member of the corporate HR team, succeeded Ganshyam Pant as the general manager of the Kanjikode factory two years after its commissioning. Vijayan's specific skill sets and his Kerala roots helped augment the foundations laid by Pant, particularly in the areas of culture building and community outreach.

Harsh was pleased with the decision to go to Kerala and the results that followed. The prophets of doom conceded that the approach that Marico adopted was refreshingly different and the returns handsome. In the first ten years of its existence, the payback from the factory was more than ten times the cost of the project. Kanjikode also set a benchmark. It created a template for Marico to use when it set up newer factories at other locations.

All told, the selection of Kerala confirmed a popular saying at Marico:

> 'The mind is like a parachute.
> It works only when open.'

Looking Back, Harsh Comments:

'There were a number of firsts and paradigm shifts in setting up this factory. The investment in training and culture-building too paid off. The factory enjoyed a union-free environment for over five years, and though the unions finally crept in, production remained uninterrupted for another five years, helping Marico reap the benefit of sales tax exemptions and saving on raw material and logistics costs.'

Harsh Goes On to Reiterate:

'In the over thirty years since its inception, Marico has seen leadership changes, capability growth, new business acquisitions and several geographic expansions, but what remains at the heart of Marico are its values and culture. These act as the guiding light for all its processes, starting from the way it hires to the way it evaluates. To sustain and constantly enhance the culture, it believes in continuous improvement through the 5E Model: Educate, Engage, Enable, Evaluate and Evolve. It starts right from the hiring, where it follows the Marico Leadership Competency Framework, which has a strong linkage with its core values. Further, when a member joins, an extensive onboarding programme is organized for enculturation and familiarization. Several interventions are planned in the form of leadership connects, mentorship programmes, townhall sessions and buddy connects to engage members by building a strong sense of belonging. Marico leaders play an important part in enabling members to unleash their full potential and act as role models. The same values are also used to evaluate, reward and recognize members for "making a difference" in the organization. Further, the continuous reflection and feedback loop in the form of engagement and value surveys ensures that we engage in constant evolution of the culture. Marico's culture continues to be its most powerful force which shapes its decision patterns, guides actions, and drives individual behaviour of all members.

'Culture is a set of shared beliefs, norms, values and attitudes that binds all parts of the organization, and is focal in driving strategy within. For values to be converted into a strong culture, they have to be reinforced on a perpetual basis. For example, if the organization has to drive innovation, it would be built on values of openness, trust, dialogue, experimentation and removing fear of failure. The larger challenge for any organization is to maintain culture long-term. In order to preserve this, top-level commitment is very crucial, and equally important is that newcomers are initiated with a strong buy-in to the culture.

The value of openness in Marico was emphasized, among other practices, through the designing of open offices as well as holding an open house or OC (Organization Communication) at all Marico locations yearly. Relationships reviews of teams were also part of the exercise. In short, culture offers a competitive advantage because it is unique to each organization.'

Says the MD of Kotak Mahindra Bank, Uday Kotak:

'I divide Indian businesses into two categories. One category is the "king and his subjects". This section comprises of Indian businessmen who believe they are king, and the shareholders their subjects. The king can do no wrong and therefore, the subjects should be accepting of what he leaves behind for them.

'The other category is a smaller one. This order believes in what I call the "value system". Here, the interests of the firm transcend those of the individual. Harsh clearly falls into the second category. He creates value for all stakeholders. Another educative facet of Harsh, which I have imbibed, is the development of HR: that, I think, is where value gets established. Which goes on to be then defined as culture.'

Prof. Ram Charan had coached a number of business leaders, advised numerous corporations and observed many organizational cultures. In his view, the largest determinant of organizational culture is the ambience that prevails in the top group of twenty-thirty managers and what they do individually and collectively. Culture is a consequence. He notes that in the 1980s and 1990s, there was very little in the form of literature or case studies on how organizations could build their culture to impact business performance. Perceptive business leaders and thinkers, nevertheless, knew that there was a linkage between engaged employees and extraordinary corporate performance. For Harsh, this knowledge was almost intuitive. He designed a culture, built ownership around it, first with five and then with thirty managers. Together, they became conduits and through their actions, they built a culture of involved employees. Regardless of the fact that nearly thirty years had gone by and his fellow forbearers had departed, the culture of employee involvement at all levels and performance remains rooted.

The professor adds, 'The way Harsh went about culture building, taking concrete steps in designing the culture, training for the culture and embedding the culture, is a master class on how to build an organizational culture of ownership and performance. He prepared a foundation for long-term growth. The company has grown and so has Harsh. He has transitioned from an entrepreneur to an institution builder, to manage big growth and large complexities.'

10

Getting Down to Business

Product Range Expansion

Post the formation of Marico, the tasks of delineating the culture, enlisting talent and synthesizing it into teams had been achieved.

Harsh now needed to address the burning issue of growing Marico's product range. The company's senior leadership had set the ambitious target of tripling revenue to ₹300 crore (US$43 million) by 1995. The need to add new brands and sources of revenue and profit was uppermost in everybody's mind.

As Marico began to acquire scale, sustainability of growth and profitability emerged as key challenges. It was critical to identify sources of competitive advantage.

The company's resource for this initiative was Dr Wayne Brockbank, a clinical professor of business at the University of Michigan. His teaching focuses on strategic human resource management.

Dr Brockbank, a thought leader in the area of delivering strategic outcomes for business, conducted a workshop with the senior management of the company.

Through dialogue and identification, it emerged that Marico's sources of competitive edge were branding, cost management, distribution and innovation.

These four identified competencies needed to be exercised, honed and excelled in for Marico's success, and various interventions were initiated to address the same.

For brand building, Marico studied the processes of a few leading FMCG companies and adapted them to its needs. Stepping up the quality of marketing professionals inducted, Marico began to peg compensation for marketing talent in the top deciles of the industry.

For sales and distribution, it was decided to leverage information technology to improve deliverables. Marico harnessed information technology and connectivity towards integration of the distributors' and company's information systems. This pioneering effort led to significant improvements in market servicing efficiencies, including outlet expansion, outlet coverage, width, depth and reach. Above all, it delivered reduced costs in the sales value chain. Instead of adding size and might to match competing FMCG companies, Marico had focused on quality of processes and trade equity.

Accenture was appointed for delivering cost efficiencies. More importantly, they also brought in an ongoing process, which was installed and improved over the years. The Total Cost Management (TCM) Process has been, since then, the mainstay of Marico's sustained success in cost management.

Innovation was taken up in a structured manner with Erehwon consultants. We also had a full-time internal facilitator to drive innovation.

Within a period of a year and a half, Marico had substantially improved its capabilities in each area of the sources of competitive advantage. That improvement has since been sustained over the years to yield consistently improving results.

Every business has to win against competition at all times. Such winning is not possible on a sustainable basis unless the business has distinct and meaningful sources of competitive advantage.

A few months prior to the formation of Marico, in the year 1990, a refined sunflower oil named 'Sweekar' was launched.

With the birth of Marico and the new team of professionals, the time had come to revisit the new products agenda. There was a frenzy of activity that followed. In the first four years, Marico had two new brand successes in hair and care (a premium, light-perfume hair oil) and Revive (an instant fabric starch). Before the turn of the decade, another niche brand was added to the range when Mediker, an anti-lice shampoo, was acquired from Procter & Gamble.

Growing Parachute

Meanwhile, Parachute coconut oil was the undisputed market leader in the branded coconut oil market with a 50 per cent market share. Dabur Anmol, Shalimar, Nihar, Cococare and Oil of Malabar were some of the other popular coconut oil brands. As Parachute coconut oil constituted a big share of Marico's revenue and profits, it was absolutely critical for Marico to safeguard this brand from all forms of competitive threats.

Parachute's success proved to be a ready market for copycats and counterfeiters. It was flattery by deceit. Fly-by-night firms copied the blue bottles of coconut oil and passed them off as Parachute. Some others would give the name a twist and call the blue bottle Paramount, Paragon and so on. The imitation and the pack graphics were so close that small town consumers couldn't tell one from the other. In one of the surveys conducted by FICCI, Parachute emerged as one of the most copied brands in the country, with over 100 copycats and lookalikes. 'We were the most copied brand in India,' recalled Harsh, 'and were losing 10–15 per cent of our sales to these counterfeits.'

The entry barriers were low. So these firms would enter the market when raw material costs were minimal and price their imitation at a significant discount to Parachute. Fighting these copycats through trademark laws and courts would be a long-drawn affair taking years, when instant justice was what was needed. Shutting them down using criminal laws for cheating would work for a while. But they would start once again in another market with another name. A huge amount of organization time was being expended in reacting to these situations, with no end in sight.

Harsh and his legal team found the exercise of stopping these counterfeiters a futile activity. There wasn't too much of a difference in the raw material. So there needed to be something unique in the packaging that would appeal to the consumer, and which would create an entry barrier. Gupte, on one of his visits to a packaging trade fair in Italy, found a solution: a combination pilfer-proof and easy to pour cap which the counterfeiters would find impossible to copy. A Dutch company helped design a mould for this cap. The capital cost involved in making this mould and the cost of manufacturing these caps would be prohibitive for the fly-by-night outfits and would act as an entry barrier. This assumption was true for a while, but it was just a matter of time before the moulds were produced locally and at more affordable prices. Harsh realized that the innovation efforts in packaging would have to be perpetual in order to just stay ahead of the copycats.

In 1997, Parachute had a 50 per cent market share of branded coconut oils, ₹200 crore in revenue (US$28 million in 2019) and was ranked among the top 100 brands in India. The only way for Parachute to grow was to drive further conversions from loose to packed coconut oils. The idea of offering the smaller 500 ml and 200 ml consumer packs, had already delivered market share and volume gains. It hoped to penetrate even further by launching 100 and 50 ml packs and even smaller pouch packs at affordable price points.

The other part of the same strategy involved contemporizing the brand Parachute. The age-old Parachute brand had stayed the same way ever since plastic packs came into vogue. The brand needed to be revitalized to appeal to the younger generation.

Marico then engaged Paris-based Shombit Sengupta's Shining Strategic Design Company for brand positioning and redesigning the packaging. Shombit held focus group discussions in a number of cities and towns. His research suggested that the brand name Parachute signified the goodness of coconut and was associated with the colour blue. He reported that the perceived values of brand Parachute were purity, nourishment, reliability and heritage. The coconut palms and the brand name Parachute on the bottle were stylized to render a modern looking graphic and font. The bottle was made more attractive with a blue pearly sheened plastic bottle and a flip-top lid, giving it a premium look and feel. The Indian tradition of breaking coconuts on auspicious occasions was rendered into an advertising commercial where a young girl performed the action of breaking a coconut with a Parachute bottle. Together, the new flip-top pack, the introduction of smaller packs and the new look of the brand continued to add new consumers to the franchise and combat competition.

The Nihar and Shalimar brands of coconut oil had a dominant leadership presence in West Bengal and, to a lesser extent, in Bihar, Orissa and eastern UP. The two brands had been around in these markets for a long time. Their heritage did not allow any room for the third brand, Parachute, to grow beyond a point. If Parachute tried to discount the market, so did the competition. Parachute had to break through the veil of their heritage. It needed to keep them busy defending their market share in West Bengal in order to prevent their expansion to other markets and pose a threat to Parachute.

So Marico created Parachute Uttam coconut oil, which was launched only in West Bengal in a green pack with Bengali graphics and commercials. The earlier tactic of discounting the original Parachute blue packs was causing the lower-priced blue packs from West Bengal to infiltrate the neighbouring states of Bihar, Uttar Pradesh and Orissa, adversely impacting net realizations from Parachute blue packs. The launch of Parachute Uttam appealed to the Bengali consumer and its attractive pricing helped nibble away at Nihar and Shalimar in West Bengal, and also arrested the erosion of price premiums enjoyed by Parachute blue packs in the neighbouring states.

Fillip for Growth – Saffola

Saffola was the second flagship brand of Marico. It had emerged as a strong health brand synonymous with heart care. The brand had leveraged scientific research on the benefits of safflower oil in the management of cholesterol. It had invested several years in building the awareness of the brand in the medical fraternity and in educating consumers through advertising. As volumes grew, so did some limitations. Availability of safflower seeds and oil was low. It was not a very remunerative crop for the Indian farmer. Despite Marico's attempts to get more crops grown through agricultural extension work, bringing more land under safflower cultivation and contract farming, the incremental volumes of raw material so generated were insufficient to meet the growing demand. There was a risk of losing sales for a brand that was built with a lot of sweat. Limited availability of safflower made the oil expensive. It was a single season crop and the raw material inventory had to be built up in three months for the entire year. Overseas sources of safflower oil were limited. Marico was the only importer of safflower oil in India, with the minimum shipment being several months' requirement at a time. Working capital turns suffered, and higher interest costs impacted the Saffola financials. The inventory carrying and brand building costs necessitated price increases. The premium price, as compared to the other brands of cooking oil, limited the market for the brand.

Meanwhile, as is often the case, medical opinion had also moved. In the past, safflower oil was preferred for its high PUFA (polyunsaturated fatty acid) content. While some continued to recommend high PUFA oils, another school believed in a PUFA-MUFA (monounsaturated fatty acid) balance.

The business challenge for Saffola was to continue to leverage the brand equity for heart and health while addressing the issue of poor availability of safflower oil seeds and oil. Up until this time, government regulations did not permit the blending of two or more different generic oils. The reason for this rule was the fear of adulteration by manufacturers. Harsh reasoned that this was not sound government policy. He gathered his team of food technologists and asked them to come up with scientific arguments as to why blending and adulterating are two different things. From an economic standpoint, placing such restrictions were counter-productive to the country. The swings in agricultural production, price volatility and frequent imports to meet shortages created conditions that benefited the traders and short-changed the consumer. The license to blend offered a chance to hedge shortages. Blended oils would help the industry offer consumer packs at stable prices and different price points, in preference to only selling generic cooking oils at volatile prices. To the government, it meant less imports and foreign exchange outflows. To the consumers, it brought affordability and more price stability. To the farmer, it offered greater flexibility to grow different oil seeds, based on soil agronomy and weather patterns. It was a win-win for all the stakeholders.

Harsh encouraged his technology team to form a task force of industry players and together represent the issue to the government. He also sought the intervention of other industry bodies to petition the government for a more sound policy for the cooking oil industry.

A team of food technologists from Marico, along with representatives from other edible oil companies, petitioned the Food and Drugs

Department, making a case for blends. The approval to market blends was finally granted in 1998. Harsh and his foods marketing team saw a big opportunity open up for Saffola.

Marico could now invest in renewing the identity of brand Saffola and its 'good for the heart' theme could be leveraged to include other healthy foods in their natural and processed forms. Once again, Shombit Sengupta of Strategic Shinning Design was commissioned to research brand values and create the architecture for brand Saffola. Research indicated a strong association between the brand name, heart and health.

The Saffola brand was then repositioned on the 'heart of a healthy family' platform. The intent was to extend the image from an excellent product for heart problems to heart-healthy foods for the entire family. Its pack graphics and shape underwent a change. From a yellow 'jerry can' kind of a plastic pack used formerly, a heart-shaped, easy-pour, glug-free yellow container was designed, with stylized fonts and graphics. Alongside, it launched the safflower oil blends with corn oil in heart-shaped green jars and with rice bran oil in orange jars. The combined volumes grew 15 per cent in the first year, followed by a 28 per cent growth the year after.

In one masterstroke, Harsh and his team seemed to have freed Saffola from the constraints of raw material availability, the PUFA tag and the stagnant volumes owing to super-premium pricing. This out-of-the-box idea to bring about change in government regulations and to revitalize the brand converted a problem into an opportunity. Saffola oil blends sold more volumes and their premium price ensured healthy add-ons to Marico's profit line. More importantly, Saffola had set itself up as a brand that could be extended to other categories of healthy foods.

In 1998, various experiments of extending the Saffola brand were attempted. Saffola Low Sodium Table Salt, Saffola High Fibre Wheat Flour mix (to be added to atta) and Saffola Rice (with a low glycaemic count) was launched. It helped add to the idea that Saffola was now a brand that was at 'the heart of a healthy family'. To the consumer, however, this was value at a higher price and they were unwilling to pay for it. With slender margins and inability to spend heavily on advertising, the new offerings from Saffola could not make much progress. The failure confirmed the doubts on commodity branding. It was an insight that would govern all future product selection decisions.

Sweekar – Growing Dilemma

Sweekar, a refined sunflower cooking oil brand, was launched at the cusp of Marico's birth. The reason for its launch was not as much a consequence of a strategic necessity, but more a tactical plan to ward off future attacks on Saffola and its profit pool.

In the eighties, the sunflower oil market was an attractive opportunity with abundant supply and large tracts of farmland under cultivation. There were already a number of traders and refiners selling labelled packs regionally. Multinationals like Hindustan Unilever, with 'Flora', and ITC with 'Sundrop', had also entered the market and established their significance nationally through high-intensity advertising, claiming health benefits. Saffola's pre-eminent health position in the market for cooking oils was being endangered. A resultant price war could erode the healthy margins enjoyed by Saffola.

Harsh had deferred entering the sunflower oil market in the past. But with Flora and Sundrop's intentions to make inroads into Saffola's franchise becoming clearer, he had to do a re-think. Marico needed a strategy to sidestep the attacks on Saffola and keep its image as a health oil untarnished in the consumer's mind. Sweekar, refined sunflower oil, was the answer.

Sweekar targeted its multinational competition, matching price, media share and distribution reach. By 1991, Sweekar and Saffola had together achieved leadership as number one brands in the refined edible oils market with a 14 per cent share, and gotten ahead of formidable competition with their single brands. Amidst price wars, Sweekar volumes grew through market expansion, share gains from the regional brands, and in part, by acting as a foil to Flora and Sundrop. The sunflower oil face-off between the various brands ensured that the Saffola franchise by and large remained protected. Continuing price wars, however, prevented Sweekar from attaining the healthy margin that Saffola had managed.

The marketing team had tried to create a brand identity for Sweekar, positioning it as an '88 per cent saturated fat-free' oil but that did not cut ice in an already crowded, price-elastic market with similar offerings. Attempts to pare down costs did not yield much. All the sunflower oil brands had the same struggle with margins. No one had a distinct brand proposition or competitive leverage. The brands sold on price and any attempt to charge a premium only had an inverse effect on volume. By the mid-nineties, advertising outlays on Sweekar were minimal and sales volumes continued to be dependent on pricing.

In 1998 and in its eighth year, Sweekar was the second largest national brand after ITC's Sundrop at revenues of around ₹100 crore (US$14 million). It was impressive in size, selling three times Saffola's volumes, but contributing only a third of Saffola's unit margin. And therein lay the rub. Debates on the brand's role in Marico's portfolio were being raised from time to time.

The foods marketing team advocated an absolute margin strategy by dramatically growing the volumes of Sweekar. It did this by creating regional extensions to the Sweekar brand. Apart from the already established and nationally distributed sunflower oil variant, Sweekar extended itself to mustard oil in the eastern parts of India, groundnut oil in the western parts of India and soya in parts of north India. The emphasis was on regional sourcing and packing through third party contracts and distribution through the Marico sales system. The Sweekar franchise grew a massive 45 per cent in the first year with the introduction of the three regional variants. However, due to a variety of issues including sourcing, product quality, logistics and the age-old issue of low unit margins, the company withdrew the regional extensions a year later.

Harsh would frequently urge the foods marketing team to not go the route of oil variants. His hunch and years of observing the edible oil business was prompting this advice. The foods team of bright young MBAs would counter the dissenting opinion with projected financials, competitive maps and strategy to reiterate the soundness of their thinking. Harsh would finally relent and hoped that these bright young guys were right. He didn't enjoy playing naysayer. Neither did he say that he was right when the regional oil strategy was abandoned. The Sweekar business continued to limp along with the sunflower oil variant, matching the price of the market leaders.

This was a classic case of an entrepreneur's intuition, honed from several years in the trade, being pitched against the classroom logic of those who had successfully steered through many a tough exam to qualify for high-street schooling. It wasn't as if Harsh knew for sure, but he had seen the business long enough to know that it was a mug's game. However, he believed in co-creation and fundamental to that ideology was being able to give space to others and take some risks.

Niche Brands: Hair & Care, Revive, Sil, Mediker

Marico launched Hair & Care, a non-sticky hair oil, in 1991. Attractively packed in plastic, it stormed into the stronghold of Keo Karpin, an old, traditional brand sold in glass bottles and popular in Uttar Pradesh, Bihar and West Bengal. Keo Karpin was the category leader in the non-sticky hair oil market. Hair & Care succeeded in repositioning Keo Karpin as an 'old-fashioned' brand and in five years, garnered a 25 per cent share of the non-sticky hair oil market to become the second largest brand next to Keo Karpin. With a healthy margin, the brand chipped away at the leader.

Marico launched **Revive,** an instant starch and a fabric care product. This was an innovation and the first product of its kind in the Indian market. The idea came from a personal insight. Harsh liked to wear his cottons starched. His inherent curiosity led him to question his wife, Archana, about the process of starching. She explained the labour-intensive and time-consuming process. Boil the water, boil the starch. Mix and stir to get a solution which was not always consistent: 'It's quite a hassle.' Meanwhile, he asked his marketing team to carry out research to test the hypothesis that 'housewives found traditional starching methods tedious'. Climatic conditions in India favour cotton as a suitable fabric as it breathes and allows absorption of sweat. However, this causes it to crumple and look limp. Starching and then pressing would give the fabric a well-groomed look. Research confirmed that housewives would prefer starch that was soluble instantly in cold water. Based on consumer insight, Harsh, yet again, resorted to innovation: pre-gelatinizing the starch enhanced its solubility in cold water. It saved energy and time and provided the convenience of starching instantly, anytime, anywhere.

The story embodies Harsh's marketing intuition that arose from a pain that he saw at home. His marketing team confirmed the consumer's pain and a reasonably sized opportunity. The findings were then used to formulate a product that addressed the pain. Revive was launched to become the pioneer in the instant fabric starch market.

In 1999, Harsh made his first brand acquisition: a shampoo brand from Procter & Gamble called **Mediker**. It had a unique formulation that was effective against lice, an uncomfortable hair parasite problem affecting women and children, particularly in small towns. The Mediker formula made the lice inactive and therefore the task of combing them out of the hair much easier. Mediker had an attractive gross margin but P&G was uncertain of the brand's growth potential and its role in the company's portfolio. After the acquisition of the brand, Marico re-tooled Mediker in a different format, with the insight that hair oiling was a tradition and a habit with deeper market penetration than shampoos in the rural hinterland. This idea came from a study that Harsh's team had conducted. The team found that rural consumers had not adopted the idea of shampooing their hair and so didn't spend on shampoos. But they still wanted a solution to the lice problem. Combining these insights, the product development team concocted an oil form of the Mediker formulation. The Mediker oil was launched within a year of the acquisition and the sales of Mediker oil matched those of the shampoo. Mediker also added to Marico's distribution muscle by acting as a bridgehead for entry into chemist and pharmacy outlets: outlets that otherwise had a low penetration for other products from Marico's stable. The acquisition soon paid for itself. Sales revenue and its consumer franchise doubled rapidly, justifying the acquisition price of ₹15 crore (US$2 million in 2019).

From a two-brand company, Marico in quick time added four more to its range and a few years later, a fifth. By the year 2000, Marico had six brands and built an impressive supply-chain network of raw material sourcing points close to the cultivation areas, four manufacturing units, two distribution centres and twenty-six finished goods stocking points or depots. The depots serviced 1,200 distributor partners who in turn retailed to 12 lakh outlets in cities and towns with a population of 20,000 or more. A distribution network that was as good as most of the other leading companies in India. Its turnover had reached ₹648 crore (US$92.5 million), a CAGR of 24 per cent over the ten-year period. It had more than doubled its profit margins in the same period despite investments into new brands, brand expansions and warding off competitor attacks.

Reiterates Harsh:

'The experience of launching so many new products/brands taught me a wealth of lessons. We were only able to win in the marketplace when we innovated or pioneered a concept or product. Our market research showed that easy-to-use starch was an unmet consumer need. Innovation won when we put on the market a powdered starch that was easy to use as well as time saving. Again, Mediker oil, yet another innovation, was waiting to be exploited in rural markets where shampoo usage was almost non-existent. Diversifying Saffola into various blends, another innovative approach, offered a range of benefits to satiate differing medical opinions.

'On the other hand, "me-too" products like Sweekar and Whistle did not make the cut in the market, since they lacked a USP. All above, first-hand experiences paid off richly and were huge fodder in pushing for innovative and pioneering future products.'

During one of his visits in 2000, Prof. Ram Charan summed up the last decade thus: 'Laying the foundations for a new company, increasing the scope of business by growing beyond what was already being done and sowing the seeds of a bigger business to follow.'

11

Agony and Ecstasy: Mariwala Family Separation

The Last Straw

By 1996, six years into its incorporation, Marico looked and felt like a different company. Sales had quadrupled and profits had doubled despite huge investments in infrastructure, factories, labs and offices. Marico's efforts at brand building and culture development had laid a foundation for future growth. Backed by these successes, Harsh was emerging from the shadow of his elders and was gaining the respect and admiration of his corporate peers. Remarking on these progressions, Harsh said, 'It was indeed a nice feeling to win recognition and laurels, particularly after years of anonymity and toil.'

Meanwhile, the other branches of the Mariwala family were grappling with the changes wrought by the demerger. While the family recognized that the changes were in the right direction for Bombay Oil, there were new realities and challenges with the arrival of winter. The

Harsh Mariwala's grandfather, Vallabhdas Mariwala

Harsh's parents, Charandas Mariwala and Hemlata Mariwala

Harsh with his mother, Hemlata, and father, Charandas

A young Harsh, when he joined the business

At Marico's new office in Bandra West, Mumbai, 1990s

Left to right: Rishabh, Priyanjali, Harsh, Archana and Raj

Harsh's four-ball team: Ashok Patel, Pradeep Shah, Rajesh Batra and Harsh Mariwala

Chaotic streets of Masjid Bander, where Bombay Oil's office was located

Copra drying yard

Parachute ad in the early 1980s

The big deal of the '70s

Launching Parachute in plastic packs highlighting benefits
over tin packaging in the 1980s

Innovations in Parachute packaging design: Tamper-proof flip top cap (*left*), wide-mouth jar with nozzle (*right*), 1980s

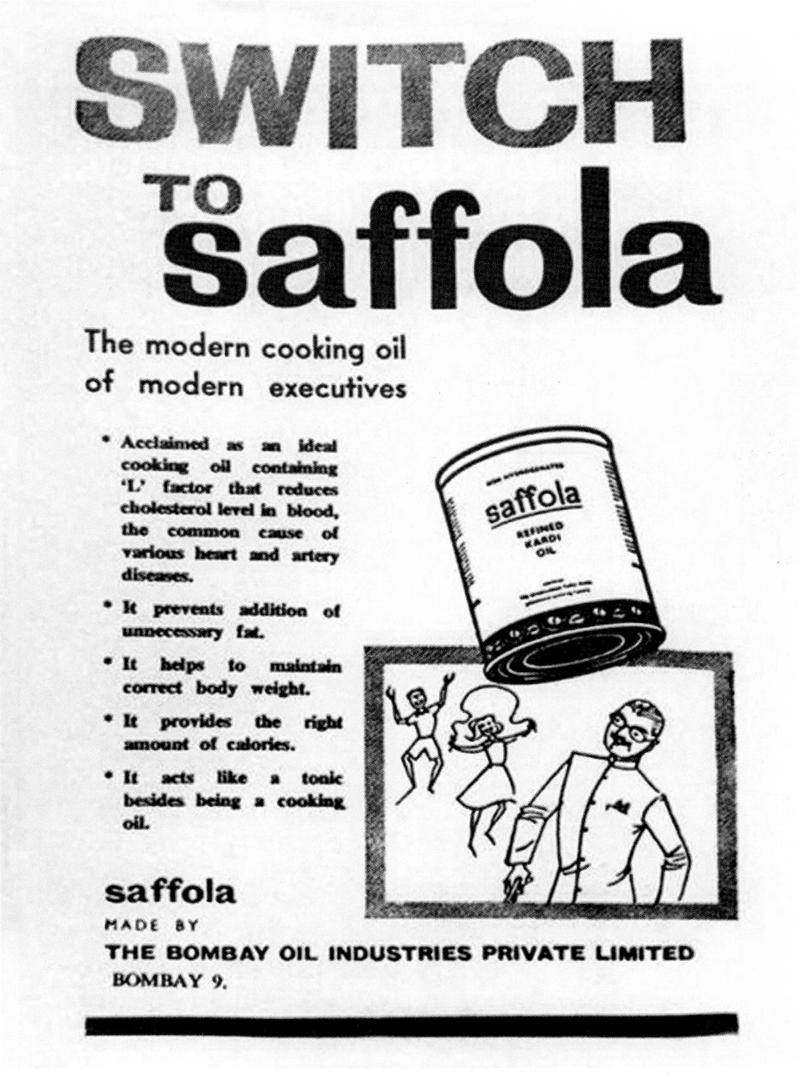

Saffola ad from the late '70s

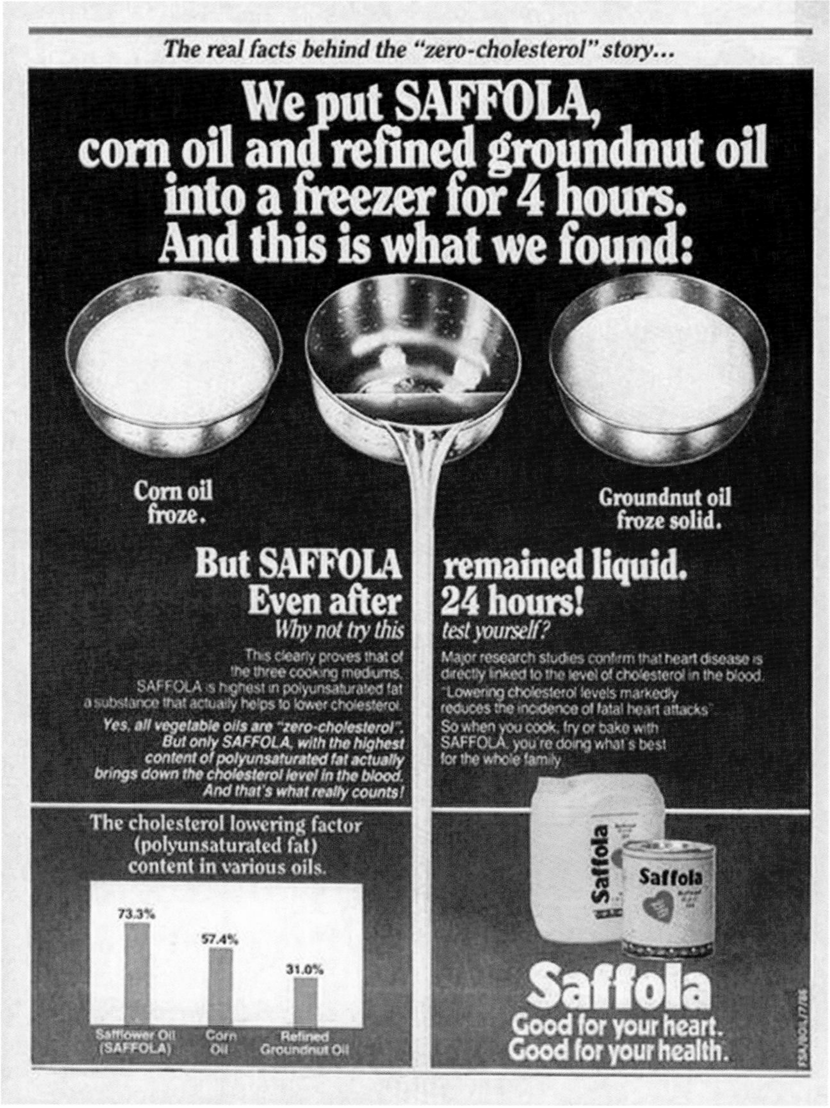

Saffola ad to counter the threat of Mazola Corn Oil, 1980s

'Shock value' ads to create awareness about the newly formed Marico, 1990

One out of 8 people reading this ad is already contributing to our bottom-line.

Marico sells over 7 crore consumer packs to over 13 crore consumers every month. Which means, one out of every 8 Indians is a Marico consumer. Our brands enjoy a leadership position in each of their categories. And we've built a powerful franchise of loyal consumers across 24 countries. What drives our successes? An extraordinary way of thinking we call *uncommon sense*.

AUDITED FINANCIAL RESULTS - MARICO GROUP

	FY' 06 Rs. Crore	FY' 05 Rs. Crore	Growth %
Turnover	1,144	1,007	14
Profit After Tax	87	70	24
EPS (for Marico Ltd.) (Rs.)	17	13	34
Dividend - Rs. Per Share	6.20	5.35	16

marico

UNCOMMON SENSE

Innovative approach to announcing quarterly financial results

Kaya clinic, the Middle East

Therapy pools at an aquacentric facility

Marico's India range

Mariwala elders had to find new ways to keep themselves engaged. The system of a common treasury was no more in practice. Each business had to generate its own resources for investment and growth. The subsidiary companies now run by the Mariwala cousins as CEOs met the family board once each quarter to apprise them of their company's performance. Harsh's cousin Rajen, the CEO of the Fatty Acids and Speciality Chemicals business, acknowledged the obvious when he said, 'Harsh's approach stood apart from that of the previous generation. Harsh had a more futuristic outlook for the company. He invested in professionals and delegated to them. He was very sensible in taking the initiatives that built long-term growth, stability and sustainability.' He was also quick to add that the changes were 'emotionally trying for some of the older family members.' Rajen's father, Kishore Mariwala, echoed the same sentiments, stating that there were mixed feelings among the Mariwala seniors but that he personally was satisfied that the demerger had happened in a professional, a systematic and, most importantly, a transparent manner.

At these quarterly meetings, Harsh gave updates on Marico and its impressive growth. But he was soon to be met with an unprecedented challenge. Trouble was brewing very close to home. Disturbing and unnerving news came to light.

The Mariwala family had stayed together, parents with children, siblings with siblings in the same mansion through generations. Their ancestors and fathers had sagaciously held the family wealth and assets in legally bound and registered cross-holding companies, much as many other business families did, in that era. They had followed the practice of crossholdings to ensure that the future generations would continue to stay together. Under the circumstances, a family break-up was very difficult, and any division of wealth could happen only via mutual agreement.

So it happened in one of the quarterly meetings in 1992 that disturbing information surfaced about one of the jointly owned businesses losing much more money than was disclosed. As would be natural, it created doubts in the others' minds. The family charter, set up in 1990, had created a framework for transparency, but the arrangement seemed to have unravelled. Family members were extremely rattled at this breach of trust. If those responsible for running the various companies in the group could not be trusted, the very basis of the business restructuring exercise stood threatened and was in danger of coming apart at the seams.

So far, all the businesses were jointly owned, in equal proportion by the four branches of the family. The rupture of trust brought to the fore the inevitability to call for a financial separation. A now distraught Harsh was resolute to sever this partnership.

Negotiations and Mediation

The quest for separate ownership saw Harsh enter into negotiations with one branch of the family to buy out their interests in Marico. As Marico was the most highly valued company in the group, any exchange of shares meant that Harsh would have to pay a very heavy consideration. Harsh learnt that he had the backing and innate trust of his uncle Kishore, who told him to also negotiate on his behalf. Through the years 1992–94, negotiations among the family members continued. With multiple family members being involved in negotiations over the various businesses and other assets such as real estate properties, the process became extremely complex. Each asset had to be listed and a fair value arrived at. The only way in which this issue could be resolved would be through the mediation efforts of an external person that all trusted.

A contemporary of the senior Mariwalas, Bipin Shah, former chairman of Lipton and an executive director on the board of Hindustan Lever, was known to all in the family. Highly respected, and as a friend of the family trusted by all, he agreed to oversee the mediation process and held numerous rounds of discussions with the family, sharing his expertise and mediating among members, guiding them towards what was equitable. Many meetings followed: joint meetings and one-on-one meetings to resolve the complexities involved in this family separation.

Two years of negotiations, and an agreement on Marico's valuation still wasn't forthcoming. Finally, the family decided to appoint a reputed third-party valuer, Y.H. Malegam. An Agreement was signed whereby Harsh and his uncle Kishore were given eighteen months to buy out the shares of the other two families at a valuation determined by the third party. Till which time, they would place their own shares in escrow as security.

It was a trying and intensely stressful period for Harsh. He was working round the clock, getting a new company off the ground while at the same time sorting out the family ownership crisis. Harsh was well aware that he and his uncle would need access to substantial capital to repay the loans incurred by the deal. The large buyout of the other two branches of the family left them little room to manoeuvre financially.

In May 1994, Malegam was ready with the valuation. A family meeting was called at the Belvedere Club located in The Oberoi Hotel, Bombay. Based on his enquiries with some finance experts, Harsh had a rough sense of how much the business was worth. However, when the third-party assessment came in at double the value he had anticipated, he was stunned. When he heard the figure, blood drained from his face.

Now, basis the very attractive valuation, the second branch of the family also decided to sell their Marico shares. This meant doubling the cost that Harsh and Kishore would have to pay in a short time frame. Both debated at length about whether such payments would be within their reach. Ultimately, they determined that, though risky, it made eminent business sense to acquire the shares of the second branch as well. They agreed that Harsh would continue as MD of Marico while Kishore Mariwala's family would serve as joint promoters without any active involvement in the business. The high valuation nearly put Harsh's future out of reach. He had to raise far more monies than he had expected he would need in order to buy out the other family branches. To top it all, this turn of events happened at an inopportune time, at a stage when Marico was still in its infancy. As per the agreement, if he was unable to come up with the money to pay for the shares of the outgoing branches, his own shares in escrow would be forfeited. Based on this high valuation, he feared losing control of the company and having to let go of what he had so painstakingly created.

Harsh's sense of hurt and injustice ran deep: it seemed that the curtain would come down on his future dream. For Harsh, Marico's birth was all about liberating himself from the cage. Fatefully, he was still caught in the same cage. What kind of irony was this?

Prof. Ram Charan Observes:

'There are incredible ups and downs and stresses in family business ownership. Most siblings in business families crave liberation, which evades them due to lack of openness and family hierarchy. The issues are held subliminally and not discussed openly enough. Instead, a stalemate lingers. Then something happens unexpectedly, and all hell breaks loose. It becomes an emergency and then a war. Time and energy are diverted to deal with these exigencies and business suffers. So it is important to think ahead and plan for any such eventuality. Arriving at a win-win is the key but not everyone will end up happy.'

Financial segregation spells the ultimate departure and parting of ways. But how do you separate financially? Pay out the others, borrow at high costs, launch an IPO? Prof. Ram Charan adds, 'The quandary is compounded by a lack of experience in these matters. The desire for liberation can lead you to take huge risks—large debts at high costs, for instance—which may then return to haunt you. A cool head is needed and finding a trustworthy set of advisers is crucial. The confluence of the stresses of business, family and debt can be overwhelming and can happen in all family businesses. Harsh was not the only one.'

He continues, 'In those days, it was common for business families to raise personal loans against their shares. For some, it worked out. In other cases, the families were destroyed. I am saying this: be cautious, because no one really controls lack of liquidity and interest rates. One of the three richest families got wiped out. And I mean *wiped out*. They put up their shares as collateral for a loan and it went the wrong way.'

Bankrolling the Buy-Out

During the darkest point of the crisis, at an offsite meeting with his management team at the Taj Fisherman's Cove in Chennai, the pressure finally took its toll. Harsh broke down. He said he couldn't understand where his fault lay. He had worked with utmost integrity and sacrificed a lot to keep the family together. Despite all his hard work, integrity and contribution to the family coffers, he was the one who had to now take on a massive personal debt. It felt like he was being sentenced instead of being rewarded. He despaired, wondering aloud if he could go on. How was he going to raise the money needed to buy out both his uncles' shareholding?

On their part, the management team, obviously in the know, had not conjectured that the valuation would be such a big stretch and so out of reach. Pranab, who was well networked in the world of finance, was partnering Harsh through the valuation process and identifying strategies to fund the buyout. He assuaged Harsh's fears, saying, 'I am confident we'll find a way out. We have a healthy business, a credible management and a very good track record. Money will not be hard to find. There are numbers of FIIs (foreign institutional investors) looking to invest in the India growth story. Only, we need to be very cautious on the terms of any such funding.' The management team, who had worked with Harsh for over five years, had never seen Harsh in such distress. He was always composed and upbeat. Upset, they reassured Harsh that they stood with him and were committed to supporting him through this difficult phase. They were sure that Marico would prevail. That as always, Harsh himself would make it happen. Recalling the moment, Jeswant Nair said, 'Seeing Harsh break down was very humanizing. Role boundaries instantly dissolved. We were touched that he trusted so completely in us.'

Harsh was between a rock and a hard place. He had barely put together a strategy to raise funds for what he imagined would be the anticipated valuation—which by itself was a big stretch. Now having to raise twice the funds was a task for which he had neither a plan nor the wherewithal . . . And the clock was ticking. With shares in escrow, if Harsh and his uncle Kishore were unable to come up with the funds in time, they risked losing the company.

Once again, Harsh turned to someone trusted to seek guidance and counsel. Harsh asked Uday Kotak, his friend and founding partner of Kotak bank, whether his bank would lend the funds needed to settle the family deal. He emphasized that he was not requesting a favour based on family ties and would pledge his shares as well as those of his uncle Kishore as collateral. As they talked, Kotak noticed the physical toll that the separation process had taken on Harsh. Kotak knew that many other family businesses faced the same difficult process of disentanglement—and quite a few had handled the separations badly. Often, decision-making bordered less on rationality and more on what the opposing party would receive. Said Uday later, 'I must give credit to Harsh for his maturity. The Mariwala separation went better than a lot of family business experiences I have witnessed.' A statement which emphasized the professional and open approach that Harsh brought to the situation.

Along with Uday Kotak, Harsh also approached Sajjan Jindal for bailing him out by loaning funds. Cognizant of Harsh's integrity,

Sajjan agreed without hesitation to stand by him. Again, as with the bank, the shares stood as collateral.

Interest rates in India during that period were exorbitant. Harsh and Kishore Mariwala borrowed money at rates ranging from 18 per cent to 24 per cent per annum in order to pay the other two branches for the shares buyout. They were required to repay the loans in a period of eighteen months, in accordance with the signed agreement. The loans gave Harsh and Kishore Mariwala a bit of breathing room, but it still put them under a big load of debt. The sum was huge and the risk one which could sink a less stern entity. But for Harsh, every hurdle seemed surmountable as long as he emerged with control over Marico. And his own master. No price was too high to attain that freedom. He had invested so much of himself in the company and its people; there was no way he would let his dream sink now.

Another option, Harsh reasoned to himself, would be for Marico to attract private equity investors. He spoke with several prospects. Goldman Sachs showed particular interest. They met with Harsh and CFO Pranab Datta at the Marico office. Post their meeting, one member of the Goldman team, Steve Remus, stayed behind to gather information for further analysis. He delved deep into the numbers to grasp the foundation of Parachute's growth and Marico's landscape of distribution and competition. 'I'm an information hog,' Remus said as he vacuumed all the data he possibly could. Goldman Sachs made an offer to acquire part of Harsh's shares so he could repay the loan. But Harsh and Datta found their valuation too low. Although they nearly came to an agreement, negotiations broke down.

It was an extremely taxing period for Harsh. On the one hand, he had to devote time towards growing the business of his new company while on the other, he had to find a way out to repay the burdensome personal loans. Harsh had to present an aura of business as usual but underneath the surface was the back-breaking fear of the debt he was carrying. Meanwhile, interest costs mounted and the time it would take the loan to be serviced stretched beyond two years.

Taking the Bull by the Horns

Another route that Harsh and Pranab discussed was to take Marico public, something they would have liked to execute much later, at a better time and not with a gun to the head. When they broached the idea with merchant bankers, they were advised that the capital markets were not conducive to announcing an initial public offering (IPO)—and at their expected valuation.

Harsh appointed Vallabh Bhansali of Enam, and Citibank, as merchant bankers. And once again, he turned to his trusted advisor, Uday Kotak. Kotak saw there were factors in Marico's favour for an offering: the company showed a clear commitment to building a strong consumer products venture. Parachute was a well-known brand and advanced the market perception of Marico as a consumer brands company. Some analysts would, however, argue that Marico was a commodity-oriented company and so would not attract valuations comparable with brand-owning companies. Some others would argue that the branded consumer space was dominated by multinationals and Indian brands could be flooded out. Getting investors to put money down on a home-grown competitor was not, at that time, an attractive proposition.

Going public also meant that there was going to be a 'new master' that Harsh was unfamiliar with. From simple financial parameters of performance, the evaluation would get more stringent as a public limited company. PE ratios, market caps and the attractiveness of Marico scrips would be the new challenges. He would also have to deal with short-term quarterly performance pressures from analysts and investors. Again, given the depressed capital market backdrop, Harsh's anxiety led to many a sleepless night over whether the public issue would get fully subscribed.

The conversations with Kotak convinced Harsh that the time was ripe to take the plunge and take Marico public, even if it meant risking a lower valuation. Harsh held extensive meetings with potential buyers, merchant bankers and FIIs, both in India as well as abroad. He decided to sell a part of his own and his uncle Kishore's shareholdings alongside the IPO. In March 1996, Kotak and Enam helped create a listing, and took Marico to the public market at what was considered a very high valuation. In a bearish market, the Marico share was priced at a premium of ₹165 (US$2.35 in 2019) per share on a face value of ₹10 (15 cents in 2019) per share. Given the need to raise funds at an extremely high premium, coupled with the sluggish state of the capital market, pressure and stress were hitting the roof among Harsh and his top team. This tension percolated through the entire Marico office as well as home fronts (of both Harsh and Uncle Kishore)—the atmosphere at both ends was taut as a bowstring. All were aware that the under-subscription of the issue would result in absolutely disastrous consequences on the future of Marico.

In a little over a nail-biting twenty-four hours, jubilation ensued. The public issue met with a rousing response: it was over-subscribed. Harsh's joy knew no bounds. He stood vindicated. All those years of unacknowledged, unrecognized efforts, tireless toil, followed by the mountain of debt, were absolved in one fell swoop. Harsh had surmounted all his obstacles. And now stood tall with the faith the public had reposed in him.

It was a simultaneous offer for sale by the promoters and an IPO by the company. The families of Harsh and Kishore sold shares worth ₹46 crore (US$6.6 million in 2019) and Marico raised fresh equity capital of ₹17.5 crore (US$2.5 million in 2019). Harsh had solved his personal debt problem and also infused some funds into Marico which were then deployed to ease working capital pressures. After the IPO, Harsh and Kishore's family together owned roughly 65 per cent of Marico stock. At the same time, his sense of fair play was gratified that the other two branches of the family received more than a fair valuation.

Post-IPO, in 1996, Marico's market capitalization was ₹236 crore (US$34 million in 2019). By mid-2020, the market capitalization had multiplied 190 times.

The success of the IPO brought a tremendous sense of relief and validation. He was grateful for the support he had received from his Uncle Kishore. An ecstatic Harsh, with his wife Archana, celebrated this landmark milestone of his life with his equally elated top team and their spouses over a champagne dinner at the Zodiac Grill, then the most exclusive restaurant in Bombay.

Although onerous at the time, buying out the other branches of the family proved to be not just a worthwhile decision financially, but also one where he was finally master of his own destiny.

FINALLY.

One Journey Ended.

Another began.

Says Harsh:

'A joint family's separation usually entails huge economic upheaval, emotional anguish and is mentally extremely unnerving. As was the case with us.

'Running all the joint family assets through legal and financial experts and allocating the same to different branches of the family took all of two years. This long-drawn process of disentanglement merited endless perseverance and the patience of Job. The decision to appoint a mediator trusted by all the branches of the family proved extremely crucial. I had known of many family splits where stances taken during negotiations would often shift from meeting to meeting or over a period of time, thereby derailing the discussions.

'Bipinbhai, as family mediator, proved a sterling choice: very just and eminently trustworthy, he paved the way for smoother negotiations. These elements are of vital importance while dealing with complex family separations.'

Prof. Ram Charan appreciated the way Harsh had navigated the family separation process. He said, 'In Indian family businesses, a family separation is almost always also a financial separation. There are a large number of stakeholders and the ownership of assets is fragmented through crossholdings. A clean cut is almost impossible to achieve without agreement. Invariably, the process generates a lot of animosity and the person in the leadership role has to absorb incredible amounts of tensions and recriminations. Building agreement across all the stakeholders and ensuring a fair distribution of wealth requires a leadership that is different from business: the leadership of a family. Harsh took that leadership in negotiating an agreement with his uncles and cousins, admirably.'

12

Organizing for Growth

Six years had gone by since the incorporation of Marico and the crafting of its mission and values statement. Values have an eternal quality about them, somewhat like personality. They cannot change too much. Mission statements, on the other hand, are contextual and can change over time. The mission statement then said that:

> 'Marico would be a highly competitive consumer-oriented enterprise; be number one or two in our chosen businesses.'

Product portfolio choices in the early years were governed by the idea of looking for a niche where a Marico brand could rapidly assume a leadership position, number one or two. Revive was a market leader and an innovation that created a category. Hair & Care moved quickly to the number two slot in the non-greasy hair oil category. Saffola and Sweekar together became market leaders in the refined edible oils category and Parachute was indisputably the number one coconut oil brand—and by a wide margin. It was then Marico's belief that market leadership would help it build scale and earn superior margins.

Harsh was deliberately playing in markets where the big guns were absent or where they weren't pushing for a dominant position. This was long before he was introduced to the concept of 'blue ocean' thinking of 'unexplored new market areas'. One of the reasons he succeeded in the coconut oil market was largely because the MNCs were absent at the time he began marketing Parachute, though Unilever did attempt to build a coconut oil brand in the later years. Likewise, Saffola refined cooking oil was another example where Harsh had made an early entry and consolidated his leadership position in the heart health market. As was Marico's entry into Bangladesh, which was ripe for the picking.

The mission statement of being number one or two was powerful but did not directly address the sources of its competitive advantage. The number one or two criterion could mean a whole host of fast-moving consumer goods businesses. It would open up frequent debates on the categories to enter. Each category required different skills, competencies and infrastructure and creating these ground-up could be financially draining. The mission statement was also silent on what Marico's ambitions would be in the international arena.

The need to revisit the mission statement was prompted by the act of becoming a publicly listed company. Marico needed to re-orient the internal mindset from longer-term returns to being accountable to external investors in shorter time cycles as well. Aspirational budgets were to be replaced by more hard-nosed budgets. Sharper questions were being asked on all big-ticket revenue expenses that did not have a commensurate shorter-term return. Some managers were unhappy with these interventions during the budget discussions, but the change was absolutely necessary as the company geared up to the sensitivities and expectations of the external stakeholders.

Harsh often lamented that it was not possible anymore to create altogether new brands, unlike in the past where time moved slowly and media reach was limited. It would take decades of effort to build a brand through repeated usage and familiarity and that was fine by the standards of those days. Media options had multiplied with a plethora of print, more attractive billboards and a saturation of television channels in local languages. Brand launch and communication costs had become prohibitively expensive. Also, there was pressure from shareholders for a quick turnaround of the brand financials. The nature of consumers had changed too. A younger India preferred variety and new experiences.

Brands had to adapt to these needs and stay contemporary and relevant. For instance, a few decades ago, Colgate toothpaste was available as a single variant. Since then, it had become available in different flavours and colours, all within the same brand, to address diverse oral conditions and tastes. Thus, a single brand had begun to satisfy a variety of needs through its variants and catered to a larger franchise of consumers. The brand owner got a better bang for the buck when the same advertising spends cross-subsidized the mother brand and its variants. Harsh would prompt his team to examine these trends as they crafted a new business direction.

Describing this phenomenon, Prof. Ram Charan says, 'There is a myth that the founders, the early starters had a grand vision of their company. They do have a picture in their mind in the initial stages. But as they grow, they widen the lens through which they look at the world and slowly the outlines of a vision evolve. I had the chance to work with Michael Dell in his early days—he didn't then say that "technology was all about enabling human potential". Yet Michael changed how technology was designed, manufactured and sold. It transformed the IT industry for ever, according Michael the title of youngest CEO at twenty-five years, to list in the Fortune 500 of 1992.

'Likewise, Harsh had a vision of going from a commodity business to a branded and packaged business. He had a vision of a local family company becoming a global company one day. But his vision was driven almost entirely by what the consumer wanted. What is the consumer's pain point? What is the retailer's pain point? He focused on solving these problems and in doing so, over a period of time, built a foundation for the future.'

Prof. Ram Charan adds, 'Visions are never static. They evolve as the world and horizons change. Some react to external changes, some shape external changes. Harsh has shown us the way in which he shaped the external landscape. He showed us that India could spawn indigenous multinationals. He did this by stepping into the Middle East through export-led distribution. Then by setting up a company to manufacture and market in Bangladesh, and later by acquiring companies and brands in South-East Asia, Egypt and South Africa.'

A New Organizational Structure

A new business direction was articulated in 1996. Marico had a coconut oil business and a refined edible oil business as its main resource engines. New categories were being added to expand the franchise of these businesses. Marico was expanding to other countries where the Indian diaspora lived. Each of these businesses needed a higher degree of specialization in terms of supply chain, product development, consumer insights and even distribution.

For Harsh there was another compelling reason. By 1997, Harsh's core team had been together through seven years of intense growth. The three senior members—Nair, Gupte and Datta—were devoted to Harsh and reluctant to ask themselves: where do I go from here? The three of them had been valued partners and with Marico's success, their work had gained notice. Harsh knew that some of them nurtured ambitions of being CEOs and business leaders. They would sometimes talk about the approaches made to them. He wanted them to be around for the long haul and worried about a time without them. A profit-centre approach to the business had been discussed between Harsh and the individual members of his top team: a way by which organizational and personal objectives could be synthesized.

Combining the organization's need for specialization and the career needs of his top team, Harsh revised Marico's **business direction** and created **three business groups.**

a. The **Nature Care** business would offer products and brands that enhanced the appeal and nourishment of hair and skin through distinctive products, largely based on coconut and other natural materials.
b. The **Health Care** business would make available a variety of branded foods needed for healthy living, drawn from agriculture and offered both in their natural as well as processed forms.
c. The **International Business** was tasked with building a franchise for company brands in other countries in the Indian subcontinent, the Middle East and other parts of the world, where significant Indian diaspora lived.

The sales and distribution of the Nature Care and Health Care range was to be organized under a common **sales group** to service the trade and consumer. **Finance** and **human resources** were two other corporate groups that glued the four verticals.

There were still questions around whether the change was conceived prematurely. Did the businesses have the critical mass to be split into three groups? Was the structure being pushed by the career expectations of the leadership team? The arguments in favour of the profit-centre structure were: growth focus, aggressive new products and consumer focus and the consolidation of specialized skills and competencies needed for each business. Studies of other consumer business organizations would support the hypothesis that the change was premature but Marico still went ahead under the premise that organizational slack, if any, was a deliberate investment for new expansion and growth.

Nair, who became CEO for the new sales group, said, 'I never, in my wildest dreams, imagined that this would happen to me. But it did.' Shreekant Gupte became CEO of the Nature Care Group. Pranab Datta became CEO of the Health Care Group and Arvind Kumar, who till then was looking after commodity purchases and the exports business, took over as CEO of the International Business Group.

In the short term, the restructuring showed significant benefits. The new CEOs took to shaping their divisions with zest. They drew up plans and shared them with the group. All three CEOs had adopted the growth mantra of growing the existing lines profitably and unleashing a clutch of new products, variants and extensions.

a. The **International Business Group** found new life as it set up and developed distribution in the GCC countries with its own team of sales managers. The emphasis had shifted from mere consignment exports to building a network of distributors, to systematizing the distributor-retail operations, in order to reach a larger number of outlets and, with well-designed in-shop activity in the modern trade outlets. Nepal and Bhutan were earlier being serviced by the East Region sales team and the small volumes from these markets were a low priority. Replicating the GCC sales and distribution model helped shore up volumes and improve market coverage. Marico then made an entry in Bangladesh with exports.
b. The **Sales Group** focused on building sales capacity and capability. There was an emphasis on going deep with rural distribution and a

separate network of around 300 super-distributors was established to serve this purpose.

The Sales and Information Technology teams collaborated to build an indispensable virtual office that provided real-time information for decision-making across the supply chain called MIDAS (Marico Distributor Application Software) for distributors and linked it to Marico's own SAP-based Supply Chain Management System. Marico became the first FMCG company to have built integrated connectivity, from the retail outlets to production units and procurement units. It did this in an interesting way to ensure the buy-in of the distributors. The key link to the project were Marico's distributors across the country, who were comfortable with their own accounting systems. Getting them to adapt to a new system was an exercise in large-scale change management. Recognizing the relationships of the salespeople with the distributors, a team of star sales executives and managers from across the country were co-opted full-time to the project team based in Bombay. They not only helped in refining the content and reports generated by MIDAS but were also being trained as change leaders for implementation. The change leaders were then assigned to train the distributors on how to use MIDAS and make them attitudinally ready for the change. Identifying the best talent for a multi-disciplinary project team, which worked full-time, was a masterstroke in preparing for the change. The implementation and the switchover were flawless. The system went live across the country all at once, without any pushbacks or fallbacks . . . The distributors now had a real-time inventory, accounting and ordering system and the inventory planners had real-time visibility of demand patterns to plan procurement, production and dispatches. The success of the project and the meticulous fail-proof plan reinforced Harsh's belief in Prof. Ram Charan's maxim of 'remove escape buttons', i.e., resisting the temptation to have people double-hat their regular and project team roles, and to build fallback contingencies should the implementation run into rough weather. MIDAS had become a new benchmark for automated information management for sales and inventory planning in the fast-moving consumer goods industry.

c. The **Nature Care Group** launched a suite of products and extensions in quick succession: Parachute Advansed Jasmine,

Parachute Advansed pre-shower hot oil and Parachute Advansed post-shower grooming oils.

d. The **Health Care Group** launched Saffola brand extensions of salt and atta alongside the repositioning of the Saffola brand. Later, with the change in government regulations, the team launched Saffola blends: safflower and corn oil blend and safflower and rice bran oil blend. The Sweekar brand too launched regional extensions of mustard, soya and groundnut oil.

There was a release of new energy as the new launches followed one after another. Marico was struck by frenetic activity, frequent and animated meetings, high-level market visits, intensity of product development work in the lab and frequent interactions with the advertising agencies. It would appear that the structural intervention of creating the profit centres had unleashed a visceral energy and a feverish pace. A likely phenomenon when people start new jobs and there is lots to learn and do.

Datta, Gupte and Nair provided able collective leadership to the company in their functional avatars as the chiefs of finance, marketing and human resources. Harsh was confident that the team would continue to collaborate as they steered their respective divisions to another level of growth and profit. Harsh's own role had changed to business reviews, as counsel and coach to the CEOs and to build altogether new businesses. Yet, the consequences of the transition to the profit-centre structure played out in unexpected ways.

Nair made his mark as CEO of the Sales Group but experienced tensions with some members of the top management team. A sense of competitiveness had crept in between the businesses. Two years into the role, in 2000, Nair decided to seek an opportunity outside Marico and gave Harsh notice of his departure.

In the early years of the new millennium, sales and earnings started to plateau after the rapid growth of the 1990s. Sales growth had begun to taper off in the years 2001 at 3 per cent and 2002 at 4 per cent—the worst it had seen through its existence. There was a sense of despondency and Harsh was a worried man.

Also true were new-product failures—a terrible blow to any FMCG company and its marketing and brand building skills. The proud record of a brand success each year in the early nineties, had been punctured. Only two of the ten extensions that were launched in the late nineties survived. The question uppermost in most people's mind was whether splitting the marketing team into two different groups in the two business divisions had diluted marketing capabilities and the synergies that existed under one roof. Brand failures apart, there was a sudden exodus of brand managers. Several years of accumulated in-depth category learnings and an entire legacy seemed lost forever.

Harsh later recalled, 'As growth slowed and new product extensions fared none too glowingly, I began to wonder whether the restructuring and the delegation to the CEOs had been premature. Had it caused a loss of focus and scale? Or could it be the recessionary trends in the economy at the turn of the century?' Harsh was mulling over whether the decision that put the careers of key individuals ahead of the organization's needs had anything to do with the growth squeeze. In any case, the fact that they were CEOs and were accountable for the lacklustre performance was reason enough to take a relook at his direction. Harsh discussed this with a few trusted business-founder peers as he pondered over a solution.

Sensing disquiet around company performance, Pranab and Shreekant told Harsh that they felt responsible for the flat performance and product failures. They offered to move on from Marico so that Harsh could build a new team. That made the task of separation a little easier. In accepting their decision to move on, Harsh told them that he was appreciative of their many contributions but was unhappy with the progress of the company in recent years. He offered them some time to decide on their future pursuits and take their final calls.

There were emotions and memories of a long association. There were several professional contributions to boot. They had been pillars of strength as Harsh navigated through the family business separation and the public offering. 'Letting them go was a painful decision for me. I was very close to them: not only at work but in our personal relationships too. We had nurtured social relationships, exchanging occasional family and team dinner evenings in each other's homes. We had gone on family retreats together,' said Harsh.

In 2002, four years after creating the profit-centre structure, Harsh reversed the decision and went back to a unified organization structure. It was time for a change and Marico needed to grow without them. The company was reorganizing into a more coherent arrangement for domestic and international businesses. He emphasized the need for fresh blood and thinking in the organization.

Pranab and Shreekant joined as CEOs in other companies of repute but kept in touch and continued to stay on good terms. For years since, Harsh could still count on their counsel and goodwill when he needed it or when they met or visited.

Harsh Reflects:

'Pranab and Shreekant, among my key anchors during the family separation (Pranab was CFO and Shreekant, VP Operations), performed admirably well in their roles. However, when their roles changed to profit-centre heads, they found themselves to be square pegs in round holes.'

Responds Prof. Ram Charan:

'That is because they were excellent in the old structure. But, with increased scale and complexity, their skills did not match. You are going to have these issues every time you grow. How do you deal with them?

'Scaling up requires the right organizational structure and right people in the right jobs. That's the lesson!' observes Prof. Ram Charan.

'And that's what I think Harsh did. Organization structure does matter for business success. Initially, you are a one-person business, then you are a ten to twenty-person outfit, then a 100-, a 1000- and later a 10,000-strong company. As the organization expands, at some point, it comes to a stage where the old structure prevents newer and future growth. For a company to remain vital, the entrepreneur must sense the points of time where stagnation or complacency sets in. Confront these, make changes, reorganize and redesign.

'Not all people grow at the same speed and required competence to manage the complexities of change. Such people may not be able to grow any further and become a hindrance to the growth of the business and the talent under them. This is one of the reasons why companies fail. They do not make changes when they are needed the most.

'For many founders, it is emotionally difficult to replace those who have played an important role in the past. But it is necessary to be straightforward and honest and work with them to show them why their journey with you may have come to an end. It may cause upheavals. Relationships may change or even get strained. But failing to deal with these issues is a recipe for obsolescence.'

Harsh, in complete agreement with Prof. Ram Charan, adds, 'The interest of the organization should always be primary. Looking back, it was an error to satisfy the aspirations of a handful of my top team.'

13

Angels and Predators

Profits Bring Predators

Being an entrepreneur, especially one disentangling from a family business, teaches one many lessons. One lesson that Harsh swore by was never to underestimate the competition. He had an insatiable curiosity regarding competitor thought process and what the consumer felt about the brand. A lesson that Harsh had learnt a long time back from his unsuccessful experience of entering the tooth powder market. It would serve him well in the years ahead, when competition from a multinational corporation grew fierce.

Hindustan Lever (now Hindustan Unilever Limited, or HUL) was and is the biggest and most respected player in the FMCG sector. Conditions seemed right for it to expand its product portfolio and get into large categories that it wasn't already in. The route it chose was acquisitions. In 1993, it acquired Tata Oil Mills Company (TOMCO), predominantly a soap manufacturing company, which also had in its portfolio a coconut oil brand, Tata—Nihar Coconut Oil, a brand with distribution mainly in eastern India. Hindustan Lever was the gold standard in FMCG marketing and distribution and the TOMCO acquisition provided it with a beachhead to enter the coconut oil and hair oil segments and expand nationally.

Hindustan Lever boasted market leadership across several categories. Brooke Bond, which had acquired Kissan and Lipton a few years earlier, was merged into Hindustan Lever in 1996, creating an even larger and more dominant company. The ice cream brands Kwality and Dollops had also been acquired in 1993 alongside TOMCO. Ponds (India) Limited was merged with Lever in 1998. They had also announced the acquisition of International Best Foods in 2000 and Modern Foods in 2002. Many in the industry saw the acquisition of TOMCO as Hindustan Lever's way of consolidating forces in the personal soaps and shampoos sector.

Hindustan Lever had already proved its mettle as a marketer by unsettling consumer categories. It had done this in oral care. Colgate entered the India toothpaste market way back in 1937. It was the market leader in the oral hygiene market with a range of toothpastes. In the nineties, Hindustan Lever upped the ante with huge investments in advertising behind its toothpaste brand Closeup. Backed by its distribution muscle, it made big strides and rapidly wrested a significant market share from Colgate. Colgate, being a multinational with deep pockets, was able to match Lever's advertising spends and survive the onslaught. Colgate, almost a monopoly till then, had now to contend with a strong competitor forever.

Keki Dadiseth, who took over as the chairman of Hindustan Lever in 1996, built his career on corporate acquisitions. Along with mergers of some of the group businesses, he knew he could strengthen Lever's position by acquiring promising companies. The company was doing extremely well, both in terms of financial results as well as accolades and recognition for achievement across several disciplines. Hindustan Lever's hunger for growth into new categories was tangible as it forayed relentlessly, executing its mergers and acquisitions plan.

Prime among these targets was Marico. Dadiseth was confident that he could add Marico to his portfolio.

War Breaks Out

When Hindustan Lever acquired TOMCO, one of the brands of that portfolio was Tata—Nihar coconut oil. Nihar's attempts to grow its share in the coconut oil market (which then stood at 7 per cent) were being thwarted by Parachute (which claimed 48 per cent) and so Lever increased their discounts to retailers dramatically, giving them a 35 per cent margin against Marico's 10 per cent. Hindustan Lever managers then outspent Marico on advertising by a 2:1 ratio. This amounted to a full-blown assault on Marico. It further turned the screws when it pre-empted Marico by acquiring Cococare, a coconut oil brand enjoying significance in the western region and Marico's core geographic territory. Gupte, by then the vice president of marketing, exclaimed, 'Hindustan Lever is after us, all guns blazing. Its sudden passion for the coconut oil market is not innocent. It is looking to gobble us up. Hindustan Lever is well aware that Nihar won't see a return on investment for a long time. Its strategic rationale is quite clearly to buy Marico by driving Parachute to its knees.'

Competing with a giant multinational seemed a huge challenge for the young company. The skirmishes in the marketplace were getting uncomfortable and Hindustan Lever was using its age-old and strong relationships with trade to spread rumours. Retailers told Marico's sales force what they had heard: your company is going to sell out. This, coupled with the heavy trade discounting by Nihar, made some of Marico's field force nervous. Lever was using strategy to create an environment of fear and uncertainty in the Marico ranks. As also among distributors. At a Hindustan Lever conference for investors, it was hinted that they would acquire Marico before long and this information was conveyed back to Marico by analysts.

While Harsh's team was confident that Parachute would ultimately come up trumps against Nihar, many outside the company believed that the direct assault by a multinational would seriously hurt Marico's long-term future and set the stage for a buyout. If Marico's management did not see the writing on the wall, they risked losing everything. Many well-wishers approached Harsh and gave him their advice: take the buyout as an opportunity to sell. At the Willingdon Sports Club where he sometimes held meetings, three bankers met Harsh individually, and all three urged him to sell. Taking on Hindustan Lever would be futile, all three reiterated. Harsh walked out of these meetings undaunted. Marico was enveloped in an onslaught of rumours and buzz in the market and disturbing messages from 'well-wishers'.

In Prof. Ram Charan's view, 'Almost all start-ups look to expand. As they do, they get noticed by the competition, for more reasons than one. The competition first notices the marketplace play and the small successes being notched up by the upstart. Then they become curious about the brains behind this success. Full of energy, innovative and changing the rules of the game, they move faster than big companies who are bogged down by bureaucracy. They become attractive and challenging places to work. And sometimes, the big daddy competition begins to lose their talent to these start-ups.' Large companies are watchful of these starts-ups for not just these reasons. Their competitive game is not only to grow organically but through acquisitions too. The start-up once grown to size can become their prey. Marico was no exception.

Over the years Harsh had been approached by big multinational consumer companies for JVs, possibly with a hidden agenda of acquisition later on. Prof. Ram Charan had known Unilever and its leaders for over thirty years. A number of them, including several chairmen of Hindustan Unilever, had been to his leadership programmes at Unilever's Four Acres Leadership Development Centre, UK. They were extremely capable, highly ambitious and he knew the way they thought.

To them, Marico was clearly a jewel. They would seek to buy not just the company but the CEO, the management team and the culture that it delivered to its shareholders, customers and employees.

They knew that in the ultimate analysis, it was the competition between the two sets of people on either side.

They knew that size did not matter in this game, neither did the financial resources.

They knew that it was the brains, the competence and the knowledge of the set of people that determined whether they could outwit and overcome the big guy on the other side.

Prof. Ram Charan added, 'You should anticipate these things even if you can't predict when. You should be prepared. Be aware of your vulnerabilities. If you own less than 51 per cent of the company, your vulnerability is going to be high. If you are a public company and if you don't have significant ownership, again, you are vulnerable. Large companies can offer incredible financial payouts. Because for them, what they give you does not materially affect their earnings per share. Hindustan Unilever was a thirty times larger predator, with humongous hunger and deep pockets. Very deep pockets.'

Goliath Comes Knocking

Dadiseth knew how to apply direct and indirect pressure, and how to skilfully stoke fear to close a deal. He was confident they could add Marico to their own portfolio.

As the weeks passed, Harsh saw that the situation had built itself to another unhappy consequence. Marico's stock price fell sharply, with the PE multiple slipping to a single digit. The market believed that if Harsh sold Marico, the share price could rise again. Undeterred, he stayed the course.

One evening, Harsh received a phone call at home. 'I am Dadiseth,' the caller announced. He had never met Dadiseth before. A startled Harsh asked, 'How did you get my home number?'

Dadiseth brushed aside the question and made his case. Hindustan Lever was making a compelling offer. Dadiseth hinted at a lucrative sale of Marico with significant benefits for Harsh's family. 'The consideration will ensure that you and the next generations will be well cared for,' he told Harsh. 'You know that we're in the coconut oil market. We're very serious about this. We have a far superior and deep penetrating distribution network,' he continued. 'I'm giving you an opportunity to sell out.' Harsh demurred, but Dadiseth would not take no for an answer. He backed up his offer with a not-so-veiled threat: if Harsh didn't sell, he would lose everything he had struggled to build. 'Marico will be history,' he told Harsh. Even worse, Harsh's family would pay the price. 'Sell,' said Dadiseth. 'If you don't, you will live to regret it.'

At the end of the five-minute call, Harsh hung up the phone. He was rattled that evening. Sleep eluded him. He had built Marico himself. His vision for it was just as long-term as any multinational's plan. He wondered about the nerve of the caller. So far, he had received only hints and innuendos. But now here was a direct threat from the antagonist himself.

Harsh woke up the next morning, his mind made up. The threatening call had had the opposite effect: there was no question of selling out. He and his uncle held 65 per cent share holdings. The only way Hindustan Lever could hurt Marico was by causing it to bleed in the marketplace. Harsh was hell-bent on taking them on, well aware that it would be a long-drawn battle. As is very human, determined though he was, waves of self-doubt assailed him every now and then. The acquisition of Thums Up (a market leader) by Coca-Cola weighed on his mind. Even in his conviction, he realized that most people would think him a fool—maybe even a proud fool. He wondered how he would convince the key people that fighting the predator would be the right step.

Harsh's conviction was further bolstered by the fact that his team, like him, believed that Marico could take on a giant like Hindustan Lever. Strong rationale lay behind this conviction. Parachute was a high stakes game for him and Marico, comprising about 61 per cent of the company's revenues at the time. A huge advantage for Harsh was his in-depth knowledge of branded coconut oil: consumer insights, sourcing expertise, a well-established distribution and marketing set-up, and the significant cost optimization achieved across the value chain. In contrast, for Hindustan Lever, this was one among several product categories that they had in India and it was far from being a significant component in their portfolio. Harsh's grip of the coconut oil business and his relationships in the trade, honed through decades of engagement, was overwhelmingly more than the knowledge of a man focused on acquisitions. He was confident that he could outmatch the high marketing spends that the competitor would throw into the game.

Parachute was a pure coconut oil and there wasn't much differentiation that Hindustan Lever could make in this category. It would be a 'me too' at best. With a combination of well-sourced copra and the right tweaks to perfect the extraction process, Parachute offered a coconut oil high on clarity—not easy to better. Also, Parachute had a distinctive aroma—also not easy to replicate. Perfected over time, this entailed selecting premium quality copra and treating it at a precise temperature in order to exude a nutty aroma. Both these features were highly regarded by consumers. The scope for Hindustan Lever to offer a superior product was limited if not altogether absent. The best Lever could do was to battle it out in the market. Marico already had plans to cover this angle too.

Still, a direct threat from a powerful opponent was deeply unsettling. Hindustan Lever intended to destroy Marico—of that there was no doubt. Hindustan Lever had an extensive sales and distribution network with the largest outlet reach among FMCG companies in India. They were known for their marketing capability and of course deep pockets to outspend and outshout most competition, most certainly Marico. Harsh was anxious at the prospect of a face-off with a pedigreed and battle-hardened Hindustan Lever team backed by big budget firepower.

Harsh reached out to Prof. Ram Charan. 'Protect your resource generating engine,' said he, referring to Parachute. 'You have the capability to take them on. You may have to increase investments in advertising, improve distribution and match Nihar's price. But at the end of it, you will have a stronger brand and a bigger reputation,' the veteran business coach told Harsh. Encouraged, Marico would ready a war chest and take a planned short-term squeeze in profits.

Marico's steepest challenge stood before Harsh. He gathered his team for a work session with Prof. Ram Charan to review whether all bases had been covered for the battle with Hindustan Lever. The professor endorsed the views held by the Marico team. He agreed with the central assumption that the Marico team knew the business inside out, including a deep understanding of the cost structure. Harsh added, 'We have twenty-five years of insight in that category—something that they lack.'

Prof. Ram Charan reiterated that Marico held an unexpected advantage in management strategy too. Dadiseth would have to delegate the fight to a manager two or three levels below him. Continued he, 'When the threat does come, do not just take the CEO's word at face value. Dig in to see: who is the person on the opposing side to wage the campaign? And find out at what level that person is placed in the hierarchy, as well as the authority and resources at his disposal.' In fact, as anticipated, Harsh discovered that his real competitor inside Hindustan Lever was two levels below Dadiseth. A manager at that level had limited flexibility over his budget—only the CEO could dedicate the budget needed for such a campaign, redirecting resources from other divisions of Hindustan Lever. That meant the multinational could not respond as nimbly as Marico to shifting conditions and tactics.

Harsh, on the other hand, could mastermind his game plan, and manoeuvre tactics as per need.

Commenting on this takeover bid, Prof. Ram Charan said, 'In the overall scheme of things, there is no such thing as a straight-line linear win; challenges and successes will come. The more successful you are, the more vulnerable you are to takeovers. India will see a trend towards more such transactions. What matters is your conviction and ability to seek help from the right people and finally, the tenacity to overcome the adversity.'

In the months that followed, Hindustan Lever intensified the brand war with Marico and aggressively upped its advertising and trade spends for Nihar. Lever acquired Cococare, a regional coconut oil brand owned by Recon. Lever had upped the Marico bid for Cococare to pre-empt a future pincer attack from Marico, showing its formidable capacity to throw money behind its threats.

Fighting Back

Meanwhile, the brand positioning and packaging re-design of Parachute with Strategic Shining Design had been completed. The rejuvenated Parachute brand was launched, backed by big ticket advertising. A massive TV campaign was aired, focusing on the relevance of the sacred coconut in Hindu religion and tradition. It centred on the symbolism of the coconut: selflessness, purity and prosperity. Offered in temples, auspicious occasions and religious ceremonies, the television advertisement associated all these values with Parachute Coconut Oil. The campaign struck an emotional chord with consumers, and Parachute not only strengthened its position, but also notched up a double-digit volume of growth. It reached 18 million households and increased market share to 52 per cent. Up by 4 per cent. Nihar too, gained share, but mainly from smaller competition.

Separately, Harsh and his sales team worked at widening and deepening distribution reach. The packaging, too, now wore a new look, with a tamper-free cap (uncommon in those days), along with a high-decibel promotion of 'Shuddhata Ki Seal' (the seal of purity). There was a single-minded focus on overcoming the brute force. Not just that. Harsh astutely turned around the Nihar and Hindustan Lever threat to augment competitive advantage for Parachute and Marico.

New Designs Parachute:

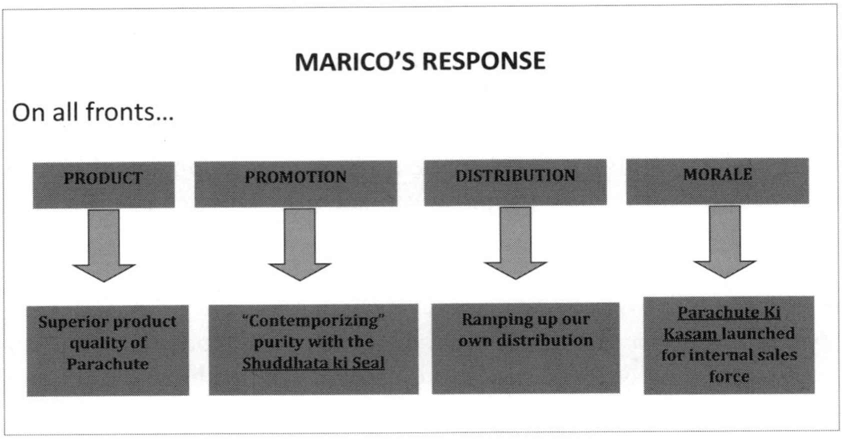

Marico's outlet reach was strong in the urban areas but was relatively weak as it went further into small towns and rural areas. It strategized a rural distribution thrust by appointing around 250 super-distributors who would sell, only to retail, in the rural markets and compensated them for the additional costs. With this structural weakness plugged, Marico would march on to build a distribution reach that matched the top FMCG companies in the country.

Battle-Ready

Another key ingredient in the mix was to enthuse and incentivize the sales force which experienced the Hindustan Lever aggression every day in the market, just like on a battlefield. A war room was created with dedicated telephone lines to get direct information from the field and respond to Hindustan Lever's moves in real time. Marico convened a sales conference with one and all attired in army fatigues. The field platoons and the platoon leaders representing each of the field sales team crawled through a tunnel into the conference venue amid the battle cry of 'Parachute Ki Kasam'.[16] The conference venue resembled a battlefield at night and acoustics included the sound and fury of

[16] Parachute Ki Kasam: swear by Parachute.

guns and cannons and a battle in progress. The general (sales manager) unveiled the threat from the enemy, Marico's battle plans and the arms and ammunition (strategic and tactical inputs) that were available for the fight. The sales force raring to go, marched off to battle with their spirits high and the determination to vanquish Nihar.

Furthermore, Marico, not undone by Cococare being stolen from right under its nose, acquired another coconut oil brand—Oil of Malabar from the west coast—and relaunched it at a lower price to direct fire at Hindustan Lever's Cococare. This effectively neutralized any tactical plan of Hindustan Lever to attack Parachute with Nihar and Cococare. The game was getting ugly as Marico too responded, salvo for salvo.

As Harsh prepared for battle with Hindustan Lever, Uday Kotak suggested that he should meet Karsanbhai Patel, the founder of Nirma, who had successfully taken on Hindustan Lever in the detergent space. He made a trip to Ahmedabad to meet him. As two Indian entrepreneurs fighting a multinational giant, there was an affinity and willingness to share counsel. Karsanbhai encouraged Harsh, telling him not to back down from the eyeball-to-eyeball fight. He added that in his experience, the Surf-Nirma fight did not result in Nirma losing. Instead the market for economy detergents expanded, with Nirma holding its own. Karsanbhai's advice was to fight on with grit, guts and tactics and a win against the colossus would definitely be within the grasp of Marico.

Marico continued to gear up and protect its resource engine. Harsh realized that the increased spends would have an impact on the company's profitability in the short run. He decided to proactively share this outlook with the analysts from the capital markets, indicating that a near-term sacrifice of profit growth was inevitable in the long-term interests of the company. Some placed their bets on Harsh, confident that he would see this through and emerge stronger. Most however, quite understandably, decided to wait and watch or conclude that this would be a long and hard phase for the company that would end with either Harsh giving up or result in a severely diminished Marico.

Yet again, the problem of the Hindustan Lever offensive was converted into an opportunity to serve numerous purposes. Advantageously, the war with Hindustan Lever led to strengthening the strategic health of Marico, i.e., modernizing the look and feel of

Parachute, exemplifying the brand with a high-decibel campaign, fortifying rural distribution and revitalizing the field sales force and finally, acquiring another brand to help it play the price game. This theme of deriving a number of spinoffs from a single problem situation was a hallmark of Harsh's thought process, and a game plan that continues to resonate with Harsh.

The multiple interventions helped Marico and Parachute, not only to hold their own but also to build for them an impregnable fortress that others would dare not invade. The fight enhanced Marico's reputation as a 'giant killer'. Harsh remembered what Prof. Ram Charan had told him: '. . . at the end of it, you would have a stronger brand and a bigger reputation'—the reputation of having bested a powerful adversary. Nihar, in the meanwhile, seemed to be limping along and losing steam, with its market share plateauing in the teens.

Since that fateful phone call, when Dadiseth threatened Marico with destruction, Hindustan Lever had seen shifts of its own. Dadiseth moved on to the Unilever headquarters in London. Hindustan Lever was also getting 'Unilever-ized'. The multinational decided to focus on global categories across its markets and not focus on local market brands. Coconut oil usage was predominantly a south Asian habit and could not form a part of Hindustan Lever's global portfolio. Hindustan Lever also began to face heightened competition on several fronts. Colgate was retaliating, P&G raised the ante in shampoos and some regional brands began making serious forays into mass market detergents.

Although Nihar had doubled its market share to 15 per cent in the early years, Marico remained untouched. Nihar's growth came at the cost of the smaller brands. The intense multi-dimensional war had actually strengthened Parachute and Marico. Finally, Hindustan Lever relented and after an assault lasting over six years, they stopped investing in the coconut oil business. During the period from 2002 to 2006, Nihar's market share in pure coconut oil plummeted from about 15 per cent to 8 per cent. The giant had lost his footing.

Goliath Steps Away

After more than six years of market encounters and threats to Marico's very existence, there were credible rumours that Nihar, Hindustan Lever's coconut oil brand, was up for sale along with some other brands in its stable. Harsh made an informal approach to Harish Manwani, the chairman of Hindustan Lever, over a game of golf.

He then asked his team, which Saugata Gupta, then chief marketing officer, was a part of, to evaluate the strategic advantages of owning Nihar in Marico's basket as also the scenario of likely competition buying the brand and the bid value of the same.

From a strategic perspective, the two brands of Parachute and Nihar had potential synergies. Nihar had a strong following in eastern India, whereas Parachute was strong in the rest of the country. Additionally, Marico's cost structure was far superior to Nihar's. This was because:

a. Parachute procured copra at a far more competitive cost by purchasing it directly from the source as compared to Nihar's coconut oil purchase, which was done through brokers.
b. Parachute bottles, which used approximately 20 per cent less plastic than that used in the same-sized Nihar bottles, and so held a far greater economic advantage.

In the value-added coconut oils market, having Nihar perfumed hair oil would make Marico a dominant player in the hair oil segment, with pricing power and economies of scale.

When Hindustan Lever decided to sell Nihar, Harsh was ready. He surmised that Lever would negotiate directly with Marico for the sale of brand Nihar. However, Lever obviously knew that they would get a far superior value if they ran the process of auctioning the brand. The stakes for Marico to acquire the brand upped immensely, since all the major Indian FMCG players had entered the fray. Marico put forth its non-binding bid. A few days later, Lever informed Marico that the latter had made the final round of the two-stage bidding process.

In 2005, the concept of a data room had not yet caught on. So Lever invited Marico to its data room at the training centre to start due diligence of the relevant documents. Meanwhile, over another round of golf at Chembur, Harish Manwani reinforced to Harsh that the others, too, were serious bidders.

Two days later, Harsh conferred with Marico's board and the directors' stand was clear: they urged him to make an aggressive bid. They averred that it would be a strategic disaster to lose the opportunity to buy Nihar. The buyout of Nihar would yield consolidated market share gains and internal synergies. Their point of view: 'Go as high as you can. Do not try to over-optimize the valuation. You should not regret later that you could have upped the bid.' Prior to the board meeting, Marico's team was inclined to put in a bid of ₹170 crore for Nihar. Post the meeting, the bid was upped to ₹216 crore. Had they quoted ₹170 crore, and had that amount been close to other bids, Lever would have been tempted to negotiate between Marico and other players.

Two days later, and with the encouragement of the board, Marico submitted its final bid. There was no contest as Marico's bid price was much higher than all others and frankly, even beyond Lever's expectations. They gifted Harsh a top-of-the-line Mont Blanc fountain pen, with which he sealed the deal.

Marico bought Nihar for ₹216 crore (US$31 million in 2019). With this acquisition, Marico achieved more than 80 per cent market share in the perfumed coconut oil market and a stronger national footprint, especially in northern and eastern India. Plus, with both Nihar coconut oil and Parachute, Marico would also become the leader in the coconut oil market in the eastern region—the only market where Marico had lagged. Marico's national share in the branded coconut oil market jumped from 52 per cent to 60 per cent. Importantly, Marico had extinguished a formidable competitor with deep pockets and shut the doors on other potential competitors from posing any new threats in the coconut oil market. The experience of this large-sized and financially successful acquisition gave Marico a new confidence and an appetite for more.

Nihar's acquisition in February 2006 marked a watershed moment for Marico. The company, which appeared to prefer incremental moves, had taken a giant step. This was a mind-altering decision for Harsh and Marico. It also marked the final bend in the story, from being hunted as a target for acquisition to acquiring the hunter's brand. Harsh continued the celebration that weekend on the golf course. His good feeling about Marico's future gave his swing an extra lift and follow-through on every fairway. Goliath had finally fallen!

Analysts were initially sceptical of Nihar's high valuation but the synergies that Harsh's team had forecast came to pass. Because the deal for acquiring Nihar involved the brand only, it didn't obligate Marico to take on new staff or infrastructure commitments and spend time and unnecessary effort to rationalize these. Integration was easy and Marico could use its own manufacturing and distribution infrastructure to deliver to the market seamlessly.

As anticipated, the battle with Lever had taken a toll on Marico's earnings. In the short term, Harsh looked for ways to recoup revenues lost in the price war of the previous years. An opportunity came later in the year when copra prices dipped. Marico kept its product pricing steady. Parachute held market share and volumes, despite holding the price line. Proof again to the naysayers that Parachute was a strong brand. Marico's operating margin grew as a consequence, from 9 per cent in 2005 to 13 per cent in 2006. The decision to buy Nihar was more than vindicated.

The Nihar acquisition cemented Marico's new stature in the Indian corporate world. Commenting on this acquisition, Harsh declared, 'It was a quantum leap for Marico. Internally, it brought a strong feel-good factor that we were good enough to succeed against a powerful company. Externally, it brought us market synergies and financial upsides in a very short time.' The Nihar deal shifted perceptions in the capital markets—of a company that not only had strong financials but also the gumption to stare down a mighty competitor.

Harsh sums up the experience of being preyed upon through four years:

'Initially, there was the fear of being gobbled up as well as anxiety over how to proceed. Weighing the pros and cons of the situation, I deducted that whereas I had been in the coconut oil market for more than twenty-five years, Lever had entered it a mere two years ago. Lever had appointed a second or third tier manager with limited knowledge to head its foray. I, on the other hand, knew the coconut oil market and its value chain inside out. Nihar was a relatively small fish in the Hindustan Lever portfolio, and hence, they were unlikely to pursue Marico indefinitely. Whereas with Parachute being my only resource engine, I had to invest all of my firepower and wherewithal towards protecting it.

'My apprehensions turned to confidence once I had sized up the battleground.

'The odds were stacked in my favour.'

Harsh continues, 'Another vital insight I derived from Prof. Ram Charan was to delve into the genetic coding of your opponent, decipher the nature of the fight that is going to unfold. My opponent, being a chartered accountant and a finance professional by training, had chosen the strategy of growth through acquisition. Along with other strategic advantages, I concluded that it would actually be a long-drawn battle to tire out Lever, ad so it turned out to be. Also, it was crucial to keep people motivated and inspired to carry on the fight. Prof. Ram Charan's advice to protect the resource generating engine and not sell out to Lever proved to be worth its weight in gold. Retaining Parachute was also a blessing in disguise as it strengthened our market share, especially in the east, where it took a giant leap. It also compelled us to consolidate our rural distribution and substantially upped our profitability. Till date, Nihar remains the best and most profitable acquisition for Marico.

'Let there be no doubt that success is a magnet for predators, particularly when there isn't ownership control,' cautioned Prof. Ram Charan. Buying Marico would have got Lever market dominance in the coconut oil market without impacting its balance sheet in any significant way—its market cap was 100 times that of Marico. The self-assurance and conviction of Harsh in deciding to stand up not only saved the company but also brought for it rich rewards: a brand, improved margins, leadership share and volumes in all the markets, and forever extinguishing another threat. It also brought home the lesson: 'When the opportunity to acquire key brands that are central to company strategy presents itself, one must go to great lengths and be aggressive.'

14

Building New Growth Engines: India

Apart from the brands of Parachute and Saffola, there didn't seem to be any other brand or idea that could help Marico leapfrog. Much of the growth and profits came from the two major brands, with new introductions continuing to be niche performers. Harsh, once again, invited Prof. Ram Charan to help ignite growth.

Prof. Ram Charan: Voice of Reason

Prof. Ram Charan attended Marico's strategic plan meeting in the early part of 1996 at The Resort, Madh Island, located on the outskirts of Bombay, to add his perspectives to the plan. Harsh was meeting him in person for the first time. Previously, they had spoken on the phone and Harsh had shared some plans and performance documents with the professor. Over lunch, they shared their life stories and how life's journey had brought them to where they were. Like Harsh, Prof. Ram Charan too had to disentangle himself from his family's shoe business in north India to carve out his own path. The two connected instantly.

Harsh was awed by the professor's immense intellectual depth and insights. This was the beginning of a long association between the two. The professor was to have a large influence in guiding Harsh's leadership and strategic thinking thereon.

The both of them met every time their travels landed them in the same city. They'd catch a meal and update each other about what had transpired in the interim. Prof. Ram Charan's obsession with leadership processes and Harsh's hunger to continue learning were complementary. Sometimes, the professor would join the Marico team for day-long strategy sessions.

He would compliment Harsh on continually evaluating and adjusting his mix and portfolio of brands, geographies and businesses. He would often say that for a company to live and thrive over long periods, it should have a culture of continuously reinventing the portfolio in tune with the times. He saw Harsh do this when the domestic business was on a steady trajectory of growth. Harsh changed his business model to build Kaya Skin Clinics. He stepped out of India to build businesses overseas and then used the acquisition route to buy out brands in India and companies in other parts of the world.

Prof. Ram Charan showed an inexhaustible appetite for work. He lived permanently in a hotel suite and travelled around the world for client meetings. One time, he took a transcontinental flight to land in Bombay and drove three hours to reach the off-site retreat of Marico's board. Although he arrived in the middle of the night, he joined their discussions early next morning and continued throughout the day, holding the group's attention with his insightful observations. After the meeting adjourned at 5 p.m., he met the board members for one-on-one sessions till 10 p.m., post which he returned to Bombay for other appointments the following day.

Strategic Funding

Prof. Ram Charan and Harsh joined the top management team and the members of the Strategy Planning Task Force soon after their first meeting at lunch. Prof. Ram Charan shared the insights that he had gathered as he coached global corporate leaders such as Jack Welch, former chairman of GE.

Prof. Ram Charan provided useful insights and critique as the task force presented their plans. One of the issues that invited a lot of discussion was the huge advertising outlays planned for the new products. Harsh broached the dilemma of having to invest heavily in an attempt to create future growth engines. The success ratio of consumer product companies on new launches was and remains about one in ten, and a gamble most times despite research and planning. Failures being more the rule, chances are that the advertising spends on new launches could erode profits for several years into the future. But a progressive company would also need to create vehicles for future growth and expansion, and that can't be achieved without advertising year after year. This dilemma needed a resolution.

The plan outlays, when summated, looked unaffordable, with each product group coming up with their own growth, product plans and input budgets. How could Marico prioritize the outlay to a critical few? Harsh did not believe in issuing diktats or slashing plans and budgets unilaterally. He would want his team to conclude what the sound direction was, given the many competing demands.

Prof. Ram Charan, who was a strong advocate of growth, impressed upon Harsh that growth was like oxygen to a company and inculcating a growth mindset in the organization was an imperative. At the same time, growth had to be sustainable and profitable.

Prof. Ram Charan introduced the concept of strategic funding, whereby Marico could earmark around 20 per cent of profits as a fund to develop new growth engines each year. This funding became a part of the annual budget with a strong discipline to ensure that it did not get cut or diverted for other short-term exigencies. The strategic fund was important to keep the pipeline of product prototypes active and also to demonstrate the company's commitment to building future growth engines. Over time, some of the new products launched earlier would turn profitable and exit the strategic funding net, making way for other, new opportunities to enter the cycle. The advantage of the strategic fund was that it paced new product engines, and at the same time, the company did not take a disproportionate hit on profits. Over the years, as profits grew, so would the capacity of the company to enlarge the pool of strategic funding. It thereby served the twin objectives of investing in future growth engines and at the same time managing shareholder expectations of sustainable and profitable growth. The strategic fund was now a gospel for all the new business ventures, new brands and extensions, or new categories, as well as entry into new international emerging markets.

Harsh had begun to feel that the consumer business was running along a steady trajectory and he had created an organization skilled enough to face its challenges and opportunities. He needed other big winners in his basket, even if it meant exploring diverse business models in hitherto untested territory.

Contrarian Move in Hair Oils

Another growth engine that Marico was banking on was a range of hair oils it was hoping to build under the Parachute Advansed brand name, a brand that was already reaching more than 50 million households. Though the concept of creating a bouquet of hair oils came late in the nineties, it stagnated at an embryonic stage till the marketing mix and brand architecture was fine-tuned. The real traction for the Parachute extensions came later, in the early years of the new millennium.

In most parts of the world, the practice of oiling the hair was unknown or had died away some generations ago. The hair oiling habit was salient only on the Indian subcontinent, the Middle East and among some of the local populations in Africa. A common view was that as India and its neighbouring markets developed and evolved, the younger generations would move away from the habit gradually and then completely replace hair oils with other products for their hair nourishment and grooming needs.

Marico's marketing team, while closely monitoring emerging consumer trends, bet on a different trajectory of change. Even as they worked with their product development counterparts on modern hair nourishment and grooming formats, they doubled their investments on building the hair oil franchise. Analysts and Marico watchers were sceptical about this strategy as they felt that the potential to grow the hair oil market would be limited. However, within the marketing team, the conviction was strong that hair oils would continue to grow, as there was still a large loose oil market, waiting to be converted to packaged products.

Contrary to the analyst opinion, Marico continues its thrust on hair oils. Harsh believed that the habit of using oils to nourish and groom hair, an age-old tradition, passed on from one generation to another, was deeply ingrained in the minds of the subcontinental population. Based on this hypothesis and the growth numbers of the already long established national and regional brands, Marico decided to enter the value-added hair oil market. The market size, at around ₹1500 crore in 2000 (US$214 million in 2019) and the expected double-digit annual growth, was attractive enough for serious consideration.

Traditionally, generic vegetable oils in their pure form or with added ingredients were being used for oiling hair. These were also being offered to consumers in packed and branded forms by some companies. Marico studied these hair oiling practices and usage patterns in India and concluded that the market for hair oils can broadly be segmented into **pre-wash** and **post-wash** categories. Typically, heavier oils were being used as pre-wash, where the oil was massaged into the hair hours before a shower to provide nourishment and pollution protection. Typical to this category were oils with herbs. The post-wash category had lighter fragranced oils that did the job of hair grooming. Both pre- and post-wash oils were formulated and positioned to offer specific benefits and solutions to the consumer.

The pre-wash category was further segmented based on the basis of the main ingredient in the hair oil. There were different leaders in these sub-segments. Dabur led the amla segment with Dabur Amla—oil with gooseberry extracts to provide thickness and darkness to hair. Marico led the value-added coconut oil segment with Parachute Advansed—for hair nourishment. Emami led the cooling oil segment with Navratna, used to massage the head and relieve stress. It was not easy for anyone to dislodge the leader in these categories, to achieve leadership across all the segments.

Dabur was making a high margin in the amla segment by charging a premium. Marico launched its own variant, Shanti Amla, at a lower price with a conscious strategy to garner volumes aggressively. As expected, it made significant market share gains and with growing volumes and modest unit margins, the absolute gross margins grew healthily. Marico followed this success by adding a range of pre-wash value-added hair oils: Shanti Sarson Amla, Parachute Advansed Aloe Vera Oil, Parachute Advansed Hot Oil and Parachute Advansed Ayurvedic Oil. The range of brand extensions addressed needs of different consumers and occupied various niches of hair oil usage.

The Parachute Advansed brand launched a number of innovative advertisements on festive occasions to infuse excitement into a seemingly boring hair oil market. For example, one of the TV commercials that ran before Holi encouraged consumers to apply Parachute Advansed to their hair before setting out to play with colours. Not only would the oil protect their hair and skin, but the colours would wash off easily as well. Another campaign which promoted the oiling of hair, and which received an extremely favourable response, advocated 'One hour—*champi kiya kya*? (did you massage oil in your hair and leave it on for an hour before shampooing it?)' Following this practice would ensure that not only would hair be protected from harmful chemicals in the shampoo, but would also retain its softness post-wash. There was yet another advertisement that leveraged Hindu rituals and beliefs—it was considered auspicious to oil one's body before bathing on the first day of the Hindu New Year. Thus, a special 'Diwali' packaging was conceived to encourage the consumer to adhere to this ritual.

The brand also introduced low-priced, single use, small packs and sachets to enlarge the branded market by driving conversions of loose oil users. These festive market interventions helped the brand increase its penetration. Marico failed to make a dent in the cooling oil segment despite experimenting with a few prototypes.

In the post-wash light coconut hair oil segment, Marico had Parachute Jasmine and Parachute Advansed Coconut Oil. The Hair & Care brand, which was a non-sticky oil, was repositioned as a youthful and contemporary hair nourishment oil for the young woman, as Hair & Care Dry Fruit Oil. Later, Marico added Nihar perfumed coconut hair oil to the post-wash basket when the brand was acquired from Hindustan Unilever and later launched Nihar Jasmine.

The somewhat staid and sleepy hair oil market had found new life as Marico aggressively pushed its hair oil extensions. Marico emerged as the market leader and Harsh's assessment was vindicated as hair oils remained among the fastest growing categories in the FMCG sector. In 2019, Marico had more than a 25 per cent share of the hair oil market in an estimated ₹8000 crore (US$1.14 billion) market. Marico had finally found another winner with its suite of hair oils that contributed significantly both to its top line and bottom line.

To ensure that the company had an early presence in the youth market, Marico went beyond hair oils and introduced a range of modern grooming products like gels, creams and serums. It launched Parachute Advansed After-shower Hair Cream, Gel and Silk-n-Shine leave-in serums. To this home-grown range was added Set Wet hair gels and creams and Livon hair serums (acquired from Reckitt Benckiser). Marico had consolidated itself in the haircare market by expanding its portfolio from traditional hair oil to pre- and post-wash hair products to serums, creams and gels, thereby targeting any shifts in trends.

The company had established its presence as a haircare marketer in the Middle East when it launched Parachute Hair Cream for Arab consumers. The acquisition of Fiancée and Hair Code brands in Egypt, Caivil and Black Chic brands in South Africa and later, X-Men in Vietnam and Code 10 in Malaysia, declared Marico's credentials as a significant haircare company.

In spite of analysts' negative opinion about the future of hair oils, the company vindicated its stand on promoting pre- and post-wash hair solutions in India as well as overseas.

Saffola Health Foods

The search for growth engines had finally begun to bear fruit. Encouraged by the success of the hair oils portfolio, Marico simultaneously started work on the Saffola range. The brand had already established its credentials as one that cared for the health of the whole family through the range of its heart-healthy cooking oils and blends. The earlier attempts to extend the brand to healthy salt and healthy atta did not attain the required critical mass and set back the plans for newer food extensions. Harsh wanted his research and innovation teams to guarantee products that would emerge winners in the marketplace.

Saffola Zest was a well-crafted snack food innovation based on the hypothesis that there was a significant market for healthy snacks for the health-conscious consumer. The past learnings of margin expectations, consumer indulgence frequency and health properties were all factored into the design. The snack foods market was booming with potato chips, *namkeens* (salted snacks) and extruded foods, to name a few categories. There were already big names in the business, like Frito Lays, Bikanerwala, Haldiram's and ITC Foods, along with a host of regional brands. The market for snack foods was growing at 15 per cent per annum and was trending to reach ₹7000 crore by 2024 (US$289 million at the 2019 dollar price). Snack foods were typically deep fried in oil and considered unhealthy. They were often referred to as 'sin foods'.

Research tracked the various snacking occasions and consumer profiles and figured that there was a growing market for healthy snack foods which were frugal in the use of oil and salt. The 'sin foods' were consumed with a lot of guilt, particularly by people in the older age groups, who needed to watch out for various lifestyle diseases such as hypertension, high blood cholesterol and diabetes. Saffola Zest was fashioned to address mainly this segment. It was a snack food made from extruded high fibre grains. The inclusion of fibre in the formulation with low oil and salt looked tailor-made for the target consumer and research confirmed this conclusion.

Launched in Bombay, the billboards screamed the comparative health benefits of this new snack. It generated interest and trials but not repeats. A product that was innovative and looked promising in research did not turn out to be quite the winner that Marico had hoped for. The reasons for failure were diagnosed. Marico learnt that launching a snack that was not tasty was a contradiction in terms. Snacks by their very definition were indulgence foods and consumers weren't too fussy about them as long as they tasted good. Marico committed an error in judgement in placing health over taste. It seemed too obsessed with the idea of Saffola and its positioning as a health brand, to the exclusion of all else. Herein was a lesson learnt. Taste comes first and consumers were unwilling to compromise taste for health—an insight that it would then carry into the next series of Saffola extensions.

Up until this point, the marketing brief was used directly by the product development team to create the product prototype. Once the product was developed, it was sent to the marketing team for consumer testing. If this product was then rejected by consumers, it would go back to the R&D lab for re-jigging. This back-and-forth process would cause major delays in the launch of a new product.

With the help of an innovation consultant, Marico re-engineered the process in order to boost success rates. This re-engineering crashed all the barriers and sources of distortion in the communication process between the marketing team, the product development team and the consumer. All the three were on the same page throughout the action research process.

Oats were a popular breakfast food in the western world, owing to their proven heart health benefits. The market for plain oats was growing in India. Marico decided to enter this segment through the Saffola brand extensions. In a short time, it gained a 15 per cent share in the plain oats category. However, owing to lack of differentiation with market leaders Kellogg's and Quaker, the market share remained at around 15 per cent. Research with consumers revealed that the Indian palate preferred a savoury breakfast—e.g., while south Indians' breakfast staple was idli-sambar, the north Indian palate opted for aloo paratha. So, based on regional taste preferences, a series of different savoury offerings were developed, like tomato oats, pongal oats, masala oats, lemon and pepper oats, etc. This again was a pioneering step in the oats category. To generate consumer trials of the new offering, Marico installed vending machines in airports, offices, gymnasiums and hospitals.

With the evolving consumer preference for gourmet dietary foods, the company rolled out **Saffola FITTIFY Gourmet,** a range of healthy foods and beverages. The range includes green tea, green coffee and hi-protein meal shakes, mainly through select outlets and e-commerce channels.

In 2019, the Saffola foods basket delivered a turnover close to ₹200 crore (US$28 million) and which amounted to 20 per cent of the overall Saffola franchise. More importantly, Marico had finally got its Saffola brand extension concept right, extending from healthy cooking oils to healthy foods.

Brand Acquisitions

The first brand acquisition of Marico was Mediker, an anti-lice shampoo owned by Proctor & Gamble. It held a small and niche market, but with very attractive profit margins. Harsh was aware that the usage of Mediker was limited as it was present only in a shampoo format. At that time, shampoos registered an extremely low sale in semi-rural and rural markets in India. There was a window of opportunity here, realized Harsh, to develop Mediker through the oil route and capture the semi-rural and rural markets. Marico bought the brand, confident that they could develop anti-lice Mediker oil. Within six months of the acquisition, Mediker oil was launched, and sales of the Mediker franchise doubled within a year.

Another acquisition was that of a regional brand of coconut oil, Oil of Malabar. This buy-over plugged emerging competition from Hindustan Lever and helped fight other regional low-priced competitors. The two-brand strategy of Parachute and Oil of Malabar helped reinforce Marico's battle with Hindustan Lever over Nihar.

Despite relaunching Nihar repeatedly over the next three–four years, Hindustan Lever failed to make a dent in Parachute's market share. Nihar's lacklustre performance resulted in the FMCG giant divesting the oil from its portfolio. And Marico reaped rich dividends, further strengthening its market share to 60 per cent.

Set Wet and Livon

Up until the acquisition of Set Wet (hair gels and deodorants) and Livon (hair serum) in 2012, Marico's mainstay hair care offerings were traditional and catered to the generations. These brand acquisitions helped Marico attain a new capability and enter a more western category that appealed to the personal care needs of the millennials and the young.

Census studies in India pointed out that 50 per cent of the population was less than twenty-five years of age and a demographic dividend was around the corner. A shift in post-wash haircare needs, towards newer formats like hair creams, hair gels and waxes among young men and hair serums among women, had already begun.

Harsh and his team decided to take a look at a clutch of 'youth brands' in the category of hair gels, deodorants and leave-in conditioners. **Reckitt Benckiser** offered these for divestment. This seemed to be a good fit with Marico's strategic plans. The brands could fill the gap of youth products in Marico's portfolio and capitalize on the tailwind behind the youth products: a category that was under-penetrated and growing much faster than Marico's existing portfolio.

Set Wet hair gels and body-deodorants were aimed at young men. Livon hair serum was targeted at young women. Livon is a light non-greasy solution that reduces hair frizz, detangles and makes it soft and silky. The addition of these brands along with Parachute Advansed After-shower Hair Cream and Gel, and Silk-n-Shine hair serums, further helped Marico consolidate its market share in the haircare market and achieve leadership position in youth segments. The team decided to make a bid.

The board, however, pushed back and asked the management to evaluate it as they found the asking price too high: could Marico not overinvest in Parachute Gel and Silk-n-Shine serum, thereby strengthening its market share instead of ploughing in a considerable sum to acquire those brands? The team deliberated over this dilemma. Had Marico not pursued the acquisition route, the brands that were market leaders would have fallen into the hands of its competitors. Would this occur, dislodging or capturing a substantial market share from these brands would be an extremely difficult proposition. Acquiring them would be far more savvy, especially given that they would ride the growth curve rapidly. Some board members still had reservations as the bid value was high at ₹740 crore (US$105 million in 2019) but eventually left it to Harsh to take a final call. Marico went on to acquire **Set Wet** and **Livon.**

In the initial years after the acquisition, things did not go as planned. Growth rates were initially at 20 per cent per annum, then suddenly began to decline. The spray deodorant market also saw a disruption with the introduction of an innovative product from Fogg, which took market share from all the other deodorants. All reassessments of the buy decision suggested that the valuations were justified, but sales continued to trail the acquisition assumptions. The board pushed the management hard for a workable plan to step up performance. The marketing team believed that the rationale for entry was right and it needed to wait for the tide to change. Then, in 2018, there was clear traction to vindicate the acquisition decision. Sales of both Set Wet gels and Livon conditioners began to move up quickly and Marico seemed to look like a more rounded haircare marketer.

Incubation Cell

Harsh was of the view that the best route to set up a new business was to seed it through an incubation cell, germinate the idea, test out prototypes and grow it in measured steps. The incubation cell would characteristically be entrepreneurial in its mind-set and culture. A two-person team of Marico managers would work together for a period of time as entrepreneurs and give traction to a specific idea. They would work directly under Harsh and thus, would be empowered to make quick decisions and move fast.

Said he, 'I was conscious that as an organization grows, work becomes more complex and so, gets structured through hierarchies, functions, processes and policies. A kind of rigidity creeps in. Decisions tend to get safer and delayed. It was also my experience that many new ideas were orphaned and postponed for another day amid the many other day-to-day work pressures.'

The incubation cell started with Rahul Koul, a well-regarded brand manager. Rahul was freed from his regular work. Rakesh Pandey formed the second member of the team. Harsh made it clear to the rest of the organization that speed was of the essence and he did not want bureaucratic procedures to act as bottlenecks.

The goal of the incubation cell was to create new engines of growth, and with the license to take calculated risks. With nothing else assigned to them but the incubation projects, there were no 'escape buttons' or the refuge of the other role as an excuse for non-delivery. The success of the project was the only determinant of performance.

The fact that this wasn't a regular role-bound job, the recognition that came with the selection to the incubation team, and the fact that it reported directly to the top, together created the impetus to succeed. Seeing the power of this concept in action, Harsh put to use the idea of 'no escape buttons' time and again, when he pioneered new initiatives that weren't operational in nature, for e.g., expanding to international markets, setting up an ERP system and leveraging infotech in sales and distribution.

KAYA

One of the early projects that seemed promising came to attention in 2001. Harsh had been approached by an acquaintance, Asif Adil (who was earlier with McKinsey), to form a JV to market laser-based body hair removal equipment to clinics and beauty parlours. These had gained popularity in clinics in the US and UK and there was a potential to market them in India. They did some dipstick research that suggested that the market had high potential. However, Harsh was not keen to enter a business that could soon get commoditized. It led him to take a closer look. They undertook a trip to the US and UK to visit such laser hair clinics and experience first-hand how these clinics offered their services to customers. He learnt that they not only offered laser hair removal services but a range of other skincare treatments as well.

Harsh's instinct told him that the Indian market was ripe and ready for a bouquet of skincare solutions that offered more than laser hair removal. Most of the clinics in the UK and US were standalone clinics, run by the doctors themselves. It was difficult to create a chain of branded clinics as dermatologists were expensive to hire in developed countries. Whereas, in India, compensation to dermatologists was far more affordable. To arrive at the best suite of solutions to be introduced, Harsh himself carried out insighting with consumers in the target segment. These were in-depth individual interactions, rather than relying on traditional market research through group discussions or formatted questionnaires.

Indian skin profile differed from Caucasian skin in that it is darker, as also Indian hair which is, obviously, not only darker but also thicker. Given these facts, it stood to reason that modifications would have to be made to suit the Indian clientele. The designated team, then, along with the equipment and machinery providers abroad, designed protocols and machines accordingly.

Marico's incubation cell assembled a prototype clinic at the office and began testing this concept of a new consumer experience in India. The first few machines were installed, and the team tested the prototype with a small group of volunteers as well as acquaintances. This model provided immense learning, grasp and insights in a range of areas, including the training of personnel, designing protocol and receiving invaluable client feedback on the effectiveness and efficacy of all the treatments. Months after getting an encouraging and positive response from all those who took trial treatments, Harsh and his team were very confident regarding the potential of this new venture. Asif Adil, who had partnered this venture from day one, also held a minority stake in this. Parallel to the trials, a search for a suitable property for the first clinic in Bombay bore results, and soon, work on the interiors was underway at a fast pace.

Meanwhile, the team identified the cities that would offer maximum potential, the number of centres, projected financials and other such relevant details. Would this new enterprise fall into the beauty space?

Along with all the luxe frills and visuals implemented in a top-of-the-line beauty salon? Or should it be positioned as an extremely clinical and hygienic doctor's premises? Many debates and deliberations later, the team concluded that it would be neither. It would be a zen space, peaceful and soothing, coupled with the highest standards of hygiene and cleanliness, and of course, cutting-edge technology.

It was named **'Kaya'**.

Kaya was primarily about skin. Recapturing the flawless skin that nature bestows at birth. And recovering that skin as best possible, years later, past the ravages of lifestyle, environment and time.

Work on the interiors of the first clinic progressed at a rapid clip. Prior to one of his site visits, Harsh asked his wife, Archana, to accompany him and share her observations. Her take on the almost complete premises disturbed him. She not only negated the location of the place, but also completely disapproved the look-feel of the same. Previous to this, she had also visited the training centre and undergone a few treatments. She found the quality of service as well as the treatments to be excellent. However, she pointed out to Harsh that there was a pressing need to hone not only the communication skills of the therapists, but also their overall grooming. Unsettled and upset by all the points she had made, Harsh insisted that she attend the next Kaya committee meeting and state her views. The committee comprised of only males, whose exposure at that time to anything close to a salon experience was, at best, a head massage and a shampoo. What she had to say was met with unanimous disapproval and censure.

Archana wanted to change the interiors completely. She visualized a very zen look and feel: rice paper-lined treatment rooms, pastel interiors, the very soothing murmur of flowing water with soft, calming music in the background. Additionally, she insisted that Kaya should offer a signature hot and cold drink along with tea and coffee. Therapists should be given customized uniforms. Appearance, hairstyling, general grooming, with very specific importance given to personal hygiene: all these were non-negotiable for her. The all-male committee was quite appalled at her list of recommendations. 'Either you're the best, or you're down with the rest,' she stated.

She stood her ground.

And won.

And so, it was. A complete change in interiors, grooming of the therapists by agencies that trained airhostesses to walk, talk, groom and carry themselves, uniforms custom-made by an established designer, and very extensive hygiene must-dos.

Archana was involved not only in the design elements of the clinics, but also ensured that they were executed as per her standards.

The first two clinics were launched in Bombay in December 2002. One in Bandra, and the other in Kala Ghoda. Within a year, six Kaya clinics opened, three each in Bombay and Delhi. Had Harsh not set up the incubation cell, he may not have entered the skincare services business. And, had he launched the venture without initiating the incubation cell, the idea would have taken far more than a year and a half to execute. Harsh knew it would take time to build scale and assess the experiment correctly. Kaya Ltd was incorporated as a 100 per cent subsidiary of Marico.

Harsh was excited by the potential synergy of trends in India as well as the overseas market. His next step was prototyping two skin centres in Dubai. And in a short period of time, Kaya expanded quickly in both India as well as in the Middle East.

Up until now, Marico's business delivery model was through a chain of channel partners, reaching vast geographies, at the end of which the consumer had a product that she and her family could touch, feel and use.

The Kaya business model of direct consumer service was hugely different with a unique set of challenges, until then unknown to Marico. It involved expensive real estate, clinic locations, personalized service and high dependence on staff for service delivery. Aware that Kaya was a completely different venture, Harsh was cognizant that it involved safety and customer service at the intersection of three new areas for Marico: hospitality, beauty and retail. Kaya had its own offices and most of its staff was recruited from other service-oriented businesses. Interchanging or co-locating staff between Marico and Kaya was avoided as the mindset required for a consumer business and a service business were dramatically different. As the business grew, it faced other challenges too. There was a higher rate of staff churn and so a system to efficiently manage this reality of frequent staff induction and product and service training necessitated a new competency to master. There were also difficulties in balancing client experience versus client volumes. The obvious pressure of growing the client base and the business per client needed to be balanced with the quality of client experience. The high capital employed in space and infrastructure was a spoiler to attractive financial returns, particularly when compared with the consumer business. The Kaya experience, and the credibility it was to build, would later become a platform to launch a range of skincare products, retailed through Kaya outlets and other non-traditional channels.

In 2019, the Kaya business had ninety-seven clinics in India and twenty-three clinics in the Middle East. Its range of skincare products was being retailed from more than 500 outlets. Kaya achieved a turnover of ₹420 crore (US$60 million in 2019).

Looking Back, Harsh Says:

'I had yearned for a long time to initiate an endeavour that would be completely of my own making. The founding of an all-India chain of skin clinics by Kaya led to a surge of medical students majoring in dermatology. In good time, a host of "me too" skin services entered the field. However, Kaya-trained therapists and Kaya services and hygiene continued to remain a benchmark. I must emphasize here that setting up an incubation cell played a vital role in establishing Kaya.

'Kaya's pioneering initiative into skincare services in India later paved the way towards creating a market for skincare products under the brand name Kaya, backed by the science of dermatology and the in-house research team: customized products especially suitable for Indian skin.'

Joint Ventures

Another way to build growth engines was through the route of joint ventures with more established corporations. Harsh had met a few MNC chiefs seeking an India entry when they called on him during their India visits. His conversations with Prof. Ram Charan spurred Harsh to think ahead and consider how best to deal with the approaches made by foreign companies.

As India opened up to world trade in the 1990s, several multinational corporations sought to enter the country's markets through joint ventures.

In those days, it was a fashionable concept to grow business discontinuously. The media used to be alive with speculations and announcements of joint venture alliances. These generated plenty of publicity and news value.

Harsh was selective in his meetings. At one point, L'Oréal, the French personal care company, approached Harsh through an investment banker. Harsh intuitively saw that, while the immediate discussion was about a joint venture, the eventual game plan was to buy out Marico. The proposal was rejected.

One day, Harsh got a phone call from Suh Kyung-bae, the CEO of the Korean company AmorePacific Corporation, the world's fourteenth largest cosmetics company. Suh happened to be in Bombay and called on Harsh. Both recognized areas of common ground for collaboration. They met again with a few members of their teams over dinner. It looked like AmorePacific could benefit from Marico's insights on Indian consumers and doing business in India. Marico, in turn, could benefit from the Korean company's experience with product development in skincare and haircare. The teams followed up with a series of exchanges. In time, they discovered differences in their positions, including who should be the majority stakeholder in a joint venture. There could be similar conflict over brand ownership. AmorePacific was roughly three times larger than Marico. Harsh realized not only that they might have different appetites for taking a loss, but that he may also end up dealing with a lower layer of management in the Korean company. Marico did not pursue the opportunity.

In 1998, at about the time of the Mediker acquisition, Marico signed two distribution agreements. One was with P&G to distribute Camay Toilet Soap, Ariel Detergent Bar Soap, Pampers, Old Spice range and Clearasil. These were small brands for P&G and they found that the time, effort and money spent on chasing sales of these brands were somewhat disproportionate to the returns. So, they outsourced the physical distribution to Marico. The other was Indo-Nissin, a Japanese company that had also approached Marico to distribute its Top Ramen brand of noodles.

The sales division of Marico had attained a reach of 1.2 million retail outlets, covering every city and town in India with a population of 20,000 or more. Structurally, it was the distribution house for the two internal businesses of nature care and health care. So distributing for the P&G and Indo-Nissin range was not going to be a structural issue. This was a clean alliance, with no conflict of interest, as roles were clearly delineated. Seen as a win-win, it was led by a nominated manager from the client company and a nominated manager from Marico.

Marico discontinued the arrangement with P&G in 2002 as its internal volumes grew. Indo-Nissin sought more time to set up its own sales force and eventually, Marico discontinued distributing the Top Ramen brand in 2008. Both Marico and the client companies of Indo-Nissin and P&G got what they wanted for the contracted time of the alliance. Since it wasn't a joint venture, unravelling from this alliance went as smoothly as it had come together.

The distribution agreement that Marico signed with P&G and Indo-Nissin was an arrangement between equal partners with a clear understanding of roles, terms and conditions, including exit—in a way, a perfect alliance.

Reflecting on these experiences of Harsh, Prof. Ram Charan cautioned that a joint venture had to be a means to a clearly defined goal. An FMCG company's most valuable asset is its brand. In a joint venture, brand ownership was often a pivotal question. The local joint venture partner could spend time and resources on marketing and building the brand of the incoming foreign company but could be unwilling to part with the brand when the JV dissolved. Where a new brand is created in the JV, the foreign company may bleed the local partner to make the shared brand strong. If it did well, the foreign company could try to take over the business. There could be win-lose dynamics at play, often to the disadvantage to the local partner.

Invariably, a multinational corporation entering India would appoint a lower-level manager in the headquarters to be the point person to deal with the Indian CEO. The power imbalance could make the process of operational decisions time-consuming, requiring the Indian CEO to negotiate across several layers of the multinational's hierarchy.

Building new growth engines, augmenting the thrust on hair oils and foods as well as the various acquisitions helped Marico multiply its turnover ten times in the space of twenty years.

Tightening the Belt

When the word 'growth' is used in the context of a business, it creates an image of going higher and further and a sense that all's well with the business. Pruning and shedding businesses that act as a drag or have no specific strategic reason to exist also cause facilitative conditions for growth engines. It helps focus on the more relevant businesses and overall financial health of a company. It unlocks mindspace and releases energies for more profitable pursuits. In that sense alone, pruning is a form of growth. Recognizing this truth, Marico conducted periodic exercises of trimming its stock-keeping units, shedding its brands and taking appropriate steps to reduce costs.

The process involved benchmarking costs with industry peers and even with allied industry companies like pharma and paints to identify opportunity areas for cost and efficiency improvement. Partners in the value chain co-operated whole-heartedly in these cost studies as it helped them build more efficient operations and also get a share of those gains.

Once in a while, Harsh would remind his team that any area of cost that had not been examined for a period of four-five years had the potential to yield a cost optimization opportunity of at least 10 per cent. One such project was the copra oil supply chain. Harsh tasked his team to find ways and means to integrate vertically and eliminate intermediary commissions. India's coconut production was spread across an estimated 7,50,000 farmers, mainly in Kerala and Tamil Nadu. The supply of coconuts from such a wide array of producers required the company to rely on the traditional way of sourcing through brokers and traders. Apart from consolidating lots, the brokers helped the farmers sell their harvests quickly and convert their crop into cash. The farmers did not have financial resources for storing or timing their sales to buyers. The intermediaries, the brokers and traders, had the resources to hold on to inventory, control material availability and wield an influence on prices. The trade practices were often at a disadvantage to Marico being the single largest buyer. Multiple intermediaries constituted the chain of middlemen, from transporters to multiple layers of brokers and the trader. The 'middleman' margins made up a significant portion of costs in Marico's supply chain.

The Coconut Oil Market

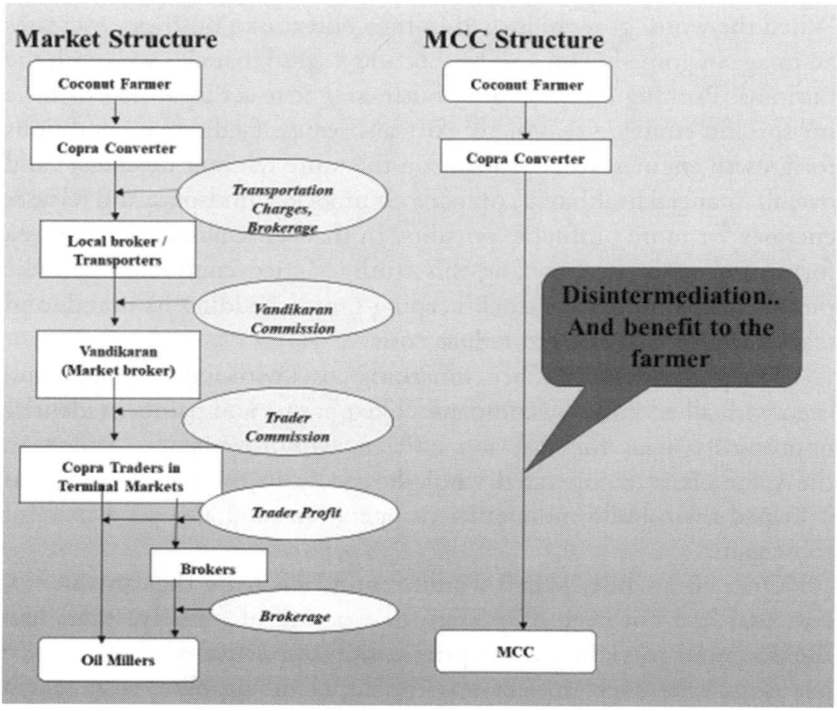

To improve the cost structure, the supply chain team came up with yet another innovation called 'gate buying'. Marico spread the word among coconut farmers in Kerala that it would buy directly from them at market prices if they brought their copra to the Kanjikode factory gate. The object of this approach was not to squeeze the farmers for lower prices but gain-share when gains accrued. The farmers received a better price for their harvest than they did from the brokers or terminal markets, thereby eliminating the layers of traders' margins and broker fees. An extension of the gate buying concept was the establishment of a network of Marico copra collection centres across Kerala and Tamil Nadu, close to the coconut growing areas. This provided farmers and marginal converters the facility of demand at their doorstep and afforded Marico a source of assured supply throughout the year. Another improvement was e-bidding. Every morning, farmers who had copra ready to sell logged in and entered the amount of copra they were offering. Marico staff responded to that estimate with bids. It was the farmer's prerogative to accept or decline the bids. The moment the farmer accepted the price, an SMS or email purchase order was sent, and Marico took delivery of the copra at its collection centres. The gate buying, collection centre buying and the e-buying: all of these brought the farmer and the company in close contact, built trust through a history of transactions and eventually culminated in the elimination of brokers and traders, as also terminal market costs. It changed forever trade practices established more than a century ago. The costs saved in the disintermediation of the supply chain went straight to the bottom line and afforded a better price to the farmer.

Says coconut farmer Muhammad Shafeeq K. from Kerala, 'Whereas earlier we sold our copra to a chain of middlemen who added their margins, we now sell directly to the Marico collection centre. Marico's buying process is open and transparent and we get a fair market rate. Again, we receive immediate payment, as opposed to others who take over a month and pay in two-three instalments. Marico buys our copra regardless of market sentiments whereas other will buy only in a favourable market.' Adds another farmer, 'We needed ten days to load a truckful of copra. Now we take a part load to the collection centre, allowing us flexibility to sell small quantities as well as saving freight costs.'

This innovative disintermediation process has been selected as a case study in IIM Ahmedabad by Prof. Saral Mukherjee and G. Raghuram.

Over time, Marico established a deep-rooted relationship with the farmers, much beyond a transactional business relationship, by imparting knowledge to them on best farming practices, which led to a substantial increase in their yields.

Divestments

The first brand to be divested was Sweekar. The refined sunflower oil category had many players, with no differentiation in any of the oils. Competition was intense, leading to price-cutting, and, therefore, very low profit margins. Harsh would often surmise that Sweekar really had no strategic reason to be on Marico's portfolio. His familiarity with the edible oil industry gave him a good sense that almost all species of refined vegetable oils sold on price. Large volumes were possible with distribution reach and trade discounts but at the cost of poor margins. It was difficult to invest continually in brand building without making a decent profit. Also, the lack of a unique or credible proposition made building a brand a futile exercise. It was not possible for Marico to do with Sweekar what it had done with Saffola: create a premium brand. Harsh never championed categories that didn't deliver a healthy margin or sold on their commodity credentials. But he had persisted with Sweekar for eighteen years due to the tactical role it played in protecting Saffola. Further, its large volumes and throughputs had helped it amortize the cost of manufacturing and selling. By 2008, Marico's other brands had built scale and the manufacturing and sales infrastructure was much less dependent on the throughputs that Sweekar provided. The brand's role in the portfolio had also diminished. In fact, margins and return on capital improved without the Sweekar business.

Looking Back

Speaking of the divestments, Harsh remarked that 'in business, there is no shame in selling off heirlooms. It is an important means of unlocking value or stopping the bleed. It helps focus on more strategic and profitable priorities.

'I have encountered many challenges in my journey. One where I am proud and gratified that I stood my ground is the challenge I took up regarding the acquisition and thrust on hair oils. Many friends and analysts from capital markets felt very strongly that I was committing a huge error of judgement in taking a big bet on a category where usage was likely to drop. The outcome in terms of market share as well as growth of the hair oil market left no doubt about who came up trumps in this challenge. Lack of substantial competition proved an added advantage in giving Marico a free run. Looking back, it proved to be a well-thought-out move.'

Harsh goes on, 'The failure of baked snacks hit home the realization that taste is of primary importance where foods are concerned, regardless of health benefits. In the plain oats segment, we reached a stagnation in market share as we did not have any product differentiation compared to the market leader, Quaker Oats. Our insighting with consumers brought home the fact that Indians prefer a savoury breakfast. Also, breakfast preferences are diverse all over India.

Each state has an exclusive taste and flavour profile. Marico conducted an in-depth study of each state's palate and eating habits, developed a range of savoury oats, then segmented them for the different markets. The launch of savoury oats was a pioneering move in the creation of a new category. Today, Marico's market share hovers around 80 per cent in this category. Over time, savoury oats were promoted as a snack and meal option to be consumed through the day in addition to breakfast.

'So for me, every failure has led to a learning. The saying, "win some, lose some," doesn't resonate with me. My belief is "Sometimes you win. But you never lose. You learn."'

15

Building New Growth Engines: Overseas

Marico's export arm had started in the early 1990s with a very small operation, mainly shipping Parachute coconut oil to the Indian diaspora overseas. A significant number lived in the Middle Eastern countries, chiefly in the UAE, Saudi Arabia and Oman, many of them originally from Kerala. For them, Parachute was a staple from back home. Marico could not cash in on the diaspora opportunity earlier due to the government's pre-liberalization policies of not exporting agricultural products.

As the liberalization policies took effect and India emerged from its 1991 currency crisis, Harsh saw new opportunities. He created a formal exports division. Hitherto, exports to neighbouring countries such as Nepal and Bhutan were managed by the regional sales manager of eastern India. However, the Indian region accounted for the lion's share of his sales volumes and so the small export business to Nepal and Bhutan would tend to get ignored. Making a manager responsible exclusively for the exports to Nepal and Bhutan would bring it the desired attention. Harsh was intuitive in his decision when he assigned a manager to open up export sales. With restrictions lifted, Marico began the export of Parachute coconut oil to the Middle East and in the process, debuted Marico's international journey.

Marico Gulf

So, in 1996, Marico set up an office in Dubai and obtained an export licence. As India's foreign exchange reserves improved, funding of overseas business development activities was liberalized.

A Marico manager was posted to Dubai to partner the local distributor in growing Parachute volumes in the Emirates. He was also responsible for driving the sales of Parachute in Oman and Saudi Arabia and the rest of the GCC (Gulf Coordination Council) through other local distributor partners. The experience of building distribution in India helped considerably in distribution to small outlets. Selling to large retail chains like Lulu and Carrefour was a new learning that would stand them in good stead when modern trade came to India. Apart from Parachute coconut oil, Marico developed Parachute Hair Cream aimed at Arab men: an innovation created in the Marico India labs for the GCC. Surprisingly, consumer research later suggested that Arab women were also using the hair cream and so the company repositioned it to include both men and women. Later, a hot oil hair treatment, Parachute Gold Hammam Zait, was introduced as a home spa product for Arab women. The three Parachute offerings in the GCC markets delivered a revenue of ₹175 crore (US$25 million) in 2019. Growth had plateaued in the past few years due to the economic slowdown, the stagnation in Indian expatriate population growth and usage saturation.

Kaya Skin Clinics set up shop in UAE in the summer of 2003. Over the fifteen years since, the network of clinics has grown to twenty-three covering the UAE, Oman and Saudi Arabia. The clinics employ twenty-eight well-trained dermatologists in a staff force of 300 drawn from sixteen nationalities to service 2,50,000 clients. This was Marico's first foray into a service-oriented business abroad and a stepping stone to becoming a multicultural employer. Kaya Skin Clinics is the only brand in its category to win super brand status six years in a row in the UAE, and an unprecedented nine across the region.

Marico Bangladesh

Bangladesh, with its Bengali-speaking population of 121 million in 1996, was a market ripe for the picking. However, there were uncertainties too. Ambiguous government business policies, underdeveloped infrastructure, weak currency, low per capita income, low purchasing power, and last but not least, a chaotic law and order scenario were major deterrents in the opening up of the Bangladeshi market for investments by international and Indian companies.

Harsh, however, saw huge potential in Bangladesh, and rolled the dice. To him, Dhaka resembled the Calcutta of ten years earlier. Much of the culture and way of life were comparable. Coconut oil was used extensively in Bangladesh, retailed in tins. It reminded him of his earlier days when tin was the medium of packaging in India. In this scenario, an important contributory factor to Harsh's gamble was the high awareness of Parachute in Bangladesh due to the spillover of TV channels, broadcast from Calcutta. Advertisements on these channels had helped create a very positive image of Parachute among the local populace.

Marico was the first Indian consumer goods company to enter Bangladesh in 1997. The branded coconut oil market then was dominated by local players. A Bengali-speaking manager was posted to Dhaka, and Marico started direct exports of packed coconut oil to Bangladesh, just as it had earlier to the UAE. Harsh grabbed the opportunity to convert the packed coconut oil market from tin to plastic, which was earlier proved a great success in India. All the earlier packaging innovations (tin-to-plastic packs, pilfer-proof bottles, mini trial packs, wide-mouthed jars and penetrative pricing), which had taken around five years in India, were launched simultaneously when Parachute entered the Bangladeshi market. Within a few years, Marico had reached 65,000 outlets directly and another 1,50,000 outlets indirectly. The process of converting consumers from tin to plastics took nearly ten years in India but thanks to the learnings in India and the similarities with the market and consumer in Bangladesh, the process of conversion was completed in a shorter period of three years in Bangladesh.

In one of his meetings, Prof. Ram Charan had underscored the importance of gaining penetration and momentum in new, emerging markets through aggressive pricing, particularly in consumer categories, as long as higher margins could be ensured in the future.

By 1999, sales had grown steadily although not dramatically. By then, Harsh had travelled to Bangladesh five times. On one visit, he had the new head of the international business group, Rajesh Jejurikar, join him. Rajesh was till then Marico's go-to marketing expert and leader of the nature care marketing team. The visit helped them update their original understanding of market potential. They felt confident of an accelerated business growth if they could fix the supply chain velocity. That visit convinced Harsh that the time was ripe for a greater investment in Bangladesh.

Harsh was optimistic that he could indeed replicate the India success—but he would want to do it faster, given the lessons Marico had already learned in India. It was time to set up a dedicated factory and a company team of managers, in a wholly owned subsidiary: **Marico Bangladesh Ltd.**

Quite against the run of play, Marico faced a setback from an unexpected quarter. The Indian government banned the export of packaged coconut oil. Prices of coconut in India had risen considerably and the government had imposed the ban as a measure to increase supply availability. Overnight, that regulatory change imperilled the entire international business.

The team scrambled to action on two fronts: the first was advocating to the government to lift the ban. It made the case that the company had introduced a branded product and non-availability would hurt an Indian brand in an export market. And, second, the team began work to create an alternative supply chain of sourcing copra from Indonesia. This seemed a fortuitous move. Parachute's sales in Bangladesh grew at a rapid clip, the demand for copra and coconut oil increased.

Marico was already the largest purchaser of copra in India. The additional demand that the team projected from the international markets was large enough to increase the pressure on demand and consequently higher procurement costs. But the copra sourced from south-east Asia did not meet the precise specifications that Parachute needed. The copra buying team set about educating coconut farmers in Indonesia, applying the best post-harvest copra-making practices from their learnings in India, to produce the right quality of copra for imports into Bangladesh. Over the years, Marico Bangladesh began procuring a substantial part of its copra requirements from Indonesia. By doing so, it protected itself from any ad-hoc bans in the future and at the same time reduced the pressure of buying all of Marico's copra requirements solely from India.

In five short years, Marico commanded a lead in the Bangladesh market. It had taken almost ten years to achieve market leadership in India, but with the benefit of experience and lessons learnt, the Bangladesh team accomplished that feat in half the time. In 2005, Marico Bangladesh acquired two soap brands, Aromatic and Camelia, in Bangladesh. The reasons were two-fold: repatriation of profits was complicated, and the build-up of capital made it tempting to look for acquisitions as a means to growth. With only the Parachute brand and volumes, the sales force capacity was underutilized and distribution costs were high. The soap brands, however, sold small volumes. In buying these brands, Marico hoped to quickly build up volumes using its distribution reach. The company was buying soap noodles to manufacture the soaps. The low volumes did not justify backward integration into the soap stock, a necessary condition for soap profitability. The brands failed to scale up and remained a low-margin, low-volume turnover. With no levers to change the fortunes of the business, Marico Bangladesh decided to pull out from the soap brands.

Acquisitions must always be the means to an end: provide market entry or consolidate market share or provide access to a new channel or acquire a new capability. The target should have a clear strategic rationale and not because it is fashionable or there is cash to acquire, or a limited objective to leverage distribution. Soap is a mass market product with many players and cut-throat pricing. Without sourcing advantages or an integrated supply chain or any other strategic advantages, and an unfavourable cost structure, it was going to be an impossible task for Marico to create a brand and grow volumes. It would seem that the move was ill-advised and not much homework went into the acquisition decision.

Marico Bangladesh had become a name to reckon with in corporate circles in Dhaka and as a company that made rapid strides in growth. Harsh wanted the local public to own equity and participate in its prosperity, thereby signalling Marico's long-term commitment in Bangladesh. It listed on the Dhaka Stock Exchange in September 2009 and offered 10 per cent of its equity to the public, the first time Marico did so in another country. Being a listed company in Bangladesh was attractive from a different angle: lower income tax rates. By 2018, Marico was the largest Indian FMCG company in Bangladesh with a market share of 82 per cent in the branded coconut oil market. Its revenues had reached ₹600 crore (US$85 million) and a market cap of ₹3200 crore (US$460 million) in 2019.

In Bangladesh, as in India, Marico found an admirer among its international rivals. Harsh had joined a customary dinner for colleagues in business from the local and international business community during one of his annual visits. As it happened, the country director for Unilever Bangladesh was seated next to him. This was during the time when Marico was facing the steady attack by Unilever's India affiliate. As they got talking, the Unilever director said in a sheepish tone that he had used Parachute as the benchmark for Unilever's distribution of Lux and Lifebuoy products. Unilever had operated in Dhaka since the 1800s. Now, this man said, they aimed to be present in all shops where Parachute was sold. Harsh smiled. He thought about how that marked a reversal from the India experience, where Marico had ambitiously aimed to place Parachute in 80 per cent of the shops that sold Lifebuoy. Leaving the dinner, Harsh understood that Marico Bangladesh had drawn level with one of the bigger players in the market.

Beyond the Diaspora

Growing overseas beyond exports to the Indian diaspora and the subcontinent to other parts of the world was a subject often discussed, but put aside for a later day. This was because Marico did not possess a brand or a business that had an appeal beyond the Indian populace. It was already present in the diaspora markets in other subcontinental countries, barring Pakistan, through exports. Cooking oils did not have a source country advantage. If Marico really wanted to enter the overseas markets in a big way, it needed another route different from the diaspora model.

Chaitanya Deshpande, a senior manager in the finance team, recalls those discussions: he had said, 'Outside the Indian subcontinent and Indian diaspora markets like the Middle East, we cannot lead with the Marico India portfolio. We will need to use M&A (mergers and acquisitions) as a strategy to enter these markets.' It echoed Prof. Ram Charan's earlier observation, 'Acquisitions are not an end in themselves but only a means to an end.'

The success of the Mediker acquisition in 1999 had a happy outcome for Marico. The idea of acquisitions as a means to grow was something to think about. Acquisition was not a significant part of the strategic maps of Indian companies then. The MNCs' successful entry approach, however changed all that. They bought into Indian companies for readymade market access. Marico decided to borrow from the MNC playbook and briefed merchant bankers accordingly. Harsh was cautious in selecting the prospects. He didn't want to be in the M&A game just because it was the thing to do. He was aware that some of his team members were enamoured by the idea of acquisitions. Acquisitions are big news as they attract press coverage and social conversation. However, they also stand the danger of becoming a millstone on the financials. The purchase had to serve a larger strategic goal, such as opening up a new market or a new geography or an entry into a new category or consolidation of market share in an existing category. He was looking for candidates that fit this bill, and was ready to experiment with different business models to enter international markets.

Another route could be to take an Indian science, something that had already caught the fancy of westerners and which could be branded and popularized—an entry strategy that would allow Harsh to leverage India globally.

US Acquisition: Sundari

With this in mind, he scoped the United States, a large and developed consumer market and a frontrunner for new trends. Ayurveda, a 5000-year-old form of medicine rooted in Indian culture, seemed to fit the bill. Going back to nature and drawing from nature was a concept that was gaining popularity and interest in the international skincare market. He already had some experience with Kaya skincare clinics in India and the Middle East. His search led him to **Sundari**.

The Ayurvedic principles of holistic balance had inspired the creation of a US-based firm called Sundari, founded in 1999 by supermodel Christy Turlington. Harsh met with the founders of

Sundari (meaning 'beautiful woman' in Hindi) in New York. He came out of that meeting excited by the possibilities. Sundari's positioning with the ancient Ayurvedic tradition would give him an entry to the US skincare market. He was conscious of the growing interest of Americans in alternative medicine and therapies. Marico acquired Sundari in 2003, with a plan to scale it up in the United States and India.

Harsh knew that he was attempting something path-breaking. Not many Indian companies had built a US business successfully, barring some pharma companies and a few enterprising youngsters of Indian descent who had made news with their technology start-ups. The Sundari business model was based on the principles of Ayurveda, an ancient Indian system of natural and holistic treatments. The five elements found in the cosmic system—air, water, fire, earth and space—as per ancient Ayurveda, resonate in the human body in differing proportions. These need to be balanced—something that Ayurvedic treatments help regulate. Sundari would send a trainer to coach high-end spa therapists in the application of different treatments—facials, body wraps, massages, poultices etc.—with the range of Sundari products. This exclusive range was also offered in retail packs to the spa client.

Rahul Koul and Mayank Bharadwaj, both bright young managers from the India operations, moved to the US to build the Sundari business. After a while, it became clear that it wasn't easy to enrol spas by the hordes and even to scale up the sales velocity of skincare products from these outlets, due to spa managements focusing more on their mainline business. Marico's legacy skills lay in mass marketing of consumer products. However, Sundari was turning out to be more of a business-to-business kind of model, which involved a different set of competencies. The problem was also exacerbated by the recession, triggered by the global financial market meltdown of 2008. Sundari's remoteness from India also meant less core management support. All of these reasons put together kept Sundari small and all attempts to spur growth were infructuous.

Harsh absorbed these lessons soberly and exited from Sundari eventually, selling it to his US management team. Summarizing the lesson, Harsh said, **'Sundari had no right to win**.' 'It was a wrong decision to enter a category of a different business model with different channel dynamics. Being far away from India meant that management support in the manner needed wasn't forthcoming. It was a courageous step to walk into the lion's den, but one that was done without too much thinking and deliberation.' Harsh was banking on Ayurveda picking up in the USA like yoga had. Unfortunately, this foray failed to get traction in that market. The failure prompted Harsh to stay with the knitting, to areas of haircare, healthcare, skincare and geographies. A new criterion that Harsh would add to his acquisition strategy would be 'markets where history and experience gave Marico a right to win'.

Africa Acquisitions

With a CEO dedicated to the international business and Marico's learnings from GCC, the African safari started with Egypt in 2006. Scoping studies done by investment bankers for acquisition threw up opportunities in Egypt and South Africa.

Fiancée

Egypt promised to be a suitable fit. As the deal progressed with Egyptian American Investment and Industrial Development Company, the seller company, Harsh joined the team in Cairo. He met with Fiancée's management. He was amazed by Cairo's density, the grinding traffic and chaotic roads. In a way, it resembled the Indian metropolitan cities teeming with people. The distribution channels too were structured in a manner similar to India.

During due diligence, Marico found that Fiancée conducted a large part of its purchase transactions in cash rather than on purchase orders. They saw a practice that left room for problematic leakages and losses. It sparked off some concerns among the Marico team; they, nevertheless, saw the long-term potential of the Egyptian market. The team investigated this issue further with business associates such as suppliers and distributors and found that they had no resistance to moving to invoiced transactions paid through banking channels. 'We were clear about staying above board,' Harsh said. The shift to sales and purchase orders had to happen immediately, even at the risk of a temporary loss of business.

In September 2006, Harsh finalized the acquisition of Fiancée, followed soon after by a second Egyptian brand, **HairCode**. Harsh reassured the local employees of the acquired company that the deal would not result in layoffs. 'We want you to succeed . . . We don't have a short-term outlook . . . We are a caring company,' emphasized Harsh to them.

Acquiring Fiancée and HairCode gave Marico a significant market share in the hair creams and hair gels segment. Egypt had a large hair cream and hair gel market and one of the highest per capita consumptions in the world.

By 2008, the Fiancée and HairCode brands performed as Harsh expected, achieving a turnover of about US$12.5 million. The same year, work started on a third manufacturing facility to supplement the capacities of the Fiancée and HairCode facilities. **Marico Egypt** got off to a promising start but soon, the political instability caused by the Arab Spring and its aftermath ground the economy into a slowdown.

After making an entry with Egypt in north Africa, Harsh shifted focus to South Africa. In 2007, Marico acquired the consumer products division of Enaleni Pharmaceuticals to create **Marico South Africa** with two haircare brands, **Caivil** and **Black Chic**, and an over-the-counter health product, **Hercules**. South Africa was considered to be one of the top emerging economies in the world and was part of BRICS along with Brazil, Russia, India and China. South Africa had long-standing and historical people-to-people contact with India, thanks to the Indian diaspora. Once again, Harsh reassured the local employees that Marico had a long-term vision for their success in Marico South Africa.

This acquisition was also a beachhead to sub-Saharan Africa. The brands Caivil and Black Chic were popular among the ethnic community as grooming products. The announcement of the Black Economic Empowerment Programme in South Africa, which promised to improve the purchasing power of the coloured population, was another silver lining. However, the recession that soon followed threw the economy into a downturn from which it is yet to recover. Sales growth has been tardy and revenues stagnant at US$13 million. The sub-Saharan dream will have to wait. In the cases of both Egypt and South Africa, the context of the buy was right and Harsh hopes that business growth will pick up as the economy mends.

South-East Asia Acquisitions

With six of the region's economies averaging an economic growth rate of 7.3 per cent in 2010, it was one of the fastest urbanizing areas of the world and one of the hottest economic regions for consumer goods growth.

Derma Rx, a Singapore firm, was acquired in 2010. It was a high-margin skincare business having close synergies with Kaya. The acquisition brought with it an impressive product range, well-developed protocols and standard operating procedures for efficacious skin solutions. Its founder, Dr Tan, was a cosmetologist and skin specialist but not an entrepreneur who could scale up the infrastructure beyond Singapore. The product range and protocols by themselves justified the acquisition price for technology transfer to Kaya.

In India, Kaya wanted to increase sales per clinic outlet and one of the routes was to increase the share of products retailed through the Kaya outlets. The acquisition of Derma Rx and the sale of its merchandise through Kaya outlets provided the necessary boost to Kaya's sales and profits. After four years, the Singapore operations were saturated, and Marico saw no further role for Derma Rx in its business portfolio. So it was hived off for a five-fold multiple: a very satisfying outcome.

In 2011, Marico acquired **International Consumer Products, Vietnam**. In doing so, it was establishing a toehold for potential expansion in the region. The acquisition added a line of grooming products for men under the brands of **X-Men** and **X-Men for Boss**, a range of shampoos, soaps, deodorants, shower gels, body wash, eau de toilette, hair styling gels and facial foams and scrubs. It gave the company a leadership position in the male shower gels and shampoos market in Vietnam. X-Men was ranked second in the male deodorants market. ICP was then owned by two PE investors, a founder and a co-founder. The PE investors and the co-founder exited the business with Marico's acquisition of 85 per cent of the equity holdings. The founder, Phan Quoc Cong, stayed on to run the ICP business as CEO for a little over three years. ICP became Marico South East Asia when all of the shareholders had exited. Harsh had a healthy respect for Cong and his insights. He remarked, 'An entrepreneur-to-entrepreneur conversation is very different from an entrepreneur-to-professional conversation.'

Code 10, a haircare grooming brand earlier owned by Colgate had a franchise in Malaysia and Myanmar. After its acquisition by Marico in 2010, it was added to the portfolio of brands managed by Marico Vietnam.

Growth through Acquisitions: A Report Card

Harsh reflects:

'As Marico grew in the domestic and overseas markets with eleven acquisitions in eleven years, my learnings were:

'Overall, the international acquisitions turned out to be a mixed bag, given the early misstep of Sundari. The failure of Sundari led to identifying acquisitions in the pre- and post-wash ethnic haircare, as well as male grooming, in emerging markets. The south-east Asia acquisitions met the intended objectives.

'Fortunately, most of the international acquisitions were self-sustaining and did not require cash infusions from time to time. Marico's international operations cumulatively contributed 23 per cent of global revenues by 2019.

'The domestic acquisitions, on the other hand, added strategic might and cash. **Nihar** helped consolidate market share and shore up coconut oil brand margins. **Mediker** was the only brand of its kind in a niche market and sold at high margins. **SetWet and Livon** were futuristic brands enjoying category leadership. The hair oil brands and the haircare formulations of creams and serums helped the combined portfolio to consolidate market share and dominate the pre- and post-haircare category.

'Each acquisition attempted to serve multiple objectives. Some succeeded from day one, others took longer. If we did make a mistake, we would have no qualms in exiting, but at an appropriate time. After all, we were new to this game of acquisitions and would learn as we went along.'

Harsh visualized another significant advantage of going international, something that most multinationals successfully did. Young managers with leadership potential from the home market could be baptized in the overseas markets, learn to operate in different markets and cultures and manage profit centres ranging from the Republic of South Africa to MENA, Bangladesh and SEA. The more such markets, the more the opportunities. It would address the appetite of bright young managers seeking career adventures. The potential for international careers would in turn improve Marico's chances of attracting better talent in the home market. Lastly, if Marico listed on stock exchanges overseas, it would have access to money in different currencies and opportunities to target local companies with attractive PE ratios.

Prof. Ram Charan summed up Harsh's foray into international markets in these words:

'Once again, Harsh and his organization were on the verge of expanding their capabilities to venture into less known territories, from the comfort of India to the complexities of doing business in other cultures. There were three principles that drove Harsh's international expansion. First, he expanded to markets with comparable consumer habits: the Indian diaspora markets, where Marico India's coconut oil found captive demand. He repeated this success in Bangladesh but went one step further to set up a company with owned manufacturing, marketing and distribution. Second, he pursued building an on-the-ground presence in altogether new markets through acquisitions in haircare and skincare. Third, he looked to reverse engineer formulations and technologies, and funnel these back for applications in India. Going international gave Marico a wider base of operations and de-risked it from economic volatility and regulatory changes in any one country.'

16

Brand Marico in the Capital Markets

Marico welcomed the idea of being a public limited company, although the timing may have been forced by circumstances. Becoming a public limited company required Marico to shift gears. Earlier, the company was accountable only to a small group of shareholders within the family. After the IPO, it had a new group of financial institutions and retail investors as its shareholders. To them, Marico would be just another avenue for investment. They would expect Marico to perform and deliver the kind of revenue growth and profitability that could earn them attractive and competitive rates of return for their investment. This investor expectation was something that needed to be factored in the strategy and plans. Harsh would use this new requirement as an opportunity to strengthen Marico's performance culture and gear up internal work processes to deliver financial results, every quarter. Milind Sarwate, the chief financial officer, would often remind the top management team that investors expected Marico to deliver on both counts, long-term and short-term. The change in focus from an internal to an externally driven metric of performance was a different ballgame altogether. Heated arguments would break out. In one such argument, addressing the finance team, a marketing manager agitatedly said, 'You accountants don't know what it takes to build brands!' To which Milind shot back, 'I may not know what it takes to build brands, but I certainly know what it takes to build value scrip. My focus is to build Marico's market cap.' These polarized arguments, though momentarily disturbing, had a purpose. They exposed issues around which an open discussion could happen and eventually, a resolution would emerge that would strengthen the quality of management decisions. Budgeting discussions grew more robust, and performance monitoring more rigorous. Sales and marketing teams pushed for volume growth, while the finance and supply chain teams focused on driving down costs. Harsh's main challenge was to make financial results more predictable and in line with investor expectations. He would often say, 'Let us not have surprises. Let's make our budgets achievable but stretched. Not too easy and not too unrealistic. And we must deliver what we tell the market.' His worry was that fluctuations in performance could reinforce the perception that Marico was a commodity company. Marico's price to earnings multiple at thirteen lagged behind other FMCG company PEs by half. He would advocate a catch-up with the industry peers saying, 'The only way to do that is to plan internal performance metrics working backwards from a chosen benchmark PE multiple.'

Harsh undertook investor meetings to help overcome the perception of Marico as a commodity-based company, susceptible to fluctuating profits and vulnerable to attacks from competition.

One request came from Arisaig Partners, an international investment management firm based in London with offices around the world. Arisaig began scrutinizing Marico in 1999 as it looked to expand its investments in the fast-moving consumer goods space. James Alexandroff, one of Arisaig's co-founders, met Harsh.

Impressed with Harsh's thought process, Alexandroff expressed his respect for Harsh's aspirations of raising Marico's valuation. They discussed several ideas, including ways to show the markets that Marico's profits were not so sensitive to coconut oil price fluctuations. They also deliberated over leveraging strong product track record and management team for strategic growth in new categories. Arisaig Partners introduced Harsh to Blue Marlin, a London-based packaging design firm that later worked with Marico on some package design projects.

Marico's record of growth was attractive to Arisaig. It helped that another private equity investor, Warburg Pincus, based in New York, had already invested in Marico's future. Marico's revenue was about US$75 million—somewhat small for Arisaig's interest—but they saw huge potential in Marico's market capitalization. So Arisaig acquired about 5 per cent of Marico stock around the year 2000.

Alexandroff and Harsh met again several times after that. Harsh appreciated that the investor did not hesitate to ask potentially awkward questions. For example, he asked Harsh about whether he should get executive compensation from dividends and market capitalization appreciation instead of a salary. Early on, Alexandroff had also advocated moving the Parachute and Saffola brands from Bombay Oil to Marico, for which a royalty was being paid to Bombay Oil: an issue that was raised by analysts time and again. This was the kind of open discussion Harsh encouraged.

From these experiences and some others, Harsh learnt that not all investors were ruthless fortune hunters in search of quick profits. They invested in companies only after thorough research on not just the balance sheets and the performance record but also the soft aspects of culture and character of the company. Once they decided to invest, they were well-meaning partners, sincere with their advice, adding value, bringing new ideas to the table and staying invested for long-term and sustainable returns: they were true partners. On its part, Marico responded to its partners by heeding their advice, being transparent with results and disclosures and giving them the returns that they expected.

There were numerous structural changes in the financials that needed to be done over a period of time. Internal climate was easier to manage and change but it was going to be very difficult to change stock market perception about Marico and make it comparable with other brand companies. Harsh knew that if the company was valued well by the capital market, its valuation could be higher and that would enable the company to raise more equity to fund both organic and inorganic growth. Besides, it would have a positive rub-off on company image and help it attract high quality talent through employee stock option plans.

Milind decided to take the initiative to reach out and be transparent in his communication with the various players of the capital markets and business media. He did not want to take an 'ask and you shall be told' reactive approach. He likened the Marico scrip to a brand and made investor relations pivotal to Marico's shareholder strategy. Harsh and he met investors at frequent intervals and communicated with a clear, unified voice. Harsh used these interactions as an opportunity to receive feedback from investors on their perceptions about the company. He was keen to learn about the changes and improvements they would like to see in Marico.

Despite being a company that delivered unfailingly on its commitments to investors, the concerns that analysts raised were issues that needed to be addressed. These were:

1. Although Marico had strong brands, the perception was that it was a commodity business with low margins, and fluctuations in raw material prices would lead to unpredictability of profits.
2. Marico was overdependent on a single brand, Parachute, for growth and profits. It had a large share of revenue and profit in its financials.
3. The hair oil category was likely to stagnate, impacting the long-term prospects of the business.
4. Since it was a promoter-led family business, it would be less professional in its approach to management, corporate governance and related party transactions.
5. The brands Parachute and Saffola were not owned by Marico but by its parent, Bombay Oil. The brand appreciation would therefore accrue to Bombay Oil and not Marico's shareholders.
6. Kaya Clinics was a retail service-oriented business and a Marico subsidiary. The business model was different from the FMCG model of Marico's consumer business. It was not in the interests of the shareholders who were invested in Marico purely on the basis of its FMCG business. To them, it was value-limiting.
7. The company was incremental in approach and did not take bold business calls.
8. Since the promoters held substantial majority holdings, the Marico scrip was low in volume.

Harsh took these concerns on board as these perceptions were causing the PE ratio to be lower than the other true blue FMCG companies. The perception that it had only pretensions of being a brands company and that it was not quite in the league of multinationals like Hindustan Lever, discounted its valuation. Harsh knew that for Marico to grow and be among the front end of companies, he needed to respond to these perceptions proactively. When Hindustan Lever had become aggressive in the coconut oil category, the share prices suffered even more, and the PE dropped to 8.

Harsh introduced the practice of periodic and transparent communication: something other family-owned businesses were hesitant to do. He appointed a manager as the point person to handle all investor communication. If there were significant mid-quarter developments, the company proactively informed the market about them. These were steps in the right direction, being taken at a time when the attention to the subject of investor relations was still at a very nascent stage in India. Marico was leading the way, at least among the FMCG companies, and the confidence of the market in Marico was growing as a performing company with a difference.

In the early years of Parachute coconut oil's growth, the company followed a pricing strategy that maintained the unit margins of the brand. Thus, when raw material prices increased, the brand had the strength to pass on this increase to the consumer and maintain unit margins. When input prices reduced, it would pass these on to the consumer and accelerate growth by upgrading more consumers of loose oil to branded Parachute coconut oil. What this meant, however, was a variation in margin, in percentage terms. A section of the investors also wondered about the strength of Parachute's brand equity, if it had to pass on the benefit of falls in raw material. Then, in 2005, when an abundant coconut crop resulted in a steep drop in copra prices, Parachute decided not to make any change in retail prices. It held on to its volumes and market share, clearly establishing its strong equity with consumers. This move also improved the overall margins of the company and set a new benchmark EBITDA (earnings before interest, taxes, depreciation and amortization) level for the company that was more in line with margins expected of an FMCG company. The ability to improve margins, while holding volumes and market share, was illustrative of the equity the brand held.

At investor meets, the company not only outlined strategy and performance but also painstakingly explained the dynamics of product categories and markets. Harsh used these interactions as an opportunity to showcase his management team, as his managers led some of these discussions. He was, in a way, letting the investors know that Marico had a depth of talented managers and the company was in good hands. These meetings also reiterated how the company balanced long-term strategic moves with quarterly performance. At a point in time, the company had recorded forty-eight consecutive quarters of revenue growth and fifty consecutive quarters of profit growth, which brought home the fact that Marico's growth was sustainable and profitable. It shifted the perception that Marico presided over a commodity business, where growth and profits fluctuated with changes in raw material prices, to being a true FMCG brands business.

On the product portfolio front too, Marico had already begun to diversify and be less dependent on Parachute Coconut Oil. It had launched brand extensions of Parachute Advansed in the pre-wash and post-wash haircare segments, to create new occasions for use of the products and to expand the market. It was also making a shift towards more value-added products that would earn better gross margins and be less susceptible to fluctuations in the underlying raw material prices. The company also added new brands to the portfolio with the launch of Shanti and the acquisition of Mediker and Nihar. The concept of strategic funding had added a new dimension to financial planning and facilitated the systematic creation of a new product portfolio. The company began to report the share of revenue from new products, to the share of total sales. Augmented by a strong and deep distribution network, the company's brands had a wide reach that improved the chances of the success of new product launches in the domestic market. Marico was building a range of strong brands. Ninety-five per cent of its revenue came from brands that were either #1 or #2 in their respective categories, demonstrating its ability to grow revenues and profits consistently. It was a signal to investors that Marico was responding to their feedback of being overdependent on Parachute. Kaya Skin Clinics had also created a new line of business. Further, the foray into overseas markets was yet another indicator that Marico was diversifying the source of its revenues and profits.

Market Leadership: Key to Category Choice

marico

Brands	Category	Indicative Market Share (%) #	Rank
Parachute/Nihar Naturals/Oil of Malabar	Coconut Oil (India)	~ 61%	1
Parachute	Coconut Oil (Bangladesh)	~ 82%	1
Saffola	Super Premium Refined Edible Oils (India)	~ 76%	1
Saffola	Oats (India)	~ 32%*	2
Parachute Advansed/Nihar Naturals/ Hair & Care	Hair Oils (India)	~ 35%	1
Parachute Advansed//Nihar Naturals	Hair Oils (Bangladesh)	~20%	1
X-Men	Male Shampoo (Vietnam)	~ 37%	1
Set Wet / Parachute Advansed	Hair Gels, Waxes & Creams (India)	~ 59%*	1
Livon / Hair & Care Silk & Shine	Leave In Hair Conditioning (India)	~65%	1
X-Men	Male Deodorants (Vietnam)	~31%*	2
Revive	Fabric Starch (India)	~64%*	1
Mediker	Anti-Lice Hair Oil (India)	~57%*	1

Over 90% of Marico's turnover comes from market leader brands (No. 1 or 2 position in respective categories)

Sep'19 /Dec'19 rolling 12 month volume market share data sourced from AC Nielsen
*Value Market Share

James Alexandroff from Arisaig Partners congratulated Harsh on the excellent consecutive quarterly results. He wrote, 'We are particularly impressed by the way you have extended your core brands into higher-margin segments and exploited export markets.' The confidence about the business outlook and its ability to grow profits and healthy cash flows prompted Marico to become the first Indian company to pay out quarterly dividends. It allayed any remaining concerns that some investors may have had about the unpredictability of profits, once again consolidating growing opinion that Marico was a thoroughbred FMCG brands company.

When Marico was formed in 1990, the brands Parachute and Saffola were retained by The Bombay Oil Industries, owned by the family. Marico paid 0.75 per cent of brand revenues as a small royalty each year to Bombay Oil. In 1996, when Marico got listed, the ownership of the brands continued to remain with Bombay Oil. From Harsh's standpoint, this served as a poison pill against potential hostile takeovers. Investors, however, expressed their concern over this related party transaction. They were uncomfortable with the brands being built by Marico but the brand ownership remaining with Bombay Oil. Responding to the feedback of investors including Alexandroff, Marico acquired the brands for a modest consideration of ₹30 crore (US$4.5 million in 2019). At that time, the brands contributed ₹350 crore (US$50 million in 2019) in sales. The acquisition price was a pittance to majority promoter shareholders but more than a fair deal to minority shareholders. The promoters were willing to forego the more handsome valuation that could have otherwise been applied to the brands. Instead, the promoters exhibited faith in Marico and were willing to wait for rewards through long-term value creation.

Once again, Harsh responded to investor concerns on the ownership structure of Kaya. Until then, Kaya was a wholly owned subsidiary of Marico. Investors were uneasy as they had invested in Marico for its brands and FMCG model of business. Kaya was an unrelated venture, with financial results much lower than that of Marico's. In 2013, Harsh demerged Kaya from Marico and made it an independent entity, listed separately on the stock exchange. Investors viewed these moves positively, both as a demonstration of good governance and also of Harsh's willingness to respond to genuine investor concerns. The capital markets responded favourably to this move with an uptick in Marico's share prices.

Investor perception around Marico's predilection to be an incremental player and its hesitation in taking risks was also dispelled when Marico made big strides in the overseas markets, first in setting up Marico Bangladesh and later in acquiring companies in South-East Asia, north Africa and South Africa. That Marico was a forerunner as an Indian multinational company and was willing to venture forth to uncharted geographies gained the respect and interest of the shareholders.

In the early years after the public listing of Marico, the free float of its scrip was small and trading volumes were low, as a majority of the holdings were held by the promoters. This meant that big-ticket investors, who found the Marico story attractive, stayed away due to the illiquidity of the stock. So, in order to provide an impetus to trading on the stock, the company issued bonus shares and also split the face value of the share from ₹10 to ₹1 per share. This generated interest among the retail investors and trading volumes began to go up. Gradually, institutional investors also stepped in as market capitalization grew and liquidity concerns abated.

Harsh also took several steps to improve corporate governance long before it became a requirement. Three-quarters of the Marico board comprised of independent board members who were also business leaders. It included a lady board member, long before it was mandatory. He took several initiatives to improve board effectiveness and outcomes by clearly laying out the agenda and in improving boardroom chemistry and professionalism. It was a front runner for exemplary corporate governance practices and any remaining doubts investors may have had with regard to its business model or professionalism, were wiped out. The hallmark of Marico's investor relations was the high level of frequency, transparency and the use of humour in its communication. It was getting more attention for its quarterly reports as very few Indian companies were issuing quarterlies then. Marico was the only company to use creativity in its reports published in the mainline newspapers. Accompanying the numbers and statistics, it used cartoons, brand imagery and other eye-catching graphics with the tagline 'Marico, Uncommon Sense'. Amid the intense pace of performance improvements, Harsh had ensured that Marico also kept the cheeky humour that had marked the company from the very beginning. When Milind moved from finance to HR, the company ran a newspaper advertisement that referred to Marico's stellar financial results with the same head-turning wit that had heralded Marico's beginnings. The headline declared:

'Our Chief Financial Officer was doing an excellent job. We moved him out.'

The text of the advertisement provided the explanation of the punchline: 'So he could move in as Chief of HR and Strategy. Most companies confine top performers to their specialist function so that they keep doing what they do best. Marico does quite the contrary. We believe, to accelerate growth, you need fertile minds that bring fresh insights and perspectives to the table.'

Pramit Jhaveri, then Citibank's India chief and an astute market-watcher, had this to say, 'During its evolution, Marico made the transformation from a small family-run trading business into what I would describe today as a highly successful, Indian multinational company.'

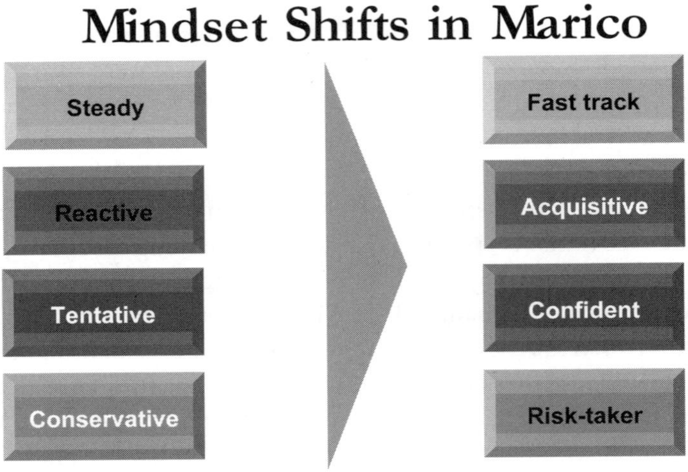

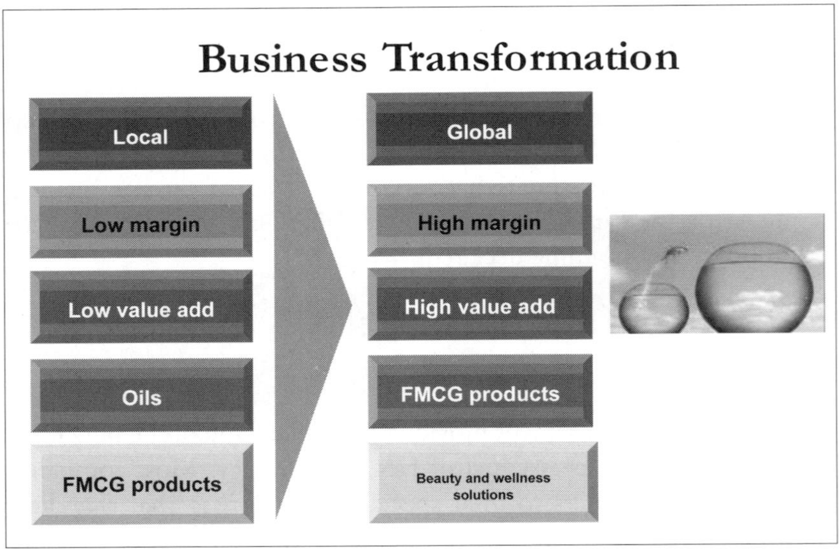

By this time, Marico's businesses had touched the lives of one in three Indian consumers. The company's products had reached people in two dozen countries, from Africa's southernmost tip to Asia's eastern coast on the South China Sea.

Harsh said that there were a number of challenges that came along the way. 'The first big challenge that I remember as significant was the way we pioneered the tin to plastics packaging change in the 1980s. It was a big discontinuity in the industry: a problem was converted into an opportunity. The higher margins earned by Parachute were then ploughed back into advertising and building the brand. It led Parachute to leadership, from 15 per cent to 50 per cent plus. This breakthrough started a cycle of innovation, investment and growth: a mantra that is followed to the day.'

Going public was one of the key events that changed the fortunes of Marico. Most promoters would do so with trepidation because of public scrutiny and the pressure to perform every quarter at a pace dictated by the markets. Harsh reflects, 'Going public placed a positive pressure on the company to perform. Not performing would have caused wealth erosion to shareholders and a loss of investor credibility. But when the company met or exceeded expectations, it was reflected in the price-to-earnings multiple and that in turn led to positive media coverage and the attendant spin-offs to the company image. Attracting talent and funds for acquisitions became easier. The benefits of being listed far outweighed the advantages of staying a private entity.

'The strategy of treating Marico's scrip as a brand and the series of actions that followed had not only worked but had become a new benchmark for progressive companies.'

Prof. Ram Charan reiterated this idea of growth when he said to Harsh, 'Growth mindset starts at the top, but the key challenge is to make sure that it trickles down all the way to the bottom. Get the growth momentum first and then work backwards to get economies of scale. Growth has to be sustainable and profitable over time. Top enterprise leaders need to keep an eye on external conditions, on changes that might affect their business, and adapt to account for these changes.

'Harsh had adapted successfully to the many changes in the landscape, by recrafting Marico's portfolio.

By maintaining a focus on growth.

By brand building.

By creating an environment where talent could flourish.

And, by delivering quarter upon quarter performance.'

17

Governance: Building the Board

The role of the corporate board today is changing.

'A corporate board is no longer a legal formality. It is a competitive necessity. The board is a source of competitive advantage. Boards must get to work. For a majority of boards, the relevant question is: how can we make a good CEO perform better? Improving managerial judgements is the new frontier for boards.'

So advocates Prof. Ram Charan.

For several years, the functioning of a board was a mere formality. It was considered weighty to have eminent personalities as members of the board: retired business leaders, bureaucrats, lawyers and accountants. Harsh himself was a member on the boards of a few companies and found that they often comprised of relatives and friends, and in fact, met only the statutory requirements of a board. These were compliant boards and rarely challenged the chairman or management.

When Marico went public in 1996, Harsh was the MD and his father, the chairman. The then Marico board reflected what was traditionally the norm.

Harsh was among the initial business leaders who sought a change. A board which was a mere formality or a rubber stamp was clearly a non-starter for him. Interactions with the professor and reading his book, *Boards That Deliver*, served as an eye-opener and Harsh saw the potential of making the board a more dynamic asset for the company. Typically, most chairmen identify an individual who would make a worthy board member. Harsh differed.

'It is important to pinpoint different competencies and skill sets to qualify a board member,' says Harsh. In the case of Marico, he identified the following:

1. Domain knowledge of fast-moving consumer goods.
2. Strong expertise in a fast-changing retail environment.
3. An HR professional who could head the nominations and remunerations committee.
4. A finance expert with capital market experience, who could also be the audit committee chair.
5. Digital prowess.

For each of these competencies, he briefed a search agency to identify options. Post-shortlisting, then meeting all of them, Harsh selected one for each capability. Bottom line is, identify competencies first, then make a selection.

The board composition process was carried forward thus:

Rajeev Bakshi, MD of Cadbury India, was chosen based on his deep marketing expertise of fast-moving consumer goods.

BS Nagesh, ex-CEO, Shoppers Stop, filled the position of retail expert.

Global head of HR at Infosys, Hema Ravichandar, earned the distinction of being the first woman to join the Marico board. 'I saw how passionate Harsh was about the HR agenda: that really resonated with me,' said she.

'He took the trouble to bring credible people onto the board so that their voices are heard and valued,' commented Nikhil Khattau, then part of Sun F&C Mutual Fund. He stepped in as audit committee chair.

Ex-McKinsey and CEO of Myntra, Anant Sanaranarayanan, drove the digital journey.

Each member brought a unique competence to the table. Harsh thus transformed the board into a body that could leverage their varied experiences and capabilities for the betterment of Marico.

The board of Marico now comprised of five independent directors: three non-executive directors including Harsh, his cousin Rajen and Harsh's son Rishabh, representing the promoters' interests, and Saugata Gupta as the managing director. The composition Harsh had chosen included a larger number of independent directors. Ravichandar found that Harsh was very open to feedback from all quarters. She saw the Marico board as refreshing in that it had a larger number of independent directors, despite the promoters controlling the board through their shareholding. Focused on deriving maximum value through the wealth of experience represented therein, Harsh wasn't defensive or shy of challenge when critique was constructive. He would steer the board to focus on crucial matters that they must be seized with. Remarks Hema, 'From a board perspective, what I find unique is that Harsh perpetually evolves. Moreover, he is known to pre-empt practices before they are mandated by the law.'

The most critical duty of a board is the selection, coaching and retention of the CEO, and when required, the CEO's dismissal. As Prof. Ram Charan had said, 'This could take up as much as 80 per cent of the board's mindshare. If the board fails to do this, the rest does not matter.' He added that the company and the board should continue after Harsh, and its involvement in selecting a new CEO as well as board members should continue as before.

Prof. Ram Charan had warned against the board co-creating strategy with the management. 'The board's role is to critique and approve the business model and strategy, and not to formulate strategy and be involved in operational decision making. Keep your nose in and your hands out. The board should be responsible for helping the CEO to select which portfolios to be in and aid him in adapting to changes in the business landscape.'

In 2013, the board gave Harsh feedback that the company's strategy and direction lacked crisp articulation. They asked for a two-page document that would spell out where the company aimed to be in the next three to five years and where it would play, which segments and geographies, and how it would win. Harsh took this advice seriously and invited the Marico leadership team to develop the two-page strategy paper. Before giving it final shape, he wanted to take the benefit of Prof. Ram Charan's inputs. As always, the professor's calendar was blocked several months in advance. He was willing to spare a couple of hours in Munich, through which he was transiting on one of his many transcontinental business travels. And so Harsh flew down to Munich just so he could get those couple of hours with Prof. Ram Charan. In a lounge at Munich's airport, the two debated and thrashed out the document.

The professor said, 'Leadership competes, businesses don't.' It was therefore the responsibility of the board to ensure quality of talent and future talent pool. As mergers and acquisitions can have a big impact on future company strategy, the board must provide guidance on its capital structure and such deliberations can take up a significant bandwidth of the board's involvement.

When Rajeev Bakshi joined the board, he made an insightful observation that board discussions tended toward reviews of past performance. They did not tackle forward-looking issues of strategy and corporate development. The five independent directors had very different styles. It could be a strength, but each one addressed topics only in their individual area of expertise. Harsh too had observed this. He found that the board's deliberations were not always well-balanced. Many discussions tended to get dominated by one individual. The board was not getting the advantage of the diverse experience in the room and the benefit of counterpoints. They all agreed that there was room to improve the effectiveness of its functioning. Harsh reached out to Prof. Ram Charan to see how they could improve the functioning of the board. Prof. Ram Charan asked the operating leadership team for feedback on the functioning of the board. Through an anonymous questionnaire, Harsh collected and consolidated the feedback to be shared with the professor. The leadership team felt that they were often being judged rather than collaborated with—and that there was room for deriving greater value.

'The board is too critical of the management and does not help it in improving strategy. Sometimes it gets toxic. We do not look forward to board meetings. It is an examination you have to pass each quarter,' said one member of the leadership team. Another shared that a couple of board members tended to dominate the meeting.

Yet another remarked, 'Some members did not appear serious enough, as if they had not read the material sent to them for the board meeting.'

The professor and Harsh discussed this feedback. To have a board work as a source of competitive advantage, they needed to create a board culture. First was a culture of openness and transparency. Second was to facilitate and air opposing viewpoints. The third was to ensure that the board got the truth from the management, not partial answers. The management then resolved these issues in a constructive manner. And fourth, the board members are engaged in improving the company collectively and individually.

Prior to conducting a one-day retreat, Prof. Ram Charan held a one-on-one session with each board member to get their individual views on the functioning of the board. At the board's retreat, Prof. Ram Charan provided guidance on board management and interactions. 'Strategy creation is the management's responsibility. Do not expect the board to co-create strategy. That leads to diffused accountability. Their job is to critique it,' Prof. Ram Charan advised. The board must also mentor management. Each team member was asked to identify areas they required board inputs on, and then paired off with a mentor from the board.

In order to keep the board informed on a regular basis, a one-page monthly summary of highlights from each profit centre and support function was shared. Ram advised that during board meetings, there should be no PowerPoint presentations, only dialogue.

The board identified an agenda of topics for in-depth discussion during meetings. These included approval of strategy and budgets, talent and succession planning, new product plans, governance and risk management. There was also a session in each meeting, a non-executive session without the management team and the managing director. Prof. Ram Charan also shared best practices of international boards and guided the chair to take feedback from dominant members. He then followed up with very specific feedback to each member individually, holding up a mirror to their strengths as well as counselling them on areas requiring improvement.

Each board meeting ended with feedback on the quality of the discussions.

marico
make a difference

Feedback on the Meeting of the Board of Directors of Marico Limited and its Committees held on (Date)

Dear Member,

We seek your feedback on today's meeting of the Board of Directors of Marico Limited.

Please tick your response in the appropriate box given alongside each element below.

Sr.	Element	Poor 1	Average 2	Good 3	Excellent 4
1	Quality of Pre-read for the meeting				
2	Presentation by Ex – Com members				
3	Degree of Participation of Board Members				
4	Openness				
5	Contribution by Board to the Company				
6	Selection of Menu				
7	Quality of food				

Any other qualitative feedback / comments:

Name :______________________________

Board members and management gave specific comments on quality of pre-read material sent for the meeting, the quality of presentations made by management team members if any, the degree of participation by board members, the openness of discussions and contributions made by the board members. This led to continuous improvement. At the annual board retreat, board members receive 360-degree feedback from their board colleagues and the management team. Prof. Ram Charan, through his interventions, helped to build balance between individual capability and brilliance, collective functioning and consensus building.

The group began exchanging views with a shared sense of Marico's strategic goals. Harsh forged the board into a more team-like dialogue rather than individuals talking from their areas of expertise. One of the contributions made by the board was to use the Marico organization to market Kaya products and leverage the synergies that lay in the channels that the two companies had. What impressed Bakshi was Harsh's style of engaging each of them individually and seeding new ideas in such conversations. Bakshi called it an 'interesting phenomenon' driven by Harsh personally. 'That has been his greatest accomplishment and his strongest suit, basically using us offline individually and collectively at the board level to stimulate discussions of the highest possible quality.'

So, as chairperson of the governance committee, Hema carried out an insight process each year. A questionnaire was given to each board member as well as the company leadership team, followed by a one-on-one insight dialogue with each member. The survey focused on a range of aspects including board processes, dynamics, succession planning, capability building, strategy and risk appetite, future readiness of company and management, and board contributions. These findings were thrashed out at board retreats. Opines chair of the audit committee, Nikhil Khattau, 'Today's market puts a premium on professionally managed, transparent companies with good corporate governance practices. I think Harsh was at the forefront of that movement.'

The board tune-ups worked. Some of the major decisions that arose from board deliberations included the decision to acquire Nihar and the advice to go as high as possible in the bid price. Likewise, the make vs buy debate on the SetWet/Livon acquisition helped clarify the reasons in favour of the same. The demerger of Kaya was another decision promoted by the board: this led to a higher valuation and market cap for Marico.

Together, Prof. Ram Charan and Harsh engaged directly with the board to keep honing the group's effectiveness. No small wonder that Marico was bestowed with awards for corporate governance.

1. Among the top five BSE 100 companies for exemplary corporate governance: 2018

2. Excellence in corporate governance at the fifteenth Institute of Company Secretaries of India National Awards: 2016
3. Silver award for excellence in corporate governance from Institute of Chartered Secretaries of Bangladesh: 2016
4. List of India's Best Boards: 2014, *Economic Times*
5. Best governed company of the year from the Asian Centre for Corporate Governance and Sustainability: 2014
6. Among top four best managed boards in the Economic Times and Aon Hewitt 'Top Companies for Leaders India Study' 2014

Harsh Avers:

'The board is a source of competitive advantage. The Marico board has contributed immense value to company strategy, talent and competencies. Any board, in perpetuity, has to take steps to keep itself rejuvenated. Thus, over a period of time, the board composition should also be refreshed, ensuring a consistent flow of "new blood" and proficiencies.'

18

Seeding Succession

Marico at a Quarter Century

In April 2015, Marico notched up twenty-five years in business. It was now valued at an impressive ₹25,000 crore (US$3.5 billion in 2019) and the Marico scrip was outperforming the BSE (Bombay Stock Exchange) FMCG Index.

Coincidently, it was only a few months earlier that Harsh had stepped down from the position of managing director and handed over charge of a healthy business to his newly appointed managing director, Saugata Gupta. A business that had improved its net margin on sales from 8 per cent to 13 per cent. A business where the dependency of its traditional businesses of Parachute and Saffola oils had reduced from 86 per cent to 54 per cent of revenues.

The professor had had a ringside view of many a succession in US corporations. He was also aware of succession dynamics in India. He remarked that successful founders who carried a larger-than-life image of themselves found it psychologically difficult to create succession.

'They can't give up their "cocaine". They have no other interests in life and fear the emptiness that follows a life without power. They haven't taken a "real holiday" because business has been their life.'

With this as a backdrop, Prof. Ram Charan once told Harsh that all founders need to think ahead about where their company would stand once they leave the scene. 'Carve this out while you are alive, designate a CEO and better still, a capable team for any later succession needs,' said he.

Harsh was keenly aware that he needed to build a succession bench and at some point, hand over the reins. He felt the need to seed succession of one or two much younger persons who were business-savvy and at the same time, shared the values he cherished. Sooner or later, this would be a question he would have to answer to the shareholders.

It was only in 2007 that Harsh began to seriously ponder the issues regarding succession. What were the competencies he was looking for in his successor? He wanted someone who had the foresight to read the changing environment and capitalize on the opportunities arising from the same. Someone who was invested in the culture and purpose of the organization. A person who would continually enhance growth, profitability and respectability of the company.

Prof. Ram Charan recommended that it was crucial that Harsh first determine the attributes the CEO should possess. He added that a significant number of successions had failed, immaterial of whether they had been recruited from within the company or externally. Prof. Ram Charan stated, 'A wrong succession could cause irreparable damage. Succession is not a science yet, it is art and intuition.' He went on to give examples of companies in the US: Hewlett Packard, K Mart and Sears. The wrong choice of successors in all these giants had resulted in huge setbacks in their performances and futures, with Hewlett Packard having repeated the blunder four times.

Uppermost in his mind were his two children: daughter Rajvi (a.k.a Raj) and son Rishabh. Raj had graduated from Lewis and Clark in the US with a double degree in arts as well as International Relations, followed by an MBA in Business Administration at Haute Ecole de Commerce (HEC), Geneva. Rishabh graduated from Hoffstra University in the US with a degree in business administration. However, he rationalized that both children were too young and not experienced enough to shoulder a responsibility as weighty as this. Regardless, he broached the subject of his succession with both children, discussing it at length. Neither was inclined to step into his shoes: both wanted to pursue diverse passions and career paths. Far from being upset, Harsh was happy. Though he had some inkling of what the outcome would be, he was very pleased to hear what both of his children had to say. He had always strongly advocated, 'Make your passion your work; you will enjoy your journey.'

Advised the professor, 'The selection of a successor is more than compatibility with the person of the founder. The successor needs to have high business acumen. He needs to have a detailed on-the-ground knowledge of business fundamentals. Also, a candidate for succession should be observed by multiple people and their feedback factored in.'

Over the next few years, Harsh initiated a process that would deliver to him one or more candidates from his existing team. Reorganizing the structure to three strategic business units, he ensured that leadership roles had sufficient room to stretch the capabilities of his team and provide a basis for identifying potential successors.

Saugata Gupta, who was till then the chief marketing and sales officer, took over as the CEO of the **India Consumer Products Business**. Vijay Subramaniam joined as the CEO of **International Business**.

While Harsh had his eye on Saugata Gupta, he also thought highly of Vijay Subramaniam.

Looking back to the day Saugata was interviewed in 2004, Harsh recalled that he had a distinct impression of a young man who showed an inner drive and a result-oriented mindset. Saugata was a chemical engineer from IIT Kharagpur and an MBA from the Indian Institute of Management, Bangalore. They talked about Saugata's work in Cadbury Schweppes (now part of Mondelez Kraft) and ICICI Prudential. Harsh was impressed with his marketing insights, his potential and ambition to go beyond. He conferred with Rajeev Bakshi, a member of the Marico board and then CEO of PepsiCo India. Bakshi was earlier the MD of Cadbury Schweppes when Saugata had joined the marketing team there. Bakshi strongly recommended Saugata.

Over time, Harsh also received substantial inputs from board members and other associates. It appeared that Saugata knew the business and 'he does learn and grow'. On his part, Saugata enjoyed his conversations with Harsh. He was impressed with Harsh's searching questions and progressive outlook. He said, 'I was looking for a marketing opportunity that would help an Indian company create consumer brands in a landscape dominated by multinational brands. Here was a company that would fit the bill.' Elaborating further on his reasons to pick Marico, Saugata said, 'Ultimately, when you join a company at a senior level, chemistry matters. Harsh came across to me as a person who implicitly trusts and gives a lot of space.' He saw that they shared a common philosophy, 'Promise what you can deliver and deliver what you promise.' Saugata joined Marico as the chief marketing officer and true to Harsh's intuition, notched up several marketing successes, displaying strategic prowess.

Vijay Subramaniam, CEO of International Business, had grown the share of International Business to 23 per cent of Marico revenues with sales of Rs 600 crore by 2010, up from a single digit share in 2005. He was entrepreneurial in growing the business beyond the Middle East and Bangladesh. Subramaniam was an MBA from Jamnalal Bajaj Institute of Management Studies, Mumbai, and had been a marketing professional with PepsiCo and Henkel before joining Marico.

In 2011, Harsh accepted the role of president of FICCI (Federation of Indian Chambers of Commerce and Industry), the apex association of business organizations in India. It is the voice of India's business and industry and influences policy by encouraging debate and engaging with policymakers. The FICCI president holds a year-long tenure. During that short period, Harsh focused on making FICCI a more execution-oriented organization. Earlier, Harsh had fought shy of networking much with the government in New Delhi, but now, he had been thrown in the thick of it and that afforded him deeper insight of how the government functioned. Harsh thus had to spend considerable time away from managing affairs at Marico. The reorganization carried out the previous year and the delegation and empowerment of his team had enabled him to withdraw from the nitty-gritty of everyday operations. In his continuing role as managing director of Marico, he met each CEO and skip-level manager once a month.

Saugata's leadership skills kept improving. One shift was that he now recognized that he no longer needed to be always in the trenches. As a leader, he could step back and delegate tasks to his team. His job was to facilitate them. With domestic and international consumer businesses operating under independent leaders, both grew rapidly. However, there were unintended consequences of the low level of synergies between the two. The opportunity to cross-pollinate knowledge, reverse-flow product opportunities to India and drive cost structure benefits through a unified supply chain did not accrue.

Early in 2013, Harsh reorganized again to merge the domestic and international business under Saugata Gupta as CEO of the Marico FMCG business. In doing so, Harsh was raising the bar for Saugata with another level of complexity. Kaya Clinics was spun off as an independent company to let it run more organically as a wellness retail business with an entrepreneurial focus. Vijay Subramaniam moved from International Business to Kaya as CEO.

One day in late 2013, Saugata requested a meeting with Harsh. He said he wished to have an open conversation about his future with the company. He had enjoyed his years at Marico. Harsh had empowered him and he had learnt and grown on the job. However, he was always cognizant that Harsh's family held majority ownership of Marico and as was prevalent in several family-owned businesses in India, it was common to bring in a family member as successor. He revealed that he envisioned himself as the managing director of a large company by his mid-forties, and he believed that he was now ready to do so. Saugata then went on to commit what he might achieve if Harsh elevated him to the role of the managing director and gave him complete charge of running the company. On the other hand, if Harsh thought differently about his succession, Saugata then would like to consider other offers he was receiving.

Succession is often one of the most contentious challenges for any family business. The issue is emotionally charged and carries long-term financial implications. Despite a company founder's deep desire for a smooth transition, succession within a family is often fraught with peril. Harsh had witnessed many such failures and wanted a smoother transition for Marico. He was well aware that if he chose a successor from outside the family, his friends and family would not react positively. Harsh had to wrestle with a very complex situation: leaning towards tradition and expectations, versus handing over the reins to a professional. It was an agonizing dilemma: emotion versus rationale. Moreover, handing over leadership is never an easy pill to swallow. Actively running a company, overcoming challenges, competing, experimenting, innovating, achieving, seeding, launching and scaling new businesses are an entrepreneur's lifeline.

Most business families in India went, and still pursue, the hierarchical route, i.e., the business is passed on from father to son. And this succession is generally expected and approved of by most others in the family.

Harsh, at age sixty-three, knew that at some juncture, he would have to relinquish his role as managing director of Marico. However, this was neither imminent nor urgent as he was in fighting fit form, both health-wise as well as cerebrally.

Meanwhile, Marico was gaining recognition in many quarters. The company ranked halfway up the prestigious Forbes 100 Most Innovative Growth Companies of India. On the cusp of Marico's twenty-fifth anniversary in business, investors expressed their satisfaction with the company's stability and growth. The commodity debate had been firmly resolved in favour of Marico being a true-blue brands company and the valuation was an index of that. The valuation of the company had soared from ₹1400 crore (US$200 million) in 2005 to ₹13,500 crore (US$1.9 billion) in 2014. Though Harsh looked back with a sense of satisfaction, he also felt that there were more milestones to achieve.

When Saugata had the conversation about his succession, it was a few years too early for Harsh to contemplate this change. Marico was his baby and he could keep things under control through ownership. Nonetheless, he introspected. Harsh knew that Saugata was very capable and wanted to retain him. He deliberated on this issue with the board. When Prof. Ram Charan was consulted, he reasoned that by waiting longer, Harsh may not get any further significant input towards making a decision about Saugata. On the other hand, he risked losing him. The board advised Harsh to step down from day-to-day operations and prepare to bring Saugata into the managing director position.

Harsh's wife Archana was unhappy with this decision. She was convinced that he should continue being managing director for much longer. Also, she was conscious of the fact that being constantly engaged and stimulated mentally were innate to him. She wondered how he would keep himself occupied given that he maintained a minute-by-minute daily schedule. Sharing her fears and misgivings with him, she commented, 'You can't possibly play golf all seven days of the week, can you?' His daughter Raj had always maintained that Marico was her father's third baby. She could not fathom how he would cope with such a momentous decision. His son Rishabh, too, could not envision how his father would handle the life-changing decision of *not* being totally involved and hands-on. All along, he had seen his father at the helm. A transition such as this would have a huge impact on him. How would he deal with it?

'You think a lot about the culture my father had created, and whether it could be sustained under someone else,' stated Rishabh. Harsh's mode had been one of a high level of empowerment. In the recent past, he had significantly reduced his involvement in an operating role.

Nonetheless, it was by no means an easy decision. Harsh battled the huge conflict in his mind. Eventually, he concluded that the perpetuity of the company he had built outweighed any other consideration. It was time his 'third baby' was nurtured by other capable hands.

The die was cast, and beyond this, he did not waver in his decision.

The board too played its role in the Marico succession and its smooth transition. It decreed that Harsh and Saugata commit to transparency in their changing roles and forge a clear and mutual understanding of the evolving distribution of responsibilities. Harsh too asked Saugata what his expectation of Harsh's role would be once he acceded to his position of CEO and MD. Both men independently penned down what they considered their own assignments and areas of operation to be and their expectations of the other. Both charters were a close match. Harsh later commented, 'That was a vital exercise. Omission of this could have led to heartburn, strained relationships and very importantly, a negative impact on company performance.' They were able to define a clear decision-making matrix. 'I think we've had a very good relationship in terms of working together and an alignment of values,' Harsh said of his involvement with Saugata. The definitions of roles and clarity of engagements were instrumental in ensuring a smooth transition. Lack of clarity in roles had upset the process in other companies around the same time. At two of India's prestigious corporate houses, the Tata Group and Infosys, changes and roles were not defined clearly, leading to avoidable chaos.

Here was a historic transaction being made: from an owner-driven and managed company to a strategic, investor-driven company. The family would have to prepare themselves for the reality of seeing a larger-than-life entrepreneur pass on the reins to a professional. For Harsh, to create Marico and painstakingly nurture it into a successful company, only to hand it over to someone else to manage, and at that, much earlier than anticipated, was a psychological sacrifice. This was perhaps the first time an ongoing and active promoter CEO was voluntarily stepping down from day-to-day responsibilities to hand over the baton to a professional.

Saugata Gupta, as CEO, MD, a professional manager and business leader, had his task cut out to profitably grow the portfolio and revenues further.

Harsh, meanwhile, would continue to play his role as Chairman of Marico. Perhaps, one of the few times in India, when management and ownership were separated. Moreover, long before the 2019 Companies Act amendment to have distinct persons in the role of Chairman and Managing Director. After nearly a quarter of a century of leading the climb, Harsh had earned the right to pause and look back at his creation with a lot of satisfaction. Harsh was planning for family continuity by inducting Rishabh onto the board. Rishabh would be the trustee of the family-owned majority holdings and also the perpetuity of the business. Both Harsh and Rishabh concluded that in time, Rishabh would be a strategic promoter investor and drive the board effectively.

In April 2014, Harsh stepped back from his managing director role, allowing Saugata to assume responsibility.

ROLE OF CHAIRMAN

1. Strategic Business Planning
    - Visionary and Strategic inputs and guidance to Top Team for the process of creation of Business Strategy.
    - Critique of the Business Strategy created by the Business/ Function. Focus on New Category Entry, New Brands, Brand Extensions, Capability and Talent & Culture.

2. Leadership Development
    - Mentor the MD and CEO.
    - Marico Top Team (MD Reports) Members – Appointment, Remuneration, Development Planning, mentoring through Skip Level Interactions, Promotions/Role Changes, Succession Planning, Disengagements.
    - LEAD Talent: Build perspective about Business Strategy, Purpose, Culture and journey of Marico for new Partners through the LEAD Talent training program.

3. Corporate Social Responsibility
    - Nurture Marico Innovation Foundation
    - Strengthen the association with CRY for spread for education.

4. Investor Relations
    - Interaction with key investors & those who are keen or insist on meeting the Chairman.

5. Image Building/PR
    - Industry Representation
    - Participation and representation in FICCI and other forums to interface with regulatory agencies.
    - Speaker at Management Forums, Institutes and other education forums.
    - Media stories on Marico, especially to highlight shift of MD Role.
    - Leverage MIF and ASCENT to build Marico's image.

6. Acquisitions & Divestments
    - Review & guide Merger & Acquisition initiatives and Divestments.

7. Board Effectiveness
    - Strengthen Marico's Board to evolve Marico to a Board Managed Company

- Creation of the Board's Agenda and anchoring the agenda of Business Strategy, Risk Reviews, Internal Governance, Vigil Mechanisms, Talent & Culture.
- Take measures to strengthen the Board through in-sighting, external benchmarks, feedback & facilitated interventions.

8. Crisis Management
   - Guide the MD and CEO and his team for resolving critical issues during crisis situations.

9. Reviews
   - Monthly Performance Review aimed adding value to the enterprise through pre-read of the MOR followed with discussion with MD and the concerned ex-com member for the function/business unit.
   - Innovation and R&D review (three times in a year)
   - Talent Interaction – talent through forums such as Corporate Induction Programme for New Partners & Managers, Popcorn with Harsh etc. (as per calendar)
   - Market Visits (India & International Units)
   - Capital Expenditure above a certain threshold (₹100 crore)
   - Fiscal Risk
   - Sustainability Initiatives

(Note: Role subject to change as needed)

Hema Ravichandar, former HR chief at Infosys and later a member of Marico's board, provided a snapshot of another key moment where Harsh's interaction with the board shifted. Harsh managed the change with keen awareness of three roles: managing director, chairman of the board and promoter. Later, as Saugata transitioned into the managing director's position, Harsh's primary focus became his role as chairman of the board. Ravichandar observed that he was 'able to gracefully and definitely give space' to the new managing director. As promoter, he ensured that his son Rishabh took on the role of a trustee of the family's shareholding interests. By doing this, Harsh was cementing a much larger deal. He was guiding Marico through the shift from a founder-owned and led company to a professionally led company: a 'transformation transition', in Ravichandar's words.

This transition involved not only a change in his functions but also a two-fold psychological shift. First, Harsh recognized at a deep level that his day-to-day identity and interactions were changing. Unlike in the past, where he had steered his own role changes gradually, from doing things himself to delegating, to influencing others, this was a sweeping one. He would have to step away from the temptation to engage operationally and find other ways to gainfully fill the void. Second, he would have to project confidence about the change and signal that the change was permanent. He would have to convey confidence to all Mariconians and other stakeholders that the company's culture was robust and secure for the long run. He would have to give his successor a free hand to act. This was true leadership at a crucial moment in Marico's journey. A succession as smooth as this was a rare and refreshing change for any Indian family-owned enterprise. And exceptional for one that had grown as fast as Marico.

Pramit Jhaveri, then head of Citibank India, made the following observation, 'We can pick up 100 very successful, home-grown, family-founded and run Indian businesses. I doubt you would be able to find even five of them that have planned, conceived of and implemented succession the way Harsh has. And if you do find more than five, then let me know.'

Saugata Gupta says of the succession, 'If one observed, Harsh had been gradually moving into a hands-off mode. It's not like it happened suddenly, one fine day. The entire process was extremely smooth.'

As Saugata took over the combined portfolio of CEO and managing director, he saw several things happening in the global business environment. One was increased uncertainty behind factors affecting growth. 'There could be political risk, economic risk, devaluation in emerging markets,' he said. Another factor was a softening of demand in the Middle East. The changing regulatory environment in food safety in India brought other uncertainties. Saugata reasoned that he may not be able to predict these ambiguities, but he had the capabilities to manage them. Marico retained its steady focus on maintaining its brand leadership and rationalizing low-margin product lines.

As chairman, Harsh stayed focused on continuously improving the effectiveness of the board and often brought in Prof. Ram Charan to share his insights.

Says Prof. Ram Charan, 'It was absolutely critical for Harsh and Saugata to clarify to each other what they would do and what they would not do in their new roles. Harsh agreed that the exercise of expectation sharing was critical in the successful transition. Communicating their new roles unambiguously to the board and to the internal organization was the next step. It was equally important for all to be conscious of the dangers of slipping back to the familiar. So they agreed to mutually share feedback periodically which further helped in cementing the new roles.

'This practice could be adopted as standard operating procedure every time a senior role change is envisaged or when a role-succession was in progress.'

Recalls Harsh:

'This was one of the toughest calls I had to take, and culminated as yet another path-breaker in my journey. Since its inception in 1990, I had helmed Marico and grown it, heart and soul, with immense determination, grit and passion. Looking back, my decision to step down has been a winner for all the stakeholders: Marico, Saugata as well as me. Subsequent to Saugata taking over as MD, the market cap has attained a CAGR of nearly 21 per cent per annum.

'This smooth transition afforded me the opportunity to pursue many initiatives that I had notched up in my "to-do" list. Not only do these keep me fully engaged, but have also enabled me to re-invent myself. Not to mention the fresh learnings that come with my new initiatives.

'The uncommon shift in my role was hailed as a pioneering move and attained accolades from the media and capital markets.'

Prof. Ram Charan Says:

'No one should underestimate the deep emotional etchings in a person who gives birth to a baby like Marico and take it to these heights.

What it takes to give it up to somebody else, even though he has control of it . . . taking that source of psychological gratification or winning every day against big giants and giving it away is the greatest sacrifice psychologically. But the win on the other hand is the perpetuity build that will live for a long time.'

19

Purpose beyond Profit

'The power of business is in its purpose. It is not *what* we do, but *why* we do it that defines us.'

Soon after the formation of Marico, one of the agendas on Harsh's mind was a strong desire to contribute to society—even when corporate social responsibility was not statutory. To that end, he asked his team to dwell on social causes that would work synergistically with Marico's business.

The thoughts that were seeded in the 1990s germinated in the early part of the new millennium. Jagdish Sheth, professor of marketing at Emory University, USA, and advisor to Marico on all aspects of strategy and marketing, had co-authored a book with Raj Sisodia, professor of marketing at George Mason University, USA—*Firms of Endearment: How World-Class Companies Profit from Passion and Purpose.* Their research led them to advocate the concept of conscious capitalism, a leadership guided by the vision of service to all stakeholders: customers, employees, associates, communities in which they operate and of course, the investors. This resonated well with Harsh. Research over a ten-year period proved that the companies that adhered to the philosophy of enveloping all stakeholders, not merely shareholders, as advocated in the book, led these to outperform the 'good to great' companies, identified in Jim Collins' book, by a ratio of three to one in the US stock markets.

Purpose of Marico

Introducing the concept of purpose, Harsh felt that Marico should now begin to think about itself as being a part of an increasingly interdependent and integral ecosystem. 'It has to be more than a mere business and become a principal agent of social change.' He spoke about Enron and Lehman Brothers, who focused singularly on shareholder return and senior manager-centric policies. This bias, to the exclusion of all other stakeholders, finally led to their downfall. A purpose achieves its greatest potential, emphasized Harsh, when a company shifts its attention from the transactional to factor in its own consciousness and inner growth. He expressed the need for Marico to build an engaging narrative that rested on a responsible, fair and ethical foundation: a purpose beyond profit. He advocated a move away from a singular focus on shareholder value.

Harsh wanted Marico members to find the eventual meaning in their work. The knowledge that their work had positive outcomes and would also benefit society would in turn add to their feelings of involvement, worthiness and meaningfulness.

Having decided on this holistic approach, Harsh engaged Alok Nanda to help arrive at and craft a purpose statement for Marico. Nanda interviewed around thirty senior managers of Marico to obtain insights regarding what they felt was unique about their company, which he then distilled into a purpose statement. Which crystallized as:

'Be More. Make a difference . . . to transform in a sustainable manner the lives of those we touch by nurturing and empowering them to maximize their true potential.'

This philosophy resonated with Mariconians as it leveraged and further accelerated what was already in practice.

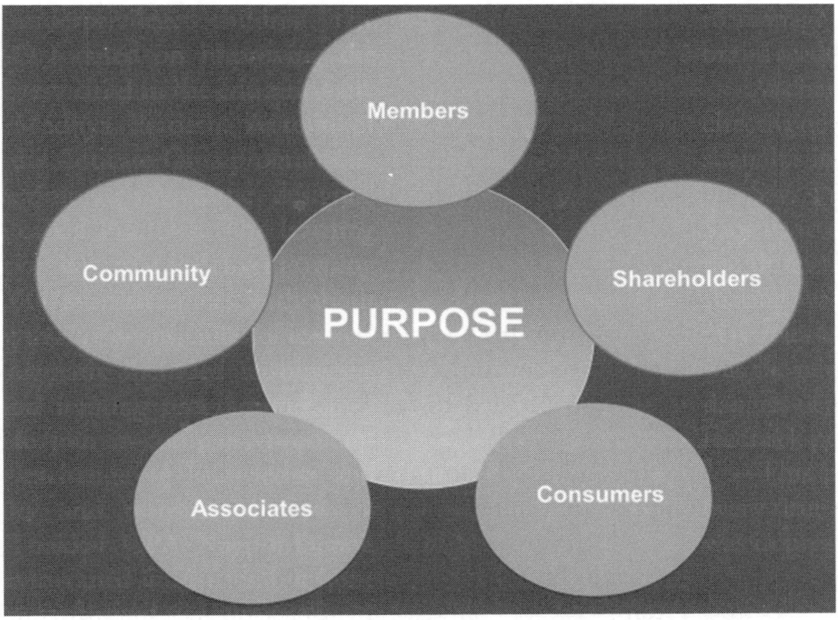

In its relationship with consumers, Marico was not merely selling them products and brands. It was creating a relationship of trust and warmth by adding convenience and quality to their life: a value that went much beyond the transaction of selling, to creating a long-term loyalty to the company. Likewise, when employees experienced a highly relevant culture, they too gave their best. Business associates with growing businesses accrued to Marico cherished their relationship with the company. Knowing that it added value to its constituents and did things innovatively attracted the best talent and business associates, and in turn, this helped Marico deliver stretched performance. Gratified shareholders received attractive returns and stayed invested in the company when they experienced raised standards of corporate governance, boosting investor confidence. All these, then, were indexed in the performance of Marico's shares. A stronger share price created more wealth for investors as well as employees who earned shares through stock option plans. It also helped the company to apportion money for improving the lot of the community around it and consumers preferred fulfilling their everyday needs by buying the company's offerings in preference to those offered by other competitors.

Each beneficial outcome fed on the other, creating a virtuous cycle of excellence and superior performance.

Brand with a Purpose

The brand team of Saffola discerned that post in-depth research, merely delivering a healthy 'heart' oil to the consumer was not adequate. They needed to capture hearts in more ways than just being transactional.

So, taking a leaf from the early 1980s, when Harsh had sown the seeds of reaching out to consumers to educate them on the benefits of heart health, the team decided to reinforce and add further value to the same.

The research conducted had thrown up grim statistics. First and most important was that India is the world capital of heart ailments as well as diabetes, which further contributes to heart disease. Every sixty seconds see the deaths of four Indians caused by heart conditions.

'Saffola Healthy Heart Foundation' was set up in 1991 with the primary objective of building cardiac awareness, educating people about risk factors, and helping them take action to lower the same. To this end, a multipronged programme was charted out. The team concluded that the basic communication to the consumer should be:

a) to provide knowledge about lifestyle, diet, nutrition
b) to drive home to the consumer the importance of routine health checks
c) to provide expert intervention.

Importantly, spreading awareness about the degree of the problem was paramount. So, to allay that, 'Heart Health Camps' were conducted in partnership with leading medical institutes such as Escorts Health Institute, Bombay Hospital and others. Talks in various fora were presented by cardiologists, and walkathons conducted to spread awareness. Free cholesterol checks were conducted across ninety cities: these netted the enrolment of 85 lakh people. Mumbai's legendary dabbawalas were also roped in to place 'I will take care of my heart' pledge cards in every dabba they distributed. Further, a 'dial-a-dietician' programme was initiated whereby people across the country could speak to qualified dieticians and nutrition experts, seeking advice on maintaining health through balanced diets and improved lifestyles.

Media campaigns further enhanced public consciousness. Commercials were aired on TV to enlighten people about four major risk factors: obesity, hypertension, diabetes and smoking. Exceptionally, for the first time in the history of world radio, in 2007, four radio stations were brought together for a 'simulcast' across Mumbai for a one-hour programme related to heart ailments and Saffola. Again, in 2008, all radio stations went silent simultaneously and broadcast the beating of a heart for one minute. Public reaction was very positive and this was touted by media as being an extremely innovative campaign. All the above resonated with consumers. A survey carried out reflected that 80 per cent of the user base would shift from other oils to Saffola. The survey also showed huge growth potential for the brand, thereby mirroring perfect economic sense to continue integrated CSR work on the brand.

On the commercial side, the commodities manager contributed to the economic well-being of the coconut farmer by sharing the gains from the copra supply chain and educating the farmer about how to improve crop yields. Higher yield meant more supply of coconut per tree and a higher earning meant that the farmer became a loyal vendor of the company. So did the human resource manager, who found greater value-add when his work helped to grow the careers of his colleagues. A factory worker loved his work when he knew that the way he and his colleagues worked prevented factory waste from damaging the environment. When, through MIDAS, Marico improved real-time information availability and fidelity, it ensured better returns through inventory efficiencies to the distributors. In turn, the sales managers experienced a newfound strength in their relationship with the distributors that then went beyond the transactional.

Marico reached out to schools in urban and rural India to teach young minds about nutrition and food safety. Messages delivered through children had the potential to usher in behavioural change and a culture of safe and wholesome food at home. The programme provided the students with practical tips and information to prevent obesity, and through them, inspired their families to start a journey of health and fitness.

Driven by the purpose, brand Nihar Shanti Amla launched a programme called 'Chotte Kadam Pragati Ki Aur' (small steps to progress) to support the education of underprivileged children. The brand funded **Educate Girls**, an NGO focused on improving the enrolment–retention–learning cycle of every child in the educationally backward districts of Rajasthan and Madhya Pradesh. A total of 2,00,000 girl children benefitted from the Educate Girls programme. Nihar **'Mobile Paathshala'** was a learning programme designed by a leading educationist organization called Pratham. The learning programme used an interactive voice response format to deliver learning modules in a fun way. There were 2,35,000 student callers, with about 2 per cent of them completing the entire thirty-five modules of lessons.

Inspired by the purpose, Marico regularly included its business partners in its conferences, seminars and training programmes on a complimentary basis. It invited them to join in-company problem-solving task forces, which facilitated exchange of knowledge and understanding, furthering their loyalty and transparent flow of information back and forth. Says Viren Thakkar, CPA, Nagpur Depot, 'We are associated with many companies in varied industries, but none match Marico. This company has always motivated us immensely . . . as associates, we have been included in many programmes like personal development etc. With their support, we have been able to improve our quality systems. Programs like "Scale the Everest", which aim to collaborate, engage and facilitate associates to constantly upgrade their performance; also, shop-floor improvement processes such as Kaizan, Six Sigma and TPM.' Mr Thakkar continues, 'A small seed planted by Mr Mariwala turned into a forest. Today, we have more than 20 lakh sq. ft of quality warehouses . . . we are forever indebted.'

Mr Nagbhusan Iyer, an ex-Mariconian and now an associate, says, 'It is amazing how Marico's philosophy remains intact in spite of attrition. I believe Marico has indirectly played a role in my success.'

A super-distributor in Jaipur reflects, 'Looking back at my association with Marico makes me nostalgic, tears fill my eyes. I have never received this warmth and comfort from any other company. Being a part of Marico has helped me to improve two important facets: look for challenges, and never give up in the face of adversity. Mr Mariwala is one of the most inspirational personalities and a true leader. Revolutionary changes brought about by Marico in their systems and processes for distribution have resulted in a manifold increase in productivity. The values of Marico, their concept of empowering others, motivating them, regularly introducing new IT tools centred on making a difference have truly enabled me to improve not only my business operations but also the way I perceive the roles of all the other stakeholders of business. All of the above steps, implemented so seamlessly and with apparent ease, talk about the quality of professionalism and persistence, requisite at this level. This is what personifies Marico: professionalism, efficiency, dedication.'

CEO of BBH and Publicis Worldwide, India, Subhash Kamath, reflects, 'I've worked with Marico now for close to twenty-four years as a communications partner across different brands, and I have always felt a part of Marico's extended marketing team. Our KRAs and those of Marico's marketing team are closely linked. Marico also involves my agency's team members in their training programmes.'

Win-win was always an integral part of leadership thought and action at Marico, from its inception. The purpose statement simply augmented and multiplied managerial action to search for more opportunities to collaborate.

Sustainability

An integral part of the purpose dialogue was Marico's commitment to the environment. A commitment whereby Marico would progressively replenish and return to nature what it drew from it, so that it would not jeopardize the planet and thereby the lives of the future generations.

Marico was among the frontrunners, leading the way with its work in sustainability. It ranked high on the list of companies in the Global Reporting Initiative (GRI) network at G4, the fourth generation of the international guidelines for sustainability launched in 2013. From energy and water management to improving farm productivity, it had shaped a more planet-friendly business.

Agro-commodities were an integral part of Marico's supply chain and constituted 84 per cent of the raw materials. Therefore, much of its share of raw material in manufacturing was renewable. To that end, Marico focused on helping farmers learn sustainable agricultural practices.

Studies showed that coconut farmers suffered from low crop yields owing to incorrect or suboptimal farm practices and pest attacks. Marico worked with agricultural universities and researchers to understand the agronomy of coconut and safflower production. They then educated the farmers on how to improve their harvest yields and reduce losses from pests and disease, through booklets circulated among them. The next step was to arrange 'farmer melas (fairs)' to demonstrate these practices. The peer-to-peer gatherings of nearly 10,000 coconut farmers, through a series of meetings, sometimes twice a month, helped improve farming practices in the coconut farming belt. Marico launched an initiative called 'Kalpavrikshya' (a divine tree in Hindu mythology). In this context, a tree all of whose parts are useful in one form or another: coconut water to drink, copra to extract coconut oil, coconut fibre to make ropes, coconut shell to make charcoal, leaves are used in the making of thatched huts and palm sugar obtained from the budding flower. In 2017, the Kalpavrikshya initiative educated 10,000 farmers through a hundred training programmes on scientific farm practices encompassing nutrients and disease and water management. It resulted in improved farming techniques, increased outputs and higher farmer earnings. It deployed agronomists and agricultural experts who travelled across villages, interacting with farmers to create awareness and provide on-field support. A toll-free advisory call centre was set up for farmers and a mobile application was developed to oversee all queries. The feedback from the beneficiaries of the Kalpavrikshya initiative was extremely positive and encouraging. Rajkumar, a farmer from Tamil Nadu, reverted: 'Based on the Kalpavrikshya Foundation feedback, carrying out soil testing and fertilizer application has increased my yield.' Adds Manikandan from Tamil Nadu, 'Through them, I have learnt about water management techniques.'

'My crop was attacked by the red palm weevil and the rhinoceros beetle. My business was at a standstill till the Foundation came to my rescue,' says farmer Natarajan from Tamil Nadu. Thus, by educating farmers, Marico had increased their yields through better irrigation and soil fertility management practices. The farmers had benefitted by earning more revenue.

A story of sustainability prevailed in the area of safflower cultivation. Marico was the single largest buyer of safflower seeds in India. Therefore, its commitment to safflower farm communities dated back to the early nineties. The safflower plant didn't need much water, fertilizer or pesticides. Fallow land could produce the crop. But the disincentive to grow the safflower crop mainly arose from the thorny nature of the plant, that which interfered with the manual harvesting that prevailed. The company collaborated with equipment manufacturers to design implements to better handle the plant's thorns during harvest. Further, company representatives worked with agricultural universities and other agencies to improve the seed, thereby promoting high yielding varieties. As a consequence, productivity rose by up to 25 per cent. Nearly 60,000 farmers across five states were positively impacted by these efforts. Their fallow lands came under cultivation and the yield per acre also increased too, improving income for the farmer and raw material availability for Marico. Through these efforts of Marico, India had become the largest safflower producing country in the world—but still insufficient to meet all of Marico's needs.

The initiatives taken to help farmers were estimated to have generated about ₹100 crore p.a. of higher income for the farmers and is expected to increase three-fold, to ₹300 crore p.a., in the near future.

Plastic was the main material used by Marico in the packaging of its products. When Harsh switched from tin to plastic packs in the 1980s, the negative impact of plastics on the environment had not yet manifested itself. Plastic had become the most popular option for packaging of liquids. There were no other biodegradable and cost-efficient alternatives available that could replicate the properties of plastics yet.

Marico's strategy for improving the sustainability profile of its packaging was to employ the 3R policy of Reduce, Reuse and Recycle. Further, through value engineering, it had optimized volume and weight of packaging material, replacing it with environmentally conscious material, improving recyclability and increasing use of recycled polymer content. Marico's packaging development team had, through computer-based simulation, lowered its polymer consumption, thus reducing the packaging weight per millilitre. Parachute coconut oil's HDPE (high density polyethylene) bottles and the hair oils' PET (poly-ethylene terephthalate) bottles are one of the lowest in weight per volume across FMCG products. In order to improve recyclability, the company took the initiative to replace PVC (poly-vinyl chloride) with PET for its hair oil products—PVC is hard to recycle. Presently, less than 1 per cent of Marico's packaging is PVC. Approximately 95 per cent of the company's packaging material by weight is recyclable.

It had also begun using 100 per cent recycled PET in the packaging of one of its large volume products. The company estimated that these initiatives had helped it to use about 500 MT fewer plastics in the past five years. Its target is to move towards 100 per cent recyclables over the next few years.

Marico had also been targeting its dependence on fossil fuels for its energy needs, aiming to shift significantly to renewables. From about 33 per cent in 2013, its consumption of energy from renewable sources increased to 72 per cent in 2018. Its manufacturing units depended mainly on biomass for their thermal energy demands. Its plant at Perundarai operates 100 per cent on wind energy. At the Jalgaon unit, 91 per cent of thermal energy requirements are met through renewable sources.

Marico's logistics team measured the 'fuel consumed per tonne shipped'. Fuel efficiency was driven by optimizing the distance travelled per trip and the number of trips made to deliver stock to its customers. It continuously worked to reduce this ratio by redesigning network routes, consolidating warehouses, up-sizing vehicles and improving vehicle utilization.

Water availability is critical for Marico and it recognizes that a water crisis is one of the top risks that plague the world today. Marico helped in dam de-silting projects, like that of the Yeldari dam in Maharashtra, to create additional storage capacity for rainwater. It had helped create check dams near its operating locations, in order to improve water table levels and irrigation. Likewise, a three-way collaborative arrangement between Marico, an NGO named the Deshpande Foundation and the farming community resulted in sixty farm ponds being constructed in the state of Karnataka. These community projects were already offsetting about 80 per cent of the water consumed by Marico and it is steadily marching towards a 100 per cent offset of water consumption by 2022.

Corporate Social Responsibility

Marico Innovation Foundation

Corporate social responsibility had become mandatory for Indian companies in 2014. These rules require 2 per cent of profits to be spent on CSR yearly.

Harsh, who had already taken CSR initiatives way ahead of the mandatory requirement, launched the **Marico Innovation Foundation** in 2003.

MIF was set up with the mission of **nurturing innovation in India among businesses, social entrepreneurs and NGOs to recognize and help them scale up the innovations for enhanced economic and social value.** At that time in India, innovation was not a valued competency and was not recognized as vital for business success.

Harsh's success as an entrepreneur and as a business leader could largely be attributed to his ability to think ahead, unconventionally and innovatively. To name a few examples: the tins to plastics packaging revolution; being the first to pioneer and market a healthy oil brand; recruiting professional and competent talent as a priority on starting Marico; designing and building an organization culture and activating board professionalism. In all these and more instances, Harsh stepped off the beaten path and pioneered new ideas to accelerate business. Knowing the power of thinking differently, innovation was close to his heart—and central to his success. Harsh had observed that whenever an innovation was implemented successfully, he had observed a quantum leap in business. He was therefore convinced that innovation could play a vital role in accelerating India's growth. MIF, then, was his way of fuelling innovation. Harsh believed that innovation could spur creation and accelerate India's economic growth.

That innovation was hardly in the public mind can be illustrated by a small event. In announcing the birth of MIF, a press conference was called in one of the south Mumbai five-star hotels. Few turned up at this event, quite unlike the experience at investor meets, where the business press participated in impressive numbers.

Dr Raghunath Mashelkar, a past director general of India's Council for Scientific and Industrial Research (CSIR), was appointed chairman of the governing council of MIF. Dr Mashelkar admired how Harsh combined talent, technology and trust to unlock disruptive innovations.

In the early years of its inception and probing its way through an abstract landscape, MIF conducted exhaustive research evaluating the journeys of businesses and social organizations that had managed to scale up through innovation. The research repository was converted into a book called *Making Breakthrough Innovation Happen* by Porus Munshi (Marico Innovation Foundation—Erehwon Innovation

Consulting), first published in 2009 by Harper Collins and now into its fifteenth reprint after having sold more than 75,000 copies. A second book with business and innovation insights from newer case studies, titled *7 Sutras of Innovation*, written by Nikhil Inamdar, was released in January 2020.

In 2006, MIF's flagship event, called **Innovation for India Awards,** was set up as a platform to identify and recognize breakthrough innovators in India. This event happens once every two years.

The preparation for the awards is elaborate. The team conducts intensive research, scoping innovations and inviting applications. The applications are screened through several layers; an external knowledge partner, an on-ground due diligence and two rounds of jury deliberations, to eventually select the next set of big innovations in the country.

The audience to the Innovation for India Awards ceremony comprises corporate chiefs, impact investors, media representatives and social sector leaders. The audience is curated with the intent of attracting business interest, funding, scale-up opportunities and publicity for the innovators. The foundation's awards have, till date, recognized sixty disruptive innovations, including businesses that have been scaled up.

Well into the second decade, MIF realized that it was not sufficient to just educate and provide a public platform to recognize noteworthy innovations. MIF expanded its interventions to help the innovators scale up with management support. The Scale-Up programme provides pro bono support and assistance to innovators by facilitating partnerships between subject matter experts and innovators. The experts are drawn largely from a pool of Marico managers and external thought leaders. Since 2016, they have addressed and helped find answers to twenty-five business situations across thirteen different industry and social sectors.

Many unrecognized heroes from small towns, with small outfits and meagre resources, have engineered path-breaking innovations that have transformed the lives of thousands, if not lakhs. One such recent innovation is **Rivigo.**

Rivigo

Sometimes referred to as the 'thirty-seventh caste', long-distance truck drivers, though breadwinners for their families, have become social outcasts in their villages and communities. On the roads, away from their families for months on end, living in rough and gruelling conditions, they have to drive for an unsafe number of hours. They often indulge in activities that cause STDs. These long periods of absence and indulgence earn immense stigma and social disrespect for them. So blighted are their jobs that their children don't want to step in their father's shoes, nor will others marry their daughters into truck drivers' families. This, then, was a sadly neglected community, never thought about, till Rivigo, an innovator with a heart, effectively transformed their drudgery into a more logistically viable, and therefore humane, job. Rivigo's unique model allows the drivers to cover a shorter distance with shorter hours. Much like a relay, the driver hands the truck to a fellow 'pilot' (as they are known) at a designated pitstop. He then drives another truck back to his point of origin, thereby returning home to family and dinner.

Technology forms the backbone of this model. From a safety point of view too, this is six times better than a regular transporter. Since 2014, Rivigo has impacted the lives of 5000 pilots and their families and aims to impact 1,00,000 truck drivers by 2025. Recognized for their innovation by MIF in February 2018, it is a matter of pride that this innovation now features in the 'Unicorns of India' list of 2019.

Genrobotics

Visualize this scenario: you return home after a hard day's work. Instead of coming forward to hug you, your kids back away. Because of the stench that clings to you. The stench of the manhole you have spent the last few hours cleaning up with your bare hands. Cleaning it of decomposed wet waste, excreta, medical waste like blood-soaked gauze, syringes and needles—and even human foetuses! On the other hand, you are lucky to return—the noxious and poisonous fumes in the sewers didn't kill you.

There are 60,000 registered manual scavengers in our country. As per a report by Sulabh International, the actual number could be as high as 4 million. In the last three to four years, over 300 deaths have occurred on the job. That apart, working in hazardous conditions such as these has a huge negative impact not only physically, but on mental health as well. The unbearable stench of those sewers forces the poor scavenger to drink at least a quart of alcohol before descending into living hell. This daily frustration leads to further addiction like gutka,[17] sometimes drugs, and often domestic violence.

One of the most inspiring innovations that could end the heinous practice of manual scavenging is an ingenious manhole cleaning robot named Bandicoot. A 50 kg remote-controlled robotic scavenger, it uses a 360-degree motion to scoop out debris. This AI-enabled robot completes the cleaning operation in twenty minutes as opposed to the four hours taken manually to finish the job. Genrobotics takes this a step further by conducting a training and rehabilitation programme that enables manual scavengers to operate the machines, thereby providing them a dignified mode of earning a living. Genrobotics' goal is to eradicate manual scavenging completely in India by 2025. A brilliant innovation where science and engineering meet social good to make a large-scale difference to an entire section of society.

Atomberg

One example that was selected for the MIF scale-up programme was 'Atomberg'.

The 350 million fans running in India today consume at least 75–100 watts of electricity, which accounts for almost 15-20 per cent of electricity consumption in each household. The Atomberg fan, fitted with a BLDC motor, consumes less than 28 watts (i.e., less than a tubelight) and saves ₹1500 per year per user. In the last four years, the total power saved by these fans is 200 GWH, or an estimated ₹100 crore. By broad estimates, if every new ceiling fan sold uses BLDC technology, India could save more than 3000 GWH per year, which would be sufficient to provide electricity for almost 80 lakh households.

Revenues of the assisted businesses grew by a factor of ten and so did valuations.

Harsh Avers:

'Much of my learning and insights come from books. My reading covers books on management, leadership, self-improvement and spirituality.

---

[17] Gutka: chewing tobacco.

As someone famously said, "The business of business, is more than business. Business is accountable not only to its shareholders but also to all its stakeholders."

'These include employees, customers, associates and society. Business needs to add value to each of its stakeholders. The role of business leaders is to create value for society by providing solutions to the challenges of the same. Each organization plays a role in improving mankind.

'No man is an island and no institution is an island either. The private sector is an integral part of society and it cannot prosper without recognizing the social context within which it operates. Inequities are a scar, a major blot on any society.

'Business has a much broader positive impact on the world when it is based on a higher purpose that goes beyond only generating profits and creating shareholder value. Purpose is the reason a company exists. A compelling sense of higher purpose creates an extraordinary degree of engagement among all stakeholders and catalyses creativity, innovation, organization and commitment.

'Every conscious business has a higher purpose, which addresses fundamental questions such as: why do we exist? Why do we need to exist? What is the contribution we want to make? Why is the world better because we are here? Would we be missed if we disappeared? A firm's purpose is the glue that holds the organization together, the amniotic fluid that nourishes the life force of the organization.'

20

Personal Social Responsibility

SHARRP VENTURES

Harsh, being a true-blue entrepreneur, invested all the dividends accrued from Marico towards increasing his stake in the company. Understandably so.

However, Rishabh, who had been studying the family finances and cash flows, felt that Harsh had placed all his eggs in one basket. He was of the strong opinion that his father must de-risk himself by investing in companies other than Marico. Though his father disagreed, he persevered. Harsh eventually saw merit in his stance, and gave him the go-ahead to float his own venture. Having already done in-depth research on family wealth management, numerous sessions followed between father and son regarding where and how their investments should be placed. SHARRP VENTURES was founded.

Today, Sharrp Ventures presents a sizeable corpus with many of the investments made by Rishabh in unlisted ventures, proving to be multi-baggers.

ASCENT Foundation

The journey of an entrepreneur is often a lonely one. There are many dilemmas, personal or otherwise, that an entrepreneur cannot share with his team. Many a time, Harsh has felt the need to communicate, to confide, to seek diverse points of view in order to learn, to find solutions.

Having lived through many such solitary moments himself, Harsh wanted to create a supportive and non-threatening environment where entrepreneurs could share and learn from each other's experiences, aspirations, dilemmas and fears. Thus, ASCENT was the vehicle that Harsh launched in 2012 as a powerful peer-to-peer platform that leveraged the power of the collective through self-facilitated groups, called 'Trust Groups'.

Each Trust Group has between ten and twelve entrepreneurs from diverse and non-competing businesses. They meet once a month in a confidential and non-judgemental environment to share experiences, ideas and insights and learn from each other. The 'Trust Groups' presently operate in Bombay and Chennai. In all, there are about 500 members in forty-two 'trust groups'. Member business turnovers range from ₹2 crore to ₹2000 crore, with a collective market cap of ₹22,000 crore. Members are selected based on their ambition to grow business, motivation to be in the group, willingness to learn, and share and invest trust in one another. They are assigned to Trust Groups based on diversity, each group having a mix of business and industry types, and gender and age profiles.

ASCENT also holds several knowledge-driven events through the year. It includes an annual conclave of 700 members (including potential members) and, once a quarter, interaction with a knowledge guru. Members can also pursue academic enhancements through tie-ups with the SP Jain and Stanford Business Schools in India. ASCENT also offers a 'PowerUp Programme' of one-on-one mentorship of entrepreneur members through its panel of industry experts.

Members find the Trust Groups stimulating and supportive, as feedback testifies. Says Vishal Shah, 'A PowerUp session with Mr Mariwala changed my perception on many key things: delegating jobs, team building, compliances and systems improvement. My life has improved on multiple levels post meeting Mr Mariwala—and my business has grown by 120 per cent.'

Nevil Sanghvi comments, 'I joined ASCENT in 2014 and was part of a nine-member group. The different backgrounds and industries in my group afforded access to successful leaders, new technologies, human resource handling and more. All of which helped me evolve a business which is futuristic, predictable and scalable.'

Mariwala Health Initiative

While MIF and ASCENT encompassed different approaches towards social responsibilities, Harsh was keen to invest in another socially relevant cause as well. Broadly interested in the field of preventive health, he aspired to an in-depth and long-term commitment. To that end, he drew in his family to ideate and deliberate on which field of health they should be engaged in.

His daughter Raj suggested a game-changer in the area of mental health. A field that was grossly under-represented, under-funded and under-served. Research divulged that 150 million Indians were in need of active interventions for mental health issues—of which less than 30 million sought care. This figure constituted 15 per cent of Indian adults (above age 18). Statistics further revealed that mental illness contributes 31 per cent to the impact of global disease. India spends 1.3 per cent of health expenditure on mental health. A mere pittance.

Conferring further with his daughter, Harsh dialogued with a few stakeholders and experts in mental health. He concluded that the need gap for services in that field was huge, especially for vulnerable communities, and that there were major voids in quality delivery service. With the guidance of mental health professional Shruti Chakravarty, the father and daughter duo carried out in-depth research on this initiative. While Harsh was keen to start and run a helpline and scale it up quickly, both Raj and Shruti believed that there was no need to reinvent the wheel. Running and helming a foundation to provide direct service delivery was rejected in favour of providing support to civil society and grassroots organizations. To this end, Shruti suggested they talk to iCALL, a national helpline based out of Tata Institute of Social Sciences (TISS), which offered free telephone-based counselling services through a team of qualified and trained mental health professionals.

In April 2015, MHI entered into a close partnership with iCALL, and an agreement was drawn up whereby MHI would wholly fund iCALL services, along with promoting them in mainstream English and non-English media in order to further their reach. With the partnership underway, MHI had the opportunity to learn from iCALL as well as plan further philanthropic engagement in mental health. Harsh and the MHI team conferred with numerous stakeholders regarding their interactions with mental health systems, their beliefs, perceived need gaps and what they would expect from a partnership with a funding organization. The aim of all this was to glean on-ground realities, existing challenges, as well as potential areas for innovation.

This exercise established the five pillars on which to base MHI as well as a framework toward accomplishing their goals. A year later, adopting the iCALL partnership as a pilot and applying the learnings from it, MHI partnered with two other organizations: Bapu Trust and Centre for Mental Health Law and Policy.

While Harsh meets partners to review and add value to their performance, his networks and connections help leverage and facilitate marketing, technology and human resources support.

Since 2017, MHI has steadily added grantees, working with a total of twenty-two organizations in diverse settings such as courts, urban slum communities, farmer communities, rural settings and schools. Parallelly, in line with the framework that was outlined in 2015, MHI has worked with state governments like Maharashtra and Bihar as well as district level governments. And very importantly to raise political commitment to work on mental health. MHI's 'Bridge the Care Gap' campaign approached political parties, raised general awareness about rights-based mental health and received multi-sectoral support and signatures for its public petition. All the above resulted in 2019 being a milestone year for mental health as it was included in political manifestos for the first time in Indian history.

MHI work also extends to international actors in mental health, being part of international collaborations such as the Global Mental Health Action Network, earlier known as 'Blue Print Group'. Raj was also invited to sit on the Lancet Commission on Stigma and Discrimination.

The father and daughter duo intend to keep growing MHI, even as he advocates for other philanthropists and CSR funds to focus on this much neglected, development-based issue of mental health.

Prof. Ram Charan Reflects:

'Many CEOs and promoters pay lip service to create benefit for society. They donate to a foundation to fulfil their societal obligations. There are, however, a few passionate business leaders who go beyond personal funding to actually commit time and leadership to a cause that is dear to them. Azim Premji is a case in point. Over the long term, he has funded and led his organization of committed professionals to address large and complex socio-economic issues. Harsh is one among them in creating the not-for-profit ASCENT and MHI. We learn from these leaders that it is possible to do both: building business institutions and being personally involved in building for society, beyond the self-interest of their business.'

21

Milestones and Maxims

Flipping through the pages of my life, I came across many colours, many textures.

Emotion defying colours. Angry reds, serene blues, calm greens . . . some grey too.

Rough textures. Smooth textures. Some glossy, others matte. The rough ones defining the often very difficult passages life churned out. Harsh realities and challenges. Smooth textures outlining achievements, successes, satisfaction, positive outcomes.

The textures, the colours, the imagery of all these pages, some jagged, some torn, reflect the ebb and flow that life has pointed out for me.

And the binding behind all these?

Transparency.

Always. The very basis of my life. My work.

So, looking back over the passage of time, the resultant experiences taught me, grew me. Led me to evolve. Founded my values and principles. Which follow . . .

My Ten Milestones

1. **Distancing from the Licence Raj**
   The then ongoing trend of currying government favour to obtain licences went against my grain, my values. Instead, I identified areas that I could leverage, and which would not compromise my principles.

2. **Modernizing a traditional product**
   Coconut oil, a traditional product used by generations, needed to keep pace with current times and changing practices. We kept abreast by revamping its packaging and advertising so as to convert consumers who used unbranded oil to a branded and packaged, and unadulterated and superior product.

3. **Founding Marico**
   Convincing an inter-generational and large joint family to carve out separate companies for each member of the younger generation, providing autonomous responsibility, and thereby, accountability. This step ultimately led to the founding of Marico.

4. **Building company culture as a source of competitive advantage**
   Creating a culture of transparency and innovation well outside standard business practice of the time was another contrarian move on which the culture of Marico was then built.

5. **Betting on hair oil**
   Many analysts, sceptical of the future of hair oils, advised against investing or acquiring brands in this category. I proceeded to do the opposite—and it paid rich dividends.

6. **Choice of portfolio**
   Identifying categories that afforded us a 'right to win' through innovative and pioneering initiatives.

7. **Setting up a factory in Kerala**
   Despite the state's reputation for bureaucracy and labour unrest, our first green-field factory operated successfully—by investing in people and cultures.

8. Investing in Bangladesh
Setting up a business from scratch in a politically volatile environment to emerge as the largest Indian company in that country.

9. From products to services
In a highly competitive category, we adopted an innovative approach by entering the market through the services route—and then launched products.

10. Pioneering move in succession planning
My decision to appoint an outsider as my successor set a rare precedent in succession planning in an extremely hierarchical Indian business environment.

My Eight Maxims

1. Leveraging strengths
All of us are born with God-given gifts which, more often than not, we are not conscious of. Brainstorming with peers and mentors helps identify and leverage your natural gifts. And then mould your future based on your leanings and strengths, whereby your chances of success would be higher and goals more attainable. Again, all of us have shortcomings and weaknesses, and pour in huge effort and time rectifying and improving the same rather than concentrating on our strengths. I believe that 75 per cent of one's efforts should go into reinforcing our strengths, and 25 per cent into overcoming weaknesses.

A strength usually converts into a passion. So, to that end, you will then enjoy what you do.

2. Be focused
Do a few things. But do them well. Being 'Jack of all trades' will not allow for success in every field you aspire to. Master of a trade can only happen when you have a focused approach. Therefore, first identify what is critical, whether it is (in terms of) the kind of business you are running, or expanding to a newer geography. Focused businesses do far better than conglomerates, which also reflects in capital market valuations.

Focus leads to depth. And depth leads to excellence.

3. Take risks

Out of failure comes learning. I have undergone many failures in my journey—and every failure has resulted in a learning. For instance, Saffola Baked Snacks had to be withdrawn. However, the learning from this non-success was incorporated in the launch of Saffola Oats. Which turned out to be a thumping success. Every failure I experienced has resulted in a detailed analysis of what went wrong and my learnings from it.

Indian society, which is very hierarchical, does not take kindly to failures. This attitude serves as a deterrent to risk-taking. It is important to take risks and not be driven by the fear of failure. Every experiment, every risk need not succeed. Can anyone point out a single individual who has never encountered a failure or a setback?

'Win some, lose some' is a common saying. However, I say 'Sometimes you win. But you never lose. You always learn.'

I quote below one of my favourite verses.

> 'To laugh is to risk appearing the fool.
> To weep is to risk appearing sentimental.
> To reach for another is to risk involvement.
> To expose your ideas, your dreams, before a crowd, is to risk their loss.
> To love is to risk not being loved in return.
> To live is to risk dying. To believe is to risk despair.
> To try is to risk failure.
> But risks must be taken,
> because the greatest hazard in life is to risk nothing.
> The people who risk nothing,
> Do nothing
> Have nothing
> *are* nothing.'

4. Evolve your vision

There is a belief in management circles that every entrepreneur should have a clear vision. My viewpoint differs. Some start with a vision. Others may not have a vision but may pursue a business opportunity. As the enterprise succeeds, a clearer picture of what one's vision should be, emerges. This vision should not be cast in stone but, instead, should continually evolve as per the environment and circumstances. For example, who could have foreseen a 'Black Swan' calamity like COVID, which would have a huge impact on the vision of any organization? Who would have envisioned the digital revolution, or the confluence of technologies which have emerged in the recent past, which include artificial intelligence, robotics, blockchain and many others? It is vital to understand that one's vision should not be set in stone but evolve constantly and be revisited every few years.

5. **Aim for win-win negotiations**
In the early stages of my journey, I always aimed to win. Especially where negotiations were key. I recollect holding out against a labour union for nine months of a strike. I emerged victorious. And was elated. However, a year later, the workers who experienced a sense of let-down and felt victimized hit back with another strike. It was then that the realization hit home that a win-lose outcome does not pay in the long run. A win-win result, where both parties meet halfway without compromise makes for a sound way forward.

6. **Reinvent yourself**
Focusing, expanding and growing your business is fulfilling the aspirations you began with. However, comes a time a decade later, maybe even more than that, when you need to ask yourself whether you will continue what you are doing perpetually or think of a new journey, a new challenge, and reinvent yourself. Continuing on the same road endlessly often causes loss of momentum—and the passion you possessed when you started diminishes. It stops providing you with newer experiences, newer challenges. It is imperative to ask yourself: 'What can I do differently? What can I now pursue?' This could be a breakaway from your current line of work, and an opportunity to reinvent yourself.

When I stepped down as managing director of Marico, it was a huge shift for me. I had to reimagine myself, exploring newer horizons and take up newer challenges. All of which led to opening up a new chapter in my life: a part of which includes writing this book.

7. **Purpose**

   At a later stage, once a certain level of achievement has been attained, it is important to delve into pegging your purpose in life. Once identified, this purpose then becomes a major fulcrum of your journey. Nothing remains the same once you discover your true purpose, your calling. The complexities of daily life, of work, change. You are able to draw upon reservoirs of energy and inspiration that you were not aware existed within you. Your journey in the progress of that purpose then becomes truly fulfilling and rewarding.

   My purpose in life is to 'Make A Difference'.

8. **Grit**

   Passion is a critical ingredient in one's climb to success. Passion brings in energy, drives behaviour. However, many a time, when a passion is pursued and success is not achieved or a setback occurs, people give up. This passion, then, has to be combined with perseverance and determination.

   So,
   Passion + Perseverance + Determination = Grit
   An imperative mix in a recipe for SUCCESS

In Between

Post stepping down as chairman, another pioneering business opportunity came my way. Research revealed the benefits of the application of water treatment in physiotherapy. Further exploration confirmed an absence of any such noteworthy facilities in India. Exploratory visits to world class set-ups in Europe and the US were followed by conceptualizing this opportunity. A team of doctors and physiotherapists was selected and sent abroad for training in this specialized field. Two best-of-class clinics were then founded in Mumbai and called Aquacentric.

The results have shown this venture to be pathbreaking. And outcomes have proved to be exemplary, for which case studies have already been written, and continue to be written. Aquacentric will further progress under the nurturing and guidance of my daughter-in-law Priyanjali, who has essayed a vital role in adding substantial value with her diligence and contributions.

New Horizons

The legacy I aspire to leave behind would envision Marico as an organization that enriches the daily lives of people in many diverse ways via our wide range of beauty and wellness products, to our foundation which fuels innovation in India. Inclusive would be the Kaya chain of skincare clinics and products. As also my personal ventures in the field of physical wellness, by way of aqua therapy, the colossal and severely neglected issue of mental health and well-being in our country, as well as our peer-to-peer platform for enhancing entrepreneurship.

All my ventures today, more than being businesses, shoulder the responsibility of defining, creating and distributing value—all of which will endure as an ongoing and perennial process. The key challenge would remain perpetual enhancement of growing scale and creating mechanisms, processes and systems. Here, my family and the boards, two very important cogs in my wheel, would play a crucial role in keeping the ball rolling and raising the bar persistently.

While looking back at my journey to date has me in a 'feel-good' and contented space, the absolute highlight of my life are my grandchildren, Saskia and Shaurya. The ultimate gift. Every day is a new dawn with them: there is an amazing amount I learn and derive from these very innocent minds, uncorrupted so far by the pre-set opinions and norms of society.

Another source of satisfaction and contentment is knowing that my children, Raj and Rishabh, including my daughter-in-law Priyanjali, have found their calling and enjoy the challenges as well as derive satisfaction from what they do. By pursuing their passions, they are enjoying their journeys forward.

My quest to 'do more, *BE* more and make a difference' continues . . .

Epilogue

Harsh joined Bombay Oil in 1971, when the consumer products division had a turnover of ₹50 lakh. This he then grew, virtually from scratch, into a leading FMCG organization with a revenue of ₹4687 crore, posting a net profit of ₹485 crore, when he stepped aside from his role as MD in 2014. Marico's market cap stood at ₹13,517 crore, with most of its brands being market leaders in their respective categories. A very strong foundation had been laid to take the organization into its next orbit with a clear strategic direction, the right set of capabilities, a well-thought-out succession, high governance standards and a value-adding board. This set in motion a flywheel effect for a purpose-driven institution that would continue to deliver sustainable profit growth.

'Only when values are lived every day and perpetually reinforced, do they convert into the culture of the organization.' – Harsh Mariwala.

And Marico walks the talk. Thus, Marico's values and culture define how it conducts its everyday business. The company's conscious investment in its culture, over the years, has enabled the organization to stay resilient and agile in the face of many challenges and winds of change.

Living by its ethos of 'Make A Difference', Marico's response to COVID extended far beyond its consumers, employees and stakeholders. The overnight urgency and shift of health, hygiene and immunity essentials, with COVID spreading its tentacles across India, saw an exceptional level of grit, innovation and collaboration across geographies by Marico members to help circumvent this Black Swan event.

The company's R&D teams broke boundaries to collaborate across international borders in launching new products to meet the pandemic challenge. Members of the manufacturing plants stretched themselves to increase production despite low staffing and supply chain teams enabled last-mile delivery through innovative partnerships. Sales teams opened up new avenues of delivery by tying up with food delivery chains, logistics service providers and direct-to-society deliveries. Marico also partnered with government agencies and food delivery service providers for meals and dry rations to migrant labourers, the police force, health workers as well as the elderly and the poor. Further, a nationwide platform called 'Innovate2BeatCOVID' was launched to invite and fund the most impactful innovations by med-tech entrepreneurs, corporations and innovators to combat a shortage of ventilators, personal protective equipment and other respiratory solutions that would mitigate the demand for life-saving supplies, along with substantial cost reduction.

Internally, Marico prioritized member safety and well-being above all else. Jobs and salaries remained unchanged, with benefits encompassing Marico's extended field force, including monetary assistance and COVID healthcare insurance. Recognizing the increasing impact on the mental and emotional health of its members, in addition to existing counselling services, the company organized sessions with experts on relevant topics.

The entire organization came together as one, with utmost passion and a renewed commitment to create value. And deliver.

The market cap of Marico crossed ₹50,000 crore in December 2020.

> 'Values lead to beliefs. Beliefs convert to behaviour—which, then, creates culture.'—Harsh Mariwala

Acknowledgements

A culmination of my journey to date, this book is the outcome of the combined efforts of numerous people contributing in diverse ways. To them all, a big thanks for all their inputs.

Prof. Ram Charan has honoured me with his blessings and support in this, my endeavour. An outstanding thought leader and guru, he stands at the top of my page of gratitude as my coach and counsel through the last thirty years. Despite a hectic travel and work schedule, Prof. Ram Charan agreed to co-author this book, readily making time for me. Sometimes even detouring via Mumbai to confer and debate over the emerging drafts, providing priceless insights and value additions that punctuate the destiny-determining moments penned in this narrative.

I thank my past and present associates—all employees, board members, business partners, investors and consultants, including those who agreed to be interviewed at short notice. They helped recapture happenings and events that anecdotally enrich the pages. I would also like to place on record my appreciation of Tatwamasi

Dixit whose suggestion it was to approach Prof. Ram Charan to co-author the book.

My thanks to Radhika Marwah of Penguin Random House for her patience and support, as also to Milind, who compiled the first contents, drawing upon my random jottings and his own historical knowledge as an executive of the company.

To Aleem Merchant, a member of ASCENT, goes the credit of suggesting the title of the book.

To Rubina D'silva, my executive assistant, for her endless patience and support. She has spent countless hours compiling reams of transcripts of recorded interviews, assembling multiple drafts for review and many, many untold tasks that add to the completeness of this project.

Chaitanya Deshpande, a Marico veteran, anchored and archived all the material, transcripts and meetings records connected with the project. Co-ordinating with internal sources and past associates as the book progressed through many versions, he too has given it his all.

I thank Jeswant Nair, ex-chief human resources officer, for his contribution in penning my thoughts. He laboured for many months, poring over drafts, annual reports as well as transcripts, collating data. Jeswant also brought to bear personal insights from his years of involvement with early Marico.

To my uncle, Kishore Mariwala, my gratitude for his support and encouragement. As also for reading through the drafts and offering me his perspectives, in particular the initial history of the Mariwala family.

My acknowledgements would be incomplete without a special mention here of the ever-smiling Pranab Datta. A Marico chief finance officer, he was my steadfast support and anchor through the family separation. I visualize him today grinning down at me from the beyond: Pranab, you were and always will remain a part of Marico. RIP.

My heartfelt gratitude to Amy Fernandes, the late Anil Dharker and Sonal and Haresh Shah for patiently sitting through many, many virtual meetings and providing invaluable inputs and perspectives to enrich the book.

As for my children—daughter Raj and son Rishabh—they were my 'go-to' islands of quiet joy and relief that I would lose myself in during those mind-bending years of family upheaval. Today, I take deep pride in saying they are my sounding boards and mirrors. And am extremely proud of the diverse journeys they have chosen, as well as the integrity and passion which they impart to their work: Raj, in her dedication to the mental health cause, while also continuing to pursue her love of animals and devotion towards her first love of being a canine behaviourist. And Rishabh for propelling and backing entrepreneurs in new-age ventures, many of which have been 'multi-baggers'.

I can't count my blessings enough as my wife and life partner Archana stood steadfast with me right from the time we got married. She supported and encouraged me through my struggles of creating an identity for myself as a young entrepreneur amid the accomplished seniors of the Mariwala joint family. Through the many dilemmas I faced, she was my behind-the-scenes counsel and sounding board. My punching bag as well as my mainstay, she endured my pique through the family separation. My pillar of strength, she would allay my rancour over the personal debts I had to fulfil by continually highlighting the positive aspects of the situation.

Archana has poured her heart and soul into this book. Researching, asking questions, pushing me, studying drafts, materials, documents, recorded conversations, then compiling and further honing her writing. She brought warmth and emotion and added huge depth to the narrative.

Cheers to the success of *her* book!

Harsh Mariwala

Awards

Under Harsh's leadership, Marico and Kaya have achieved significant recognition. They have garnered more than 300 awards across different categories. Some of the prominent awards are:

<table>
<tr><th></th><th></th><th>Year</th><th>Award</th><th>Category</th></tr>
<tr><td rowspan="6">MARICO</td><td>1</td><td>1992</td><td>National Award for Best HRD Practices.</td><td>HR</td></tr>
<tr><td>2</td><td>2005</td><td>Saffola's entry into the Limca Book of Records for generating the highest number of health-related pledges.</td><td>IT</td></tr>
<tr><td>3</td><td>2005</td><td>Gold Award for the 'Most Trusted Brand'—voted by Consumers for Saffola in Cooking Oil category.</td><td>HR</td></tr>
<tr><td>4</td><td>2006</td><td>Featured in the top-100 companies in India, for creating fastest wealth for shareholders in the last five years.</td><td>Supply Chain</td></tr>
<tr><td>5</td><td>2007</td><td>Harsh Mariwala awarded 'CEO with HR Orientation' at the Global Excellence HR Awards.</td><td>HR</td></tr>
<tr><td>6</td><td>2007</td><td>Marico won the NDTV Profit Business Leadership Award in the FMCG (Personal Hygiene) category.</td><td>Manufacturing</td></tr>
</table>

	7	2009	Harsh Mariwala won the Talent Management Award at the CNBC TV18 India Business Leader Awards.	Leadership
	8	2009	Marico won the NDTV Profit Business Leadership Award in the FMCG (Personal Hygiene) category.	Leadership
	9	2010	Marico awarded the most prestigious and keenly contested Nasscom CNBC TV18 IT User Award 2010, for excellence in IT application, in the manufacturing category.	Leadership
	10	2014	Harsh Mariwala awarded the Best CEO by *Business Today*.	Communication
	11	2014	Marico recognized as the 'Best Governed Company' by the Asian Centre for Corporate Governance and Sustainability.	HR
	12	2014	Marico featured in the List of 'India's Best Boards 2014' by *Economic Times* and Hay Group.	HR
	13	2014	The 'Best Governed Company of the Year' award by the Asian Centre for Corporate Governance and Sustainability won by Marico.	Leadership
	14	2016	Marico recognized as the Best Domestic Company on Corporate Governance by Asiamoney's Corporate Governance Poll 2015.	Leadership
	15	2021	Harsh Mariwala bestowed the IMC Juran Quality medal for 2019.	
	16	2021	Harsh Mariwala awarded Ernst & Young (EY) Entrepreneur of the Year Award 2020.	
KAYA		**Year**	**Award**	**Category**
KAYA	1	2014	'ET Best Brands 2015' at Economic Times Best Brand 2015.	Communication/ Media
KAYA	2	2017	'National Award for Marketing Excellence', Times Network.	Marketing
KAYA	3	2018	Kaya recognized as the National Best Employer Brand at the World HRD Congress.	HR
KAYA	4	2010–2020	Kaya is the only brand in its category to win 'Superbrands' ten years in a row in the United Arab Emirates.	

Websites

Entity	URL
Marico Ltd	https://marico.com/
Marico Innovation Foundation	https://www.maricoinnovationfoundation.org/
Marico Sustainability	https://marico.com/make-a-difference/sustainability
Parachute Kalpavriksha, CSR	https://www.parachutekalpavriksha.org/
Kaya India	https://www.kaya.in/
Kaya Middle East	https://www.kayaskinclinic.com/uae/en/
Mariwala Health Initiative (MHI)	https://mhi.org.in/
ASCENT Foundation	https://ascentfoundation.in/
SHARRP Ventures	https://sharrpventures.com/
Aquacentric	https://aquacentric.com/